HIPPIE
HOMESTEADERS

For Denise
10-8-14

Carter Taylor Seaton

HIPPIE HOMESTEADERS

Arts, Crafts, Music, and Living on the Land in West Virginia

CARTER TAYLOR SEATON

West Virginia University Press
Morgantown 2014

West Virginia University Press, Morgantown 26506
First edition published 2014 by West Virginia University Press
Printed in the United States of America

21 20 19 18 17 16 15 14   1 2 3 4 5 6 7 8 9

ISBN:
PB: 978-1-938228-90-2
EPUB: 978-1-938228-91-9
PDF: 978-1-938228-92-6

Library of Congress Cataloging-in-Publication Data:
Seaton, Carter Taylor.
Hippie homesteaders : arts, crafts, music and living on the land in West Virginia / Carter Taylor
Seaton.
        p.   cm
Includes bibliographical references and index.
ISBN 978-1-938228-90-2 (pbk. : alk. paper) -- ISBN 1-938228-90-1 (pbk. : alk. paper) -- ISBN
978-1-938228-91-9 (epub) -- ISBN 1-938228-91-X (epub) -- ISBN 978-1-938228-92-6 (pdf) -- ISBN
1-938228-92-8 (pdf)
1. West Virginia--Biography. 2. Artisans--West Virginia--Biography 3. Hippies--West Virginia-
-History. 4. Handicraft--West Virginia--History. 5. Arts--West Virginia--History. 6. Urban-
rural migration--West Virginia. 7. Counterculture--United States--Biography. 8. Youth protest
movements--United States--Biography. 9. Country life--West Virginia. I. Title.
F240.S43 2014
975.4--dc23
2013035012

WVU Press gratefully acknowledges financial support for this book from Robert and Molly Lehman
and the Fetzer Institute.

Photo credits: Carter Taylor Seaton (top) by Rick Lee.
Back flap and cover photos, from left: V. C. and Damienne Dibble clearing land, 1972 (photo
courtesy of the Dibbles); Norm Sartorius carving; Joe Lung at the wheel; Connie McColley
weaving a basket (photos by Ric MacDowell).
Cover illustration by Liz Pavlovic. Cover design by Liz Pavlovic and Than Saffel.
Book design by Than Saffel and Nathan Holmes.

For Allison, who first asked the question.

Contents

Preface

I am a daughter of the hills—born and bred, as we say in West Virginia. Yet until 1970, I did not realize I was an Appalachian as well. I'd grown up in the city but ridden horseback through the woods behind my grandparents' home. I walked blacktop streets to school, then escaped on weekends to the outskirts of my neighborhood to play in caves. The tug of those hills was strong, the comfort in them complete.

One autumn weekend at Hawks Nest State Park, in the company of those who already knew, I found my roots. I'd recently become the director of a craft cooperative and felt I needed a quick orientation into the culture I'd be serving. Hammered dulcimer music touched my soul. A lecture on the roots of Appalachia-speak explained why my refined grandmother always said, "He don't." In a display of Scottish tartans I found the one I could claim as my own, and I understood: I am a daughter of the Appalachian immigration of the seventeen hundreds and eighteen hundreds.

For nearly fifteen years, I worked with scores of rural women to help bring their beautifully handcrafted quilts and clothing to sophisticated markets all over the United States. The experience enriched me and showed me a simple, rural life I'd disdained as a girl. It's true that an abiding love of the land often kept their families on now non-productive farms, and that a lack of education kept the breadwinners in low-income jobs. In some instances, the women had never been outside their community their entire lives. Nevertheless, their honesty, integrity, and pride were as true as the stitches in their quilts. If these women agreed to do a job, you could count on it. I came to love these wash-dressed women, their hair pulled back into a severe knot at the nape of the neck or permanent waved into a mass of tight curls every three months. And I came to know the voices of Appalachian women—those of many generations in the mountains.

During this period, as Appalachian Craftsmen, Inc. exhibited at the annual Mountain State Art & Craft Fair in Ripley, and the semi-annual Mountain Heritage Arts & Crafts Festival in Harpers Ferry, West Virginia, I began to see a different cut of artisan. Scattered among the scores of homegrown craftsmen were candlemakers, basketmakers, potters, wood sculptors, weavers, photographers, stained glass artists, leather crafters, and print makers who didn't speak with the twang I'd become accustomed to in rural West Virginia voices. I soon learned they were not natives but had chosen to make West Virginia their home. Why they came mattered not; we were simply West Virginia artisans trying to eke out a living.

Fast-forward to 1996. I returned to West Virginia after a ten-year absence, grateful to be back in the comforting mountains. I discovered Tamarack and learned that when it was built, West Virginia was the only state in the country with an entire facility dedicated to showcasing the work of its artisans. As I wandered through the displays, I excitedly recognized the names of many of my old show-mates—now highly successful, nationally distinguished artisans whose work had put West Virginia on the map in a positive manner. I remembered when they were just beginning their careers; now they formed the core of West Virginia's reputation as a fountainhead of fine art and handcrafts.

Suddenly, I began to wonder: what *had* brought those immigrant artisans to West Virginia? After several inquiries, I discovered that many were part of the back-to-the-land movement. Why West Virginia? How did they find the state? What drew them? Did they love the hills like the state's natives? Was there something unique about their West Virginia experience that contributed to their success? Curious, I began a two-year journey visiting forty-five artisans, musicians, and performers—most of whom I'd known during our years together on the craft circuit—to learn their answers.

I discovered that they came for various reasons, but found the same charm in those ancient hills. However, it's the totality of their arrival that made such an impact on the state. One or two would not have created a movement—they'd have been an anomaly, either accepted by those around them or run off—but the hundreds who came and those who stayed, because they found support from their neighbors or the state itself, have made a positive contribution to their adopted state. There are hundreds more—environmental lawyers, community activists, restaurateurs, hoteliers, directors of nonprofit organizations, archivists, and social workers—who have done the same. Here, I've chosen to highlight just the artisans, musicians, and performers. They are a slice of the whole, but each one is important. Listen carefully to their stories.

Acknowledgments

First and foremost, I could not have written this book without the exceptional cooperation and willingness of the artisans and other members of the artisan community to share their stories. They trusted me with them and I am honored by that trust. Although there were other back-to-the-landers who told me of similar adventures of the period, they were not included, either because they were not transplants to West Virginia, or they weren't artisans or musicians. The tales of those who became physicians, hoteliers, restaurateurs, social workers, teachers, lawyers, environmental activists, and more will have to wait for another day.

Many thanks go to the West Virginia Humanities Council for their belief in my project and the grant that enabled me to conduct over forty interviews. Patty Slack did an outstanding job of painstakingly transcribing those conversations. She saved me countless hours of typing, and for that I'm truly indebted. And to my hollow-born husband, Richard Cobb, goes my heartfelt gratitude for accompanying me up hollows he didn't know existed, as well for as his patience in enduring the years it took to distill the stories we heard into this book.

All writers need the encouragement and reasoned critiques of their fellow writers. I've been fortunate to have a whole group of them—The Patchwork Writers. They listened to stories, offered suggestions, and were my cheerleaders. To my "gang" of dedicated writers—Eddy Pendarvis, Gwenyth Hood, and Charles Lloyd—I offer special kudos. They read, dissected, corrected, and critiqued every word of the manuscript. If it was put back together well, they deserve the credit.

1

Traditional Handcrafts in Appalachia

W
hen the back-to-the-landers came to West Virginia in the 1960s and 1970s, their arrival couldn't have been more serendipitous, but that is only obvious in hindsight. They came seeking a place to live simply, to be free from the trappings of urban materialism, and to be allowed to mind their own business. No doubt, when they learned basketry, blacksmithing, wood turning or broommaking from their neighbors, most of them were unaware of West Virginia's long held handcraft tradition. They simply wanted to master a skill they hoped would be of practical use, provide an income, or both. Little did they know they would have a role in saving the state's craft heritage and ensuring its future.

Since the Appalachian region was settled in the late seventeen hundreds and early eighteen hundreds, handcrafts have been woven as tightly into the fabric of daily life as the rivers that wind through its mountains. The English, Scots-Irish, and German settlers who migrated to the hills looking for land, freedom, and a chance for a new life brought many practical skills with them. Their ingenuity allowed them to develop the handcrafts now considered central to the Appalachian tradition. Unlike the gentry who had settled near the coast, the mountain folks created handcrafted objects that were, for the most part, practical in nature. Aristocratic ladies who practiced any of the more delicate arts—tatting, bobbin lacemaking, embroidery, painting, and drawing—did so primarily as a time-passing hobby, to perfect their skills, and to adorn their homes, not because they had to for survival. In the mountains, women sewed out of necessity, making clothing for their families and linens for their homes. Men took up woodworking and metalworking to build and furnish their homes, and to fashion necessary farm tools.

This is not to say the products weren't also beautiful—often, they were highly decorated—but functionality was usually uppermost in the maker's mind. In fact, this combination of functionality and beauty often made the objects a pleasure to look at as well as to use. While the tools and implements of everyday life were critical, the Appalachian transplants found time to satisfy their aesthetic sensibilities as well. Blacksmiths forged essential items like wagon tongues and door hinges, but they also formed decorative fireplace tools and wrought iron candlesticks. Tinsmiths fashioned kitchen utensils like plates, ladles, and cups, as well as delicately pierced lanterns.

These hardscrabble pioneers who chose to tame the Appalachian Mountains turned to the plentiful natural resources they found to supply their everyday needs, and excellent craftsmanship was a hallmark of their work. Leathersmiths tanned hides and made carrying sacks, harnesses, saddlebags, belts, and even the blacksmiths' bellows, but they also used their talents to fashion beautiful vests and jackets. Craftsmen felled the magnificent hardwoods to build furniture, fences, and log cabins, or whittled them into bowls and cooking utensils, musical instruments, gunstocks, and even toys for their children. They split oak into thin strips, soaked them, and wove them into baskets. Coopers bent wood into barrels for storage of grains and whiskey.

Farming provided more than just sustenance. Straw and cornhusks became brooms and often dolls. Vegetables and nuts provided the dyes to color wool and cotton fibers. Carding sheep's wool, spinning yarn, and weaving it into cloth were at the heart of the pioneer woman's day. Precious little went to waste. Quilts were often made of scraps from outgrown clothes or leftover cloth, padded with worn-out blankets or cotton batting, then closely stitched together in layers. They evolved into works of art, as decorative as they were practical. Indeed, some of today's most precious antiques are the woven coverlets and patchwork or appliquéd quilts of that era.

No doubt in some places, traditional handcrafts have been practiced without interruption since the immigrants' arrival on our shores; however, by 1890 many of the old ways in this country had been abandoned as the Industrial Revolution mechanized processes formerly done by hand. However, in West Virginia, as in much of Appalachia, these skills persisted as part of daily life longer than in other parts of the United States because of the relative isolation of the region. Over the years, though, both the need for these practical skills and the public's appreciation of them have ebbed and flowed.

Beginning in the 1820s, the tools of everyday life in most of America could be bought from a traveling salesman or ordered from a catalog. Soap, candles, belt buckles, brooms, and eating utensils found their way to the shelves of the general store. Only those without cash or access to shopping—as in the mountains—continued making these necessities by hand. Owning store-bought goods gave a family a certain elevated status by signaling a measure of prosperity, while families that still made their own were seen as quaint and old-fashioned. Therefore, following the Civil War, when local-color writers for the monthly magazines that had sprung up during this time "discovered" Appalachia, they noted traits, customs, and even lifestyles that were markedly different and anachronistic in comparison with the rest of America. They viewed and wrote about this abiding craft tradition by describing Appalachian culture as primitive, simplistic, and a marker of how much progress the rest of the nation had made.

Then, like a pendulum swinging from one extreme to the other, the appreciation for handcrafted products revived as the days of the Industrial Revolution waned and the Arts and Crafts Movement took hold. Influenced by England's John Ruskin, who in 1851 bemoaned the sameness of manufactured goods and championed the creativity of handcrafted products, this movement grew in influence from the 1880s to the 1930s. William Morris followed Ruskin in establishing a firm in England for the creation of craft designs in the decorative arts. Interest in the idea espoused by these two, as well as by Gustav Stickley—that craft was a moral force in society—took root in America in the 1870s. The three men argued that because handcrafted goods demanded creativity and showed individuality, they embodied an essential humanity that manufactured goods could not.[1]

By now, Appalachia's quaintness had begun to be a niggling problem for a nation looking to celebrate its unity following Reconstruction and in the face of the upcoming centennial. Defined as "different," Appalachia needed to be brought into the modern era to become part of the mainstream. It needed to be helped. In the 1890s, in reaction to the all-male patriotic societies that were founded in anticipation of America's 1876 centennial, women began forming their own civic organizations. The Daughters of the American Revolution, the United Daughters of the Confederacy, and the Colonial Dames were concerned with issues of women's rights, education, and health care. Not surprisingly, they turned some of their attention to the Appalachian region. Accepting widespread thought that it was an impoverished and culturally backward region, they willingly offered to help improve Appalachian lives.

During the ensuing settlement-house era, teachers and missionaries began to move into Appalachia to bring education and culture to the region, and teaching craft skills became a staple in their settlement and industrial schools. Soon the sale of locally made crafts became the standard means of raising both income and recognition for the mountain settlement schools while providing financial assistance to the producing families. Although the list of well-meaning reformers who descended on Appalachia is long and well documented, few if any seem to have settled in West Virginia. In 1892, William Goodell Frost, the president of Berea College in Kentucky, began a successful fundraising campaign for the college by suggesting that making handmade objects contributed to the betterment of good moral character and education in the mountain folk. Following Frost, Frances Goodrich established Allanstand Workshop in Asheville, North Carolina; Katherine Pettit and May Stone founded the Hindman Settlement School in Hindman, Kentucky (although Pettit eventually broke away to establish her own school, Pine Mountain Settlement School, in 1913); Mrs. George W. Vanderbilt started Biltmore Industries; Olive Dame Campbell established the John C. Campbell Folk School; weaver Lucy Morgan founded the Penland School of Crafts; and O.J. Matil of the Pi Beta Phi sorority founded a settlement school near Gatlinburg, Tennessee.[2]

Each of these schools taught craft techniques of the past to the mountain folk. The founders believed that the "methods, aesthetics, and community of preindustrial labor offered an antidote to the ills of industrial society, as well as a foundation for social and economic uplift."[3] However, they often have been criticized for designing the products they taught local people to make. More than one writer has charged that they were tainting the true heritage craft tradition instead of perpetuating it, as they claimed.[4] Moreover, the women who performed the work had little or no say in what they produced, or the price for which it was sold. None of their work was made for their own use, but rather for sale to consumers with "high average buying power"[5] and urban tastes. This sales savvy often motivated workshop directors to further alter many traditional craft designs to meet the perceived market demand.

As directors of these schools became aware of each other, they formed the Southern Industrial Educational Association to provide a common meeting ground. In 1909, the association established an annual sale of mountain made crafts called The Exchange in Washington, D.C. From it, national interest in Appalachian crafts grew, attracting the attention of Allen H. Eaton of the Russell Sage Foundation. A longtime supporter of craftwork, he began organizing craft cooperatives in Appalachia that became, in 1930, the nucleus of the Southern Highland Craft Guild, which is still active today.[6]

Then came the Depression, when purchasing ground to a near halt. American citizens could ill-afford food, let alone consumer goods. Eleanor Roosevelt came to West Virginia in 1931 and saw the destructive poverty. Following the creation of three West Virginia experimental communities—Eleanor, Arthurdale, and Tygart Valley—that were founded under the National Industrial Recovery Act of 1933,[7] she suggested that groups of women band together to produce furniture as an economic development project. Although the project ultimately failed, the town of Eleanor was a model community founded on her principles. Rather than bringing an outside designer to West Virginia to oversee production, Roosevelt employed a Hardy County chair maker, Samuel Isaac Godlove, to teach the miners to make a simple chair that his family had produced for years. The project provided work for too few people, however, and without the infusion of other industries, the model community experiment was abandoned.[8]

It is interesting to note that, save for the Eleanor experiment, the outside influences exercised on the indigenous crafts in other Appalachian states—Kentucky, North Carolina, and Tennessee—are largely absent in West Virginia. While that fact left crafts there unchanged, the heritage crafts still practiced as handed down through families were in danger of disappearing less than twenty years later. During the 1950s and 1960s, the state's youth left in droves for more fertile job markets both north and south, often leaving their elders with no one at home to take up the craft skills they'd been practicing for several generations. Therefore, when the back-to-the-landers arrived in the state in the late 1960s and early 1970s, their arrival proved to be fortuitous for both the incoming artisans, the heritage crafts tradition, and, ultimately, the state.

Copycatting the flurry of patriotic activity that surrounded America's first centennial, West Virginia's state government began, in 1960 and 1961, looking for ways to mark the state's upcoming 100th birthday in 1963. The West Virginia Department of Commerce (WVDOC) wrote to counties, municipalities, civic organizations, and other groups, asking them to develop projects that would showcase West Virginia's history and culture. They wanted to know what the state's people did well that could be put on display for the world to see. Out of the surveys came word that the Department of Agriculture had been besieged with requests from rural women who wanted to sell their baskets, quilts, and other handcrafts at the county fairs. However, from the perspective of the Department of Agriculture, the county fair was for selling products of the farm, not the hearth.

Simultaneously, the folks at the WVDOC were looking for new economic development engines for the state, other than coal mining, timbering, or farming. Following European models that showed tourism and crafts were mutually beneficial to the economy, they began to look for ways to use crafts to promote the state during the centennial. With the nation's poverty level at 19 percent in the early 1960s, President Lyndon Johnson launched his War on Poverty by creating the federal Office of Economic

Opportunity to develop solutions that could be implemented on a state-wide basis. Similarly, the Appalachian Regional Commission formed and began looking at ways to stimulate the economy in its thirteen-state region. Since West Virginia was in the center of this depressed area and the poverty level there was almost 35 percent,[9] federal dollars began to pour in. When several national studies, including one conducted by West Virginia University, showed rural economic development was best achieved through cottage industries, savvy community organizers set out to establish craft cooperatives.

By the late 1960s or early 1970s, several strong regional organizations were operating. Mountain Artisans, a non-profit sewing cooperative, was formed by Sharon Percy Rockefeller, Florette Angel, designer Dorothy Weatherford, and others to provide income to rural families in the counties around Charleston through the sale of quilted and patchwork wearables and home fashions. In Parkersburg, another co-op, Rural Arts and Crafts, specialized in making stuffed toys and provided income to Wood County families. VISTA workers James Thibeault and Colleen Anderson formed Cabin Creek Quilts at the insistence of the women in that area who wanted a market for their handmade quilts and pillows. In Hamlin, the Lincoln County Artisans cooperative, started through the local community action council, grew into Appalachian Craftsmen, Inc. in 1971, with the support of the Junior League of Huntington and Southwestern Community Action Council. This group, with headquarters in Huntington, sold women's clothing, toys, and home furnishings based on traditional quilting patterns and designs.

According to Don Page, who worked for the WVDOC during those early years, this development of cottage craft industries was right up the department's alley. Under the direction of Hulett C. Smith, the first director of the WVDOC and later governor of the state, and David Callaghan, his arts and crafts coordinator, a plan was implemented. "They found out that where tourism flourished, crafts developed; and where crafts were flourishing, tourism increased. They went hand in hand," Don says. With the knowledge that the state had people who made handcrafts well, the department applied for and received a federal grant to send technical representatives into the field to find them. Don was one of those hired in 1963, along with Jane Cox George, John Harper, Jr., and K. Carl Little. Their task was to find folks who were making arts and crafts, evaluate the marketability of their work, improve their skills and techniques where necessary, and develop markets for them both inside and outside the state. "We went everywhere," he recalls. "I took a West Virginia map and a black magic marker. I blacked out every road I drove that was on that map. Each time, I would take a different route."

What Don and the others expected to find were indigenous people making crafts that had persisted in the area since its settlement—quilting, basketmaking, broom making, or whittling—but what he recalls discovering, along with the old-timers, was a cadre of college-educated young people who had escaped the establishment, had settled in West Virginia, and were living off the land. These artisans were producing a different level of handcrafted goods. Their work, while often based on or learned from the indigenous folk, was more non-traditional in design and in its level of sophistication. Hand-carved rocking horses became braying donkeys. Baskets had, not wooden, but forged metal handles. Brooms might be dyed purple or scarlet. One artisan's pots had gained such a level of artistry that a shop owner asked him if he could rough them up so they would look handmade.

Some—already craftsmen when they arrived—had brought training and skills that put them in a different league, like the studio glass blowers he found. Others, Don says, "just looked at what people were doing here: baskets, and blacksmithing, and woodworking, and they wanted to learn it. A lot of them hung out with the older people or went to the craft fairs. They began to emulate and copy and try to become proficient in traditional work. There was a marriage of the traditional craftsman and the ones who came in." While some of the older artisans pushed the design envelope and experimented with new color combinations or designs, many preferred to stick with the traditions that had been handed down to them. All co-existed peacefully. Craftsmen of the old school were not threatened by the newcomers' designs. As long as each was happy with their work, they could and did exhibit side by side.

This in-migration coincided with the out-migration of the state's young people to the better job markets in Detroit, Cleveland, Charlotte, and Atlanta; and to some extent, its opportune timing explains the general acceptance of these back-to-the-landers. Unlike their own children, these young people appreciated the elders' old ways and wanted to learn their skills. Furthermore, their friendships grew because the newcomers were very respectful of the mores and the traditions around them, says Don. They were like-minded folks who learned from their elders and valued their advice. He believes that crafts became a valid way for the newcomers to take the skills they had or could acquire and be welcomed in the marketplace. "I never saw a traditional craftsman, like say a person who was third-generation or fourth-generation basketmaker, have any problems wanting to teach this new person how to make what he did and sharing his information with him," he says. In the same manner, the locals often were all that kept the naïve newcomers from starving or freezing during their first winter in West Virginia. Don, a native of the state, now says, "I don't say they are exactly like us, but I can say this: they became West Virginians. They *are* West Virginians. They're still here and they're proud to be called West Virginians."

While most of these artisans prefer to characterize themselves as back-to-the-landers, the term "hippie homesteader" also fits. And the reasons they came are as varied as the names they prefer or their individual stories. Although it's the collective impact of this influx that matters, why they came is equally important and perhaps instructive for the future of the state.

2

The Serendipitous Timing of West Virginia's Arts Outreach Program

Unraveling the tapestry of efforts that culminated in West Virginia's strong reputation for supporting its arts is tricky business. Pull one agency thread, and you'll find it tied to others. Although Don Page and the West Virginia Department of Commerce (WVDOC) seem to have been the very earliest proponents of handcrafts as an economic engine, others took up the cause in short order. In addition to Don, artisans of that period give credit for help in launching their careers to Tim Pyles, then coordinator of the Crafts Center at Cedar Lakes Conference Center at Ripley, West Virginia; Norman Fagan and Jim Andrews at the West Virginia Division of Culture and History; and Rebecca Stelling, manager of The Shop at the Cultural Center in West Virginia's state capitol complex. The Mountain State Art & Craft Fair (MSACF) and the West Virginia Art & Craft Guild that formed at the first fair, while not actual state agencies, also were entwined in the state's efforts. They provided another valuable layer of marketing assistance to the emerging craft community.

When the WVDOC sent Don and his fellow staffers across the state to find these folks who made arts and crafts, they did so knowing that of all their tourism-marketing efforts, craft events were the most lucrative. Thus their mission was to encourage the artisans, offer additional training, if necessary, and find markets for their work, often through the craft fair venue. For the upcoming 1963 centennial, they either identified or encouraged the creation of over one hundred fairs, festivals, and celebrations statewide that included arts and crafts as an essential component.

One of these was the MSACF, which was conceived by several folks involved with the Cedar Lakes Conference Center. When Cedar Lakes was created in 1950, it was dedicated to providing educational opportunities for students and adults. Situated on a former farm, the 360-acre venue originally included four groups of cottages, an assembly building, dining hall, and chapel surrounding a 4-acre lake. A Crafts Center offering "training in the craft field to anyone in West Virginia interested in learning to make craft items for fun or profit"[1] also was part of the initial plan. Therefore, during the run-up to the state centennial, employees Ron Thomas, Larry Cavendish, and Margaret Pamalon decided the best thing they could do for the celebration was put on a craft fair, and that Cedar Lakes was the ideal location. They wanted to showcase the work of some of the people who had been taking workshops at the facility's Crafts Center. With the joint support of the Departments of Agriculture, Commerce, and Education, the MSACF opened in July of 1963 with fifty-four exhibitors. They intended it to be a one-time event. Invitations to come see what the state had to offer were sent nationwide. Huge crowds attended, including folks from the Smithsonian Institution. Faced with such success, it became an annual event, which celebrated its fiftieth anniversary in 2013.

Although its first exhibitors were indigenous artisans, it didn't take long for word of the MSACF to spread to the back-to-the-landers who were arriving as early as 1965. Don Page was eager to help them get accepted by the fair. A former industrial arts teacher, Don had operated twenty-six craft workshops while he was in the military. Each offered a different discipline. He knew his stuff. "I was receptive to those people because they often had a background in design and could move vertically in the craft medium, whereas sometimes the traditional people could not break themselves from their old molds," he recalls. This honing of a traditional craft is often what made the back-to-the-land artisans so successful.

(Overleaf) Mountain State Art & Craft Fair Family, circa 1976. (Photo by Ric MacDowell)

Some began to exhibit at the fair after adopting both West Virginia and their new craft. Others, like potter Brian Van Nostrand, who landed in Webster County three years after the centennial celebration, were already practicing artisans. Don learned about Brian after reading a letter the artist had sent to the WVDOC seeking sales outlets. Van Nostrand was typical of the new breed of artisan, according to Don, and he reached out to the young man. One day, Brian looked up to see Don and wood sculptor Wolfgang Flor walking up his road. Surprised to see any visitors at his remote homestead, he was even more amazed when Don told him the department would pay his expenses to come to the MSACF. He recalls thinking it was a dream come true. "I went, and remember making about four hundred dollars, thinking, 'Oh man, we're going to be making big money here—not big money, but maybe I can make a living doing this,'" he said as we sat chatting at a picnic table outside McDonald's near Flatwoods, West Virginia.

After nearly thirty years, I'd been thinking about this reunion for several days, knowing I'd recognize him instantly. His engaging smile and steel blue eyes were indelibly imprinted after fifteen years as his tent-next-door neighbor at the MSACF. I was just as certain he would remember me. We had talked by phone, planning the meeting. Finally, the day arrived. I found him sitting inside McDonald's, bent over the table, his hands enveloping a coffee cup as if it were an unformed ball of clay. Only the top of his head was visible. Brian is no longer young, but he remains lithe and wiry. Bearded like most of the artisans of that earlier day, he still dresses in a tie-dyed T-shirt and jeans. He hasn't changed, except for the graying hair. As I approached, he looked up, his blue eyes smiled, and crow's-feet formed. "It's been a long time, Carter," he said. After we chatted a moment, we moved outside into the sun and he continued his story.

New Jersey-born Brian Van Nostrand was studying art and philosophy at Furman University in South Carolina when he met Montie, his future wife. While waiting for her to graduate, he apprenticed with a nearby studio potter and discovered that ceramics was something he really loved. The experience set the course for his future career. When Brian learned that West Virginia was hoping to attract artisans for tourism and promotion purposes, the couple decided to look there for their future home. They knew crafts held a strong tradition in the southern highlands and had learned from Brian's mentor that other artisans were building successful careers in the mountains. After working for about six months in New Jersey to save start-up money, the young, eager couple headed south to look at West Virginia. Within eleven days of leaving home, they'd bought land in Hacker Valley, Webster County, where they currently live. It cost twenty-six dollars an acre—cheap even then—and they were debt free. They'd brought a year's worth of canned food, basic materials, and foodstuffs, including potatoes, and were determined to have no overhead from the beginning.

It was a brutal first year. Brian had few, if any, building skills, much to Montie's dismay. Arriving in October, they slept on the ground under a makeshift canvas lean-to until the weather turned so cold Brian's beard froze when he breathed. Neighbors gave them a miniature wood stove and they moved into a structure built for drying corn that was still standing on their property. Although he knew next to nothing about construction, Brian did know about the basic materials, having worked at a building supply store in New Jersey. Soon, he began building their home by reading an instruction book one chapter at a time: "Chapter One—How to Frame," "Chapter Two—Rafters," etc. By spring, they had moved in, although the house still lacked windows. Once they were under roof, he set up his studio and began making pots.

A bit older than some of the back-to-the-landers who came a few years later, Brian had served for six months in the Army National Guard. When the war in Vietnam was in full force, he was in the reserves and was never called. Furthermore, he'd never heard the term "hippie" until the back-to-the-landers began streaming into the state three or four years after he arrived. Yet, like others who survived their own naiveté, he credits much of his success to being debt free and owning his land. That alone allowed him to live a simple life while making and selling his pottery. Being able to sell his entire winter's production at the MSACF helped, too. As demand for his work grew, he sold to shops and galleries as well. Finally, in the early 1980s, after eighteen years, his family could no longer help him staff the show and he gave up the July event. By then, his wife, Montie,

had graduated from West Virginia University College of Law and was a practicing attorney.

Clearly, Don Page's initial invitation paid off for both Brian and the state of West Virginia. For many years, he annually sold a full pickup truck load of pots to a souvenir shop along US Route 60 near Rainelle, West Virginia, that also offered rubber snakes for kids. However, many of its customers were well-heeled folks on their way to The Greenbrier resort in White Sulphur Springs, West Virginia. They spread the word of his work, and now his outlets are more upscale. He doesn't have to search for them. His work is in such demand that galleries and shops approach him. Heavily incised and fired in a wood kiln, his designs carry flashes of color unattainable with other firing methods.

Currently, one of Brian's major outlets is Tamarack, a state-run arts and crafts facility where he was on the artisan advisory board before they broke ground. He helped set up the jurying process and believes the facility has done more for the image of West Virginia than almost anything else the state has to offer. As Brian points out,

It says, "We appreciate our cultural arts and we celebrate that on the interstate for the world to see." It's a wonderful venue and the most democratic art jurying system you're ever going to find anywhere, because the criterion is basically craftsmanship. If there are design issues, there are always six or seven of us in our fields to talk one-on-one to the person and say, "Hey, your craftsmanship is good here, but you need to work on this. There are some problems here coordinating the elements of design here, so we want you to work on these things and jury again." They even have a mentoring program where they pay a person to come visit a studio and work with a master craftsman. You couldn't ask for more. It's a great venue for young people starting out. Tamarack is a wonderful project. It's an artistic thing in itself because it grows and evolves, too.

By encouraging and mentoring aspiring artisans, Tamarack is ensuring that the state's heritage craft tradition can continue.

Brian Van Nostrand slip trails a platter. (Photo by Ric MacDowell)

Don Page and the others from the WVDOC helped spur a similar evolution in the crafts field after finding the new artisans. Out of the MSACF came the fair's apprentice program, which both helped preserve some traditional crafts that were in danger of extinction and allowed the new artists to explore ways to go beyond the old designs. Those eager young folks built upon the traditional styles they found, while stretching their art in new, exciting directions the old folks had never considered. Interestingly, there seems to have been little or no resentment on the part of the old practitioners to the changes being made to their favorite craft. Brian agrees. "I think West Virginia was just the perfect fertile ground," he says. "There might have been other places, but this was really just about the most perfect place." Don also served on the Tamarack board of directors and was instrumental in its formative years. "Now we have some twenty-five hundred people represented at Tamarack; they are juried, and their work is of the highest quality. There were probably only four thousand producers in the whole state of West Virginia back then, and we were trying to unearth them," he muses.

Don also connected Tim Pyles with the Crafts Center at Cedar Lakes. While the facility had offered craft workshops in its early days, the program had fallen into a slump. Tim was hired in 1976 to revive it. He says the facility had good equipment but few classes. Although Tim was previously an accountant, his heart and his natural abilities lay in the field of arts and crafts. He went to work immediately to bring in expert instructors to revitalize the program.

At first he offered one-day classes with in-state master craftsmen. Soon, he was branching out to find the very best national instructors in each field and offering longer workshops. Tim says he was never interested in merely offering classes he knew he could fill. Instead, he asked burgeoning artists like Norm Sartorius what they needed and wanted to learn. "Norm was one we offered a couple of different workshops that just hit him straight-on and changed his life," Tim recalls. Interestingly, basketmakers Tom and Connie McColley went for classes and later became regular instructors in the program. While these classes were available to everyone, newcomers eager to further refine both their skills and their designs flocked to them.

Tim wasn't just the Cedar Lakes crafts coordinator. Like Don Page, he was involved in the entire crafts community. He served on the MSACF board for twenty-one years and helped build the West Virginia Art & Craft Guild into a strong artisan-led organization. When Tim left his Cedar Lakes position in 1996, he went to Tamarack, where he served as events director until his retirement in 2007.

The second widespread effort to connect with artists and musicians in those early years materialized after the federal government recognized the importance of supporting the arts. In 1967, the state legislature created a new agency, the West Virginia Commission on the Arts, to accept and disburse federal dollars from the newly formed National Endowment for the Arts (NEA). Although artists of all disciplines had been paid for their creative efforts during Roosevelt's New Deal era, no permanent federal agency had ever been established to provide ongoing recognition or support of the arts. That is, until John F. Kennedy took office in 1961. Recognizing the importance of the arts to society, Kennedy appointed August Heckscher, grandson of a museum founder, as his special consultant on the arts. In that role, Heckscher completed a report, "The Arts and National Government," six months before Kennedy's death. This report led to the formation of the president's Advisory Council on the Arts in May 1963. The previous January, West Virginia's own congressman, Jennings Randolph, had joined several fellow members of the House and Senate in introducing bills to establish the National Council on the Arts and a National Arts Foundation, but their efforts had failed.[2]

During this same period, the Arts Councils of America—later the National Assembly of State Arts Agencies—was expanding its efforts to bring local business and arts communities together. One of its initiators, Nancy Hanks, who later served as chairman of the NEA, pushed this enterprise, as it paralleled the sudden federal interest in the arts. As with several other Kennedy initiatives, however, it fell to President Lyndon Johnson to carry out the slain president's dream. The earlier bills to form a federal agency for the arts re-surfaced and were blended into new agency-creating legislation that Johnson signed into law in September 1965. It recognized in its purpose that encouraging and supporting national progress and scholarship in the humanities and the arts were not only matters for private and local entities, but also for the federal government.[3]

After President Richard Nixon appointed Nancy Hanks to head the NEA in 1969, she brought her state-level experience from the Arts Councils of America to bear on the relatively new federal agency. Preferring local and regional arts support to placing all grant funding power in the hands of the central government, she committed to working with state arts agencies. By the end of her second term, state legislative appropriations for state arts agencies topped $55 million dollars, more than half the entire NEA appropriation that year.[4] During her eight-year tenure at NEA, funding for the arts increased from $8 million to $114 million.[5] The West Virginia legislature quickly positioned the state to receive a share of this largesse by creating the West Virginia Commission on the Arts in 1967.

Although the commission has been a part of the West Virginia Division of Culture and History since 1976, initially it was attached to the WVDOC. Early on, the department adopted Nancy Hanks' Artists-in-the-Schools program, which sent more than three hundred artists into elementary and secondary schools in thirty-one states.[6] It provided support to the state's visual artists and musicians—Bill Hopen and Ron Sowell among them—as well as those in the performing and literary arts. Bill Hopen credits the teaching fellowships he received with making him into a sculptor and Ron Sowell says that if Jim Andrews hadn't trekked up their hill to listen to them rehearse, The Putnam County Pickers would still be playing for themselves. The West Virginia Artists Showcase and the subsequent in-school residencies provided much of the group's early support, he freely admits.

Following a transition period when the WVDOC's arts programs were moved to the new agency, the division went through several name and programming changes to emerge as the Division of Culture and History. Nonetheless, the agency's purpose—to accept and disburse the federal arts dollars being filtered down the funding stream from the new NEA to state entities—remains today.[7] In fact, its stated mission—"to identify, preserve, protect, promote, and present ideas, arts, and artifacts of West Virginia's heritage, building pride in our past accomplishments and confidence in our future"[8]—could have come from the days when the two agencies merged.

One week after the United States unfurled its bicentennial celebration in 1976, Governor Arch Moore dedicated the West Virginia Science and Culture Center, which soon became known as The Cultural Center. Proudly, he could have boasted that West Virginia was second in per capita arts funding—behind Massachusetts—and had the only cultural center in the country designed to house and showcase a state's arts efforts. The Division of Culture and History moved in immediately.

Under the direction of Norman Fagan, its first commissioner, the division expanded the earlier efforts of the WVDOC's arts programs. While heritage crafts were still seen as important, the new staff began to search for and work with artists, craftspeople, art institutions, schools, local governments, and community groups across the state to stimulate the arts and the citizens' interest in them. Not surprisingly, however, many of those discovered by Mack Miles and the others hired by Fagan to promote art's "wow factor" were part of the back-to-the-land wave. When Mack and Rebecca Stelling, who worked in the division's programming department, began to take a professionally designed exhibit show booth to national trade shows, the work of these artists was an integral part of the display. Woodworker Joe Chasnoff recalls that Rebecca's introduction of his work at the Baltimore Winter Market resulted in thirteen new wholesale accounts. Spoonmaker Norm Sartorius also praises the consistent assistance given him by the agency—from purchases by The Shop at the Cultural Center to the West Virginia Juried Exhibitions—for aiding his success.

Indeed, The Shop at the Cultural Center was designed to showcase the best arts and crafts West Virginia had to offer. Rebecca was ideally suited to do that. She's a striking woman. Her straight, raven hair cascades to her hips, nearly reaching the hem of her long skirts. Vivid colors infuse her wardrobe. A lipstick-red jacket, its lapels so heavily adorned by her handcrafted pins that it's hard to focus on a favorite, contrasts with a purple skirt or a pair of thigh-high magenta boots. It's not a fashion statement with Rebecca, but rather an art statement. When she's not wearing her clothes, they adorn her walls.

Rebecca's early roots fed her interest in arts and crafts. This child of medical missionaries came to Romney, West Virginia, from India at age eight when her father learned that the rural citizens needed a doctor and abandoned his plans to return to the land of Gandhi. The precocious Rebecca, who had seen the people of that country win freedom from the British and begin to make their own goods, quickly discovered the heritage craft industry in her new state. She recalls knowing older, master craftsmen who practiced their art as a way of life, for survival. She wanted to know what they knew. She started doing craftwork, making and selling fabric dolls and stuffed animals at twelve. Enter Don Page once again. He discovered Rebecca at a small Romney craft fair and offered her an apprenticeship at the MSACF.

Now a gifted artist in several fields, Rebecca learned to recognize quality work as she mastered each skill. From porcelain doll making—taught her by Edna Henderson—she moved to jewelry. The popular magazine for teens, *Seventeen*, featured her work before she herself was seventeen. Weaving attracted her attention next, so she sought out all the state's master weavers for lessons. Next, she studied weaving and spinning with two Mennonite women near Moorefield. Lynn and Ora Tusing lived off the land, raised all their farm animals, did all the old handwork, and taught her what they knew. It wasn't long before she was a regular exhibitor at the MSACF and the Mountain Heritage Arts & Crafts Festival at Harper's Ferry, two of the largest shows in the state. Soon, she opened a retail shop in Romney for her own work and that of other West Virginia artists.

That's where she was when Norman Fagan hired her to do the same at the Cultural Center. Here, however, the premise was different, Rebecca says. "The whole focus was not so much product oriented, but showcasing the artisans and their product lines, which I think is very different. That was the primary element, but it was also to be a way to generate revenue for the artisans in the state." She contacted some of the artisans she knew and sought out those she didn't, always with an eye for artisans on the cutting edge of design. Many, she found, were back-to-the-land artisans. Those college-educated folks often represented what was new in the crafts field. The Shop carried traditional crafts as well, but its clientele—often collectors—wanted the work of artisans like potter Duke Misenkowski, whose tableware graced the White House during the Carter administration, or the jewelry of Carol and Jean-Pierre Hsu.

Rebecca managed The Shop at the Cultural Center for fifteen years, from 1976 to 1991, until she left to begin a similar project near Beckley, West Virginia—Tamarack: The Best of West Virginia. Looking back, it's as if all these early efforts were directed toward the creation of West Virginia's first-in-the-nation artisan showcase. That's not true, of course. Instead, Tamarack grew from the vision of people who simply loved their state. Located on the West Virginia Turnpike, the facility includes fifty-nine thousand square feet of retail space, working studios, a fine arts gallery, a theater, and a food court featuring cuisine from The Greenbrier resort.

In 1991, West Virginia native Cela Burge, the newly recruited director of economic development and tourism for the West Virginia Parkways Authority, had an idea to connect West Virginia craftspeople with some of the millions of travelers who drove the turnpike each year. With the vision and support of then-Governor Gaston Caperton, a dedicated board of directors, and artisans across the state, the now much-envied facility opened on June 19, 1996. Artisans also were involved in Tamarack's construction, according to the tenth anniversary history written by Colleen Anderson. If any element of the building could conceivably be handcrafted, it was. West Virginia woodworkers, blacksmiths, textile dyers, stained glass artists, potters, quilters, and sculptors began to create its structural elements and were paid for their work. By the end of its maiden year, 1,300 artisans were selling their work at Tamarack, over 450,000 people had visited, and sales had topped $3.3 million. Now, the Tamarack artisan family includes more than 2,500 producers from all 55 West Virginia counties.[9]

3

Pacifists, Protesters, and Draft Dodgers

The Times, They Were A-Changin'

From the perspective of distance, 1968 can be seen as a seminal year in the United States. Much like other years in our country's cultural DNA—1941, 1945, 1963, and 2001—it evokes the question, "Where were you?" As in, "Where were you when the Japanese bombed Pearl Harbor? When FDR died? When they shot President Kennedy? On 9/11?" For those whose memories are indelibly stamped with the turmoil of 1968, often dubbed "The Year the Dream Died," the questions become, "Where were you when they killed Dr. King?" or "Where were you when they shot Bobby?"

While 1968 was only the climax in a decade of growing unrest, it marked the turning point for a generation of kids born during or post-World War II to parents who had lived through the Great Depression. They were raised during the affluent 1950s, and thus were teenagers when President John F. Kennedy told them not to ask what the country could do for them, but to ask what they could do for their country. Poised to go to college, many took it to heart, joined civil rights protests, and questioned whether their country was headed in the direction they had hoped Kennedy could take it.

According to well-documented social histories by Judson Jerome, Timothy Miller, Irwin and Debi Unger, and Todd Gitlin, the youth of America lost heart following the tumultuous 1960s. Unable to sense that their activist approach to civil rights had been effective, disheartened by the assassinations of Martin Luther King Jr. and Bobby Kennedy, and shaken by the violent riots and urban fires that followed King's death, young people across the country began to drop out. Disgusted by the brutal attacks of the Chicago Police Department during the Democratic National Convention, and horrified by the intensification of the Vietnam War and the bombing of Cambodia, they set off to create a new world for themselves. Despite mainstream stereotypes, it wasn't necessary to take drugs to drop out; their way consisted of a new way of life, a philosophy, a rejection of the current state of affairs. It was, for them, a matter of survival. If they couldn't change things, they could simply stop participating.

To the dismay of their parents, many sons and daughters were drawn to urban centers like New York City or San Francisco—the bicoastal meccas for many a flower child—where some spent dissipated years in a purple haze of marijuana or harder drugs. Others chose a rural life for their self-made utopia. While this dream was hardly a new one in our history, the 1970s back-to-the-land movement was one of the largest.[1]

Nationally, the numbers of those who went back to the land are staggering, even if the counting methods were somewhat imprecise. Jeffrey Jacob, in New Pioneers, and Timothy Miller, in *The Hippies and American Values*, both reported that by the end of the 1970s the number of those living on the land, either in communes or as independent homesteaders, topped one million in rural North America.[2] Enclaves of homesteaders dotted the U.S. map in rural areas of California, Oregon, Washington, New Mexico, North Carolina, Tennessee, Virginia, and Maine, among others.[3]

This migration contributed to a dramatic population shift in West Virginia as well. Census figures from the West Virginia Department of Health and Human Resources's website reveal that the only decade in the state's last fifty years to see a significant increase in population was the 1970s, when it swelled by more than 200,000. Of those, 110,000 were added through the influx of newcomers. While one might assume an increased demand for coal production accounted for this population growth, the West Virginia Coal Association reports employment in coal production in West Virginia actually decreased from a high of 125,669 miners in 1948, to only 41,941 by 1969. During this period, coal production did climb steadily, no doubt because of more sophisticated mining equipment and the advent of strip mining. Yet, in the 1970s, less than 10,000 names were added to coal mine employment rosters, only 0.05 percent of those new arrivals.[4] Although at least 10,000 of the other newcomers who came in the late 1960s and early 1970s were predominantly middle-class and college-educated young people searching for a better life in the hills,[5] many are those whose contributions made a significant impact on the state's cultural climate. Were they back-to-the-landers? No doubt a large number were.[6] And although this influx cannot be attributed solely to the back-to-the-land movement, it did help reverse an alarming trend of out-migration by the state's youth that had begun in the 1950s and continued unabated in the 1960s.

But why West Virginia? Until John F. Kennedy swept through the state's hills and hamlets on his way to the White House, the characteristic but geographically ignorant rejoinder, "Oh, I have a cousin in Richmond," usually followed a resident's admission that he or she was from West Virginia. The Mountain State only hit the consciousness of most folks after President Lyndon Johnson "discovered" the poverty that still exists in many quarters of the state. Suddenly swarms of reporters came in search of poignant scenes of deprivation for the evening news. But along with the poverty and hardscrabble lifestyle, they showed the country another side of the state as well. Those rural scenes of remote hollows, old-growth forests, dirt or gravel roads, and clapboard farmhouses looked to some like a safe place to live if the world went to hell in a handbasket, as many thought it might. Many of those who came cite the Vietnam War as the impetus for their flight from the cities. Some talk of the rise of crime in the cities or their disillusionment with an increasingly materialistic society.

For others, it was the beauty of the place where they had vacationed as children. Once they'd camped under the stars, fished in a pristine stream, canoed the swift waters of the New River, or seen the tender spring-green trees that give rise to the annual hope that life will be better next year, they were hooked. They threaded their cars along narrow two-lane roads, where mountains rise up protectively on one side and valleys drop off precipitously on the other, to begin a new life in the hills.

The romantic ideal of leaving a lighter footprint on the earth by living off the land drew the majority of those who came as part of this national movement. Their dreams were bolstered by the 1968 debut of the *Whole Earth Catalog*; by articles in the new publication, *Mother Earth News*; or by the homesteader's bible, Helen and Scott Nearing's *Living the Good Life*. Dedicated back-to-the-landers, searching for a place to build their alternate lives, found a story touting cheap land in West Virginia in the third issue of *Mother Earth News*. Its May/June 1970 feature article, by Lawrence Goldsmith, boasted "much inexpensive acreage" in West Virginia and described newly purchased land in Lincoln County for which he paid only twenty-nine dollars an acre.[7] The story prompted many to give the state a look, and they liked what they saw.

Joe Chasnoff – Furniture Maker

About two hundred yards off the hard road, at the end of a winding, bulldozed trail, a truck sits in the clearing. More rust than paint covered, it seems destined to dissolve eventually into the mud. It is March on Peter's Mountain in Monroe County, West Virginia, where spring days often begin with sun-filled promise and dissolve into a cold drizzle. This is one of those days. The cool, fertile scent of forest loam fills the air, a hint of the ferns and mayapples that will soon reappear.

As I walk toward the house at the edge of the clearing, two mixed-breed dogs rush into the rain, defending the gate with furious, discordant yapping. As one dog's bark partially overlaps the other's, it sounds like a canine version of "Row, Row, Row Your Boat." Within moments, the screen door squeaks and then slaps shut. A man appears on the porch and gives a sharp, one-note whistle through his fingers. The staccato barking ceases immediately. The quiet that replaces it is as complete as if I've gone deaf; then, as the woods' creatures regain their composure, the delicate trilling, chirping, and foraging in the leaves begins anew.

The gate, cobbled together from metal rods and chicken wire, is clammy and cold. Inside the yard, the dogs dance around my legs, flipping mini-mud balls on my pants from their thick plumed tails. The alpha dog, an overly friendly black Shepherd–Lab combination, reeking of wet dog and dirt, bumps me several times with his butt while the small terrier type trails behind. Despite my efforts to sidestep his furry bulk, the big guy steps on one of my sandaled feet, his toenails leaving four red streaks on it. In a few steps, I reach the modest frame house, but my feet are soaked, my shirt is sticking to my back, and I'm beginning to shiver.

"Hi, I'm Joe," says the slight man, taking my cold hands in his very warm, rough ones. "Sorry about the dogs. Let me get you a towel."

As I follow Joe Chasnoff inside, I silently bless him for leaving the dogs behind. Joe is dressed for work, not a social call, although it occurs to me that the outfit is probably a daily choice, regardless of what he's got planned. His knee-stained and slightly hem-frayed khakis look as if they've never seen the flat side of an iron. Under his unbuttoned tan poplin shirt, the faded *Tree Huggers Ball 1999* T-shirt marks him an environmentalist. Despite his thick-soled boots, he crosses the kitchen to get me a cup of coffee with a tread so light that he hardly makes a sound. It's a cat's walk, or that of one who prowls the woods.

He sits and faces me across the silk-smooth table, which he humbly admits building, and slides the mug of coffee in my direction. I cup my hands around its warmth and lean into the rising steam. It holds a hint of chicory. His smile, under his grizzled beard, is broadly mischievous, his voice high-pitched and nasal. "So, tell me again what we were going to talk about?" His inflection rises to a question mark at the end of what should have been a sentence. As I explain why I want to hear what brought him to West Virginia, Joe drinks his coffee with measured sips, as if to savor each drop.

Then it is his turn. As he leans toward the tape recorder between us, I catch the fragrance of his soap and notice that his collar-length hair—thick and curly, but neatly tucked behind his ears—is still damp.

"Granddad was a lawyer, Dad was a lawyer, and my uncle was a lawyer. It was like, you're going to grow up and join the law firm or something. I had looked at the world and thought that things really needed to change. I thought that the values were screwy. The Vietnam War had a huge impact upon me." He has a flat-vowelled accent that screams midwesterner; however, with his receding hairline, rimless glasses, and grey-streaked beard that curls beside his ears, he looks more like the Hassidic Jews in New York than one of West Virginia's preeminent furniture makers.

I interrupt, "Did you protest at Columbia?"

"Yeah," he admits matter-of-factly. For two hours, I listen to his story, unmindful of the cold breeze from the open door blowing across my legs, the drizzle outside, or the mud stains on my pants.

To put his story in its historical context, consider that in 1968, spring fever largely went missing on New York's Columbia University campus. It was as if the dark clouds of unrest had disturbed the natural order of things. During the last week of April, rather than turning their thoughts to love or final exams, many students spent their days engaged in protests. Their attention was focused both near and far, and they saw plenty to protest. As a slim, dark-haired boy of eighteen, Joe had left suburban St. Louis to study English literature at Columbia and to see what metropolitan life was all about. However, he soon found himself responding to a different vibe and joined the campus protesters.

The country was in political turmoil, to say the least. Less than a month before, facing an almost overwhelming antiwar sentiment, President Lyndon B. Johnson had announced to the nation that he would not seek re-election. On April 4, Martin Luther King Jr. had been assassinated in Memphis, where he had gone to rally support for the striking garbage workers. Subsequently, black neighborhoods in more than one hundred cities had exploded in violent response. Now Bobby Kennedy was traversing the country stumping for the job his slain brother had held, and Senator Eugene McCarthy was attracting the support of young people everywhere in his bid for the presidency. Some even shaved and cut their hair, going "Clean for Gene."

By the time Joe arrived on the campus, two groups, Students for a Democratic Society (SDS) and the Students' Afro-American Society (SAS), and others not affiliated with any group, had been demonstrating against several issues: the Vietnam War, the university's defense contracts, and the CIA recruitment of Columbia's upperclassmen. One recent protest had been in direct violation of a new university prohibition against demonstrating indoors. In the newest affront to the upstart radicals, as they were

called by President Grayson Kirk, the administration had announced plans to build a gymnasium on a public park between Morningside and Harlem, against the wishes of the nearby area's predominantly black residents. In February, when ground was broken at the site—a park in Morningside Heights customarily used by the Harlem youth as a recreation spot—the neighborhood protests began.[8] The two student groups, SDS and SAS, took up the cause.

Although the gymnasium construction project was the initial issue that sparked campus-wide chaos, it soon burgeoned into much more. In late March of 1968, Mark Rudd, who went on to help form the militant breakaway faction, Weatherman or Weather Underground Organization, was elected as Columbia's SDS chapter chairman. That same semester, Joe Chasnoff shared a fencing class with Rudd. The radical Rudd had been tagged earlier as a rabble-rouser for leading a demonstration in the offices of President Kirk. The previous week, he had snatched the microphone from Kirk's hand during the Martin Luther King Jr. memorial service on campus. After railing against what he considered the hypocrisy of the administration over the gymnasium affair, he walked out of the service, accompanied by about fifty other sympathetic students.[9]

Now, at an April 21 meeting, Joe and nearly one hundred other SDS members listened while Rudd agitated for action instead of consensus building. While Joe agreed with the chapter's positions against the war and against the plan to build the unpopular gymnasium, he thought the action under consideration that night—taking over the campus buildings in protest—was a very bad idea. And, although he had been right in the center of previous protests, this time he was the chapter's lone dissenter. "I was the one voice saying, 'No, we shouldn't take over the buildings,'" Joe recalls.

Nonetheless, his involvement in the Columbia campus protest movement proved to be a life-altering experience for Joe and his roommate, who wasn't an SDS member. Despite his non-participation, Joe was caught

Columbia students occupy Low Library, April 1968. Courtesy of Columbia University Archives, Columbia University in the City of New York.

in one of the buildings that the protestors barricaded when the campus takeover occurred. After the eight-day standoff ended when Kirk called in more than a thousand New York City police, university officials dismissed school for the rest of the semester because they believed if they put the students back together, violence would erupt again. Students who were enrolled in any class were given a passing grade.

Joe was terrified when the NYC police attacked. "I was involved in the whole protest scene and watched while students and professors who were in those buildings got brutalized by the police. It was a violent scene. The police rampaging through the buildings and through the campus, riding their horses, cracking professors over the head with their nightsticks from horseback as they ran to get out of the way. It was awful," he says. When the police approached wearing gas masks and carrying nightsticks, he realized that a very thin thread divides law and order from chaos. Seeing Americans beating other outraged Americans suddenly made him want to stop living in the city. He wanted someplace safer, somewhere he could survive if law and order broke down completely, as he was afraid it might.

When the school was closed, Joe left Columbia and went home for the summer. He married and returned in the fall, but lived off campus. The events of the previous spring had made him and his wife, Judy Azulay, think more seriously about what their lives would be like. Upon graduation, they longed for a place that would be safe, a good place to raise kids. Joe still had some form of military service facing him, however. They eventually wanted to be away from the city, but in the meantime, they moved to Philadelphia.

"When I graduated, I moved to Philadelphia to be near the American Friends Service Committee. It looked like the right place for me to find work as a conscientious objector," he says. Although Joe was prepared to serve two years as a CO in lieu of military service, the implementation of the national draft lottery system changed all that. His birthday provided him a lottery number that put him out of range of the draft and eliminated his need to serve at all. Because he had spent his senior year expecting to be a CO, he hadn't given much thought to a career. Therefore, when he graduated with an English degree but no teaching certificate, he decided it was the perfect chance to do whatever he wanted to do. And what he wanted to do, he realized, was build furniture.

As an adolescent in Illinois, Joe was taught to work with wood by a German violinmaker who held woodworking classes at the local Jewish temple or in people's homes after school. For two years, Joe studied in his basement with the old man, learning all about hand tools and the old-fashioned ways. "I loved the time that I spent and I loved what I learned there. I hadn't thought about it for a long time, but in my senior year of college I had built, with these little simple tools, a table that I needed for that apartment." When he moved to Philadelphia, he took the opportunity to start buying tools and making simple furniture reproductions. "I spent three years there looking at handmade furniture and antiques. I would go into antique shops and just crawl around underneath the desks and cupboards. I pretended I was going to buy something and take notes on it. I really learned. I was right out of school. I was still in that frame of mind of absorbing things and studying things, and it was a great environment for it."

He started making pine reproductions of dry sinks and nightstands and was able to sell them through connections with the psychology department at the University of Pennsylvania. The married graduate students couldn't afford to buy much, but they needed basic furniture. Joe started making the pieces they needed and put every penny back into more tools. In three years, his business was making a little money, although he discovered that the price of hardwood in the city was almost prohibitive.

On a chance camping trip to West Virginia, he started buying wood from farmers who had a stash of lumber rotting outside their barns. Sometimes they just let him pick through it and have the good stuff, free. At an old-fashioned circular sawmill in Franklin County, he met a young man, Allen Ritzman, who was raised in the area. They started talking about the future and how to make a living from wood. Ritzman—later a prominent wood-turner himself—told Joe about the relatively inexpensive land in Monroe County. Subsequently, Ritzman came to Monroe County, found a homestead, and encouraged Joe to join him. Joe and Judy traveled around, looking like nouveau-pioneers in a Jeep truck with a canvas-covered back-end, until they found the land they wanted to buy.

Joe still lives on one of the two tracts, totaling 160 acres, which they bought. The couple is divorced now, but Judy still lives on the other. When they arrived, there was no house on the land. Joe recalls, "A local old-timer West Virginian from this area, Lo McMahan, took us in. He lived adjoining that land we were trying to buy. We had met him when we were camping, and he was great to us. He said he knew where we could live in an old farmhouse in exchange for working on it and fixing it up." They moved into the one hundred-year-old farmhouse in 1972 and lived there for six years while they worked on it. The house burned just after they moved into Joe's current home in 1979. By then, he and Judy had a daughter, Jessica.

Anticipating that they might not be able to sell as much furniture in Monroe County as in Philadelphia, the couple had begun making kitchen gift items that were carried by galleries and shops between West Virginia and there. Spice jars were a particularly big seller. They also participated in the Mountain State Art & Craft Fair for a few years, but managing that with two small children proved difficult. Mostly they relied on wholesale orders from established customers, making the work on the porch of the old house and shipping it by UPS. Joe admits, however, "The only way we survived was because of the McMahan family. They started teaching us how to survive, how to live out here—what you can eat, how to skin a deer, trade vegetables. In turn we helped them tie up tobacco. Lo McMahan pedaled vegetables out of the back of his pickup truck around the neighborhood. At the end of the day, he'd come and drop off some stuff that didn't sell." The Chasnoffs gardened too, and Lo helped here as well, telling them not to plant their garden under a walnut tree. Joe still gardens, although keeping the deer out is a bigger problem than where to put the tomatoes and corn.

They spent the first winter without a wood stove, electricity, or running water, cooking in one of the farmhouse's two big fireplaces while they worked to insulate and wire it. They hooked up a plastic pipe to the spring across the road and got their water there. But they didn't have a bathroom.

Joe Chasnoff, 1975.

Although Joe was very engaged in his woodworking career when he came to West Virginia, it was definitely all about coming here to own a piece of the woods and to have material to work with. It was a plan in progress, he admits. "Get some timber land, learn about a milk cow, make hay, raise tobacco," says Joe, ticking them off on his fingers. He tried raising the latter to supplement his woodworking income, but lost most of the crop because the barn he built in which to dry the leaves didn't have sides. A high wind tore through, shredding it until it lost most of its weight and value.

For the most part, their wholesale business sustained them fairly well, but when the Cultural Center in Charleston opened with its shop, things picked up. Joe got an invitation to make something for a reception following the 1976 election of Jay Rockefeller as governor. He chose to make a big cherry trestle-style dining room table. It didn't sell, as he hoped it would, but it did provide a foot in the door with Rebecca Stelling, then the director of The Shop at the Cultural Center. When she began to buy their work, each order meant a payment on the land they were buying. Soon they were getting commissions for furniture and increasing their wholesale line to include butter trays, sandwich boards, and salt and pepper sets. Many of those items are still included in his current product line.

Again, he credits Rebecca Stelling with introducing his work to retailers in the northeast. She took one of his pieces to a large wholesale show, the Baltimore Winter Market, and came back with orders for Joe from thirteen new stores. "Many of them reordered for several years, so that was big," he says.

When then-Governor Gaston Caperton was considering the concept that became Tamarack, he was introduced to Joe. He recalls the conversation. "He was like, 'Okay, so you're a woodworker down here in Monroe County. Are there very many people like you?' I said, 'Gaston, there's hundreds of us. This is really big. You're really on to something.' I was so delighted for his questions, and I was like, 'You wouldn't believe how big an economy there is, people doing some kind of version of what I do. They're all over the place.'" Joe's work was some of the first to be sold when Tamarack opened in 1996. He was also asked to bid on making the benches in the chapel at Cedar Lakes Conference Center and won the bid. He and Judy designed and built them and the pulpit, despite the fact that, although asked, he had never taught woodworking there.

Suddenly, Joe asks if I'd like to see his studio, and of course I say yes. We head for his truck—the one I thought was rusting away in the rain—and head across the hillside. I hold on tightly as the road sometimes disappears and we cross the fields, mowing down weeds in our path. In a grassy clearing sit two buildings. A vine-covered former barn that nature will one day claim now holds some of Joe's wood. Across the clearing is his studio, filled with more wood, tools, works in progress, and sawdust, which swirls around our feet as we walk. Joe uses a lot of mahogany in his products, but because of environmental concerns and his desire to leave a light footprint on the land, he buys it only from importers who harvest in forests where the amount taken each year is limited.

As we continue our conversation, Joe waxes philosophical about how he succeeded in his quest to live on the land. "I think you had to be kind of tough. I think you had to be willing to tough it out. If you're willing to go out and spend some time, you can find something that you can sell and something that you can eat. You had to really . . . really not want to be a part of the mainstream or not care about money. A lot of us are making a good living now. It's just taken a long time to develop it, and the state has helped." He believes his constant search for knowledge has been his key to success as well. "It's worked out the way I wanted it to because I wanted to keep on learning how to do different things. I like to learn new things and this lifestyle has worked for me. I've had the freedom I wanted to have, and the culture here promotes it. It's not something I have to explain to people. My neighbors around here . . . if I'm doing something different, they're different too," he says as we part back at his home.

In the early days, retirement was never on Joe's mind. Now, instead of making land payments, paying off his truck, or putting his two daughters through Sarah Lawrence and Vassar, he's putting some of his income back each year. At least he was until a devastating fire while he was out of town completely destroyed the workshop I visited and a large unfinished order. With the help of grants from the Tamarack Artisan Relief Fund and the Craft Emergency Relief Fund in Montpelier, Vermont, he rebuilt. He spent every penny of the grants on tools to complete the unfinished work that burned up with the rest. Friends gave him free workspace for eighteen months. Completing those contracts saved his business. Now, although he still maintains his woodworking business through orders from Tamarack and other shops, with a little more time and freedom, Joe is also writing poetry, carving sculptures, experimenting with making wooden jewelry, and becoming the driving force behind a First Day Festival in Lewisburg, West Virginia, which celebrates diversity through performances and provides outreach and education in local schools. "I'm very proud to have helped to build a socially conscious, relevant, grassroots volunteer organization from the ground up, including 501(c)(3) tax status," he says. It's a good life, and it's exactly the one he dreamed of over forty years ago.

Tom Rodd – Potter and Attorney

The Columbia campus takeover in 1968 was by no means the first antiwar protest in the country. In 2006, when I interviewed West Virginia attorney Tom Rodd, the grandfatherly senior law clerk for West Virginia Supreme Court Justice Larry Starcher, recalled the mid-1960s vividly. "People forget that long before there was any Vietnam War movement there was an antiwar movement. At the time of the civil rights movement there was a peace movement," he says as he talks of his tortuous trip from passionate young draft resister to homesteading potter to the Capitol Complex in Charleston, West Virginia.

While Tom's office—full of books, papers, photographs, and mementoes—looks like many other governmental cubicles tucked under the capitol's gold dome, it holds one unusual framed document that recalls his past: a pardon for his draft resistance signed by President Jimmy Carter. And, as I listen to Tom recount those days, I can see the idealistic teenage protester behind the silver beard and crow's-feet-lined, but still intense, eyes. At sixty, the boy rebel is still visible. His dress of choice is jeans and Birkenstocks, albeit it is "casual Friday" in the state's halls of justice. No hint of regret tinges his voice. Instead, he counts his actions as Gandhian.

"I had been hanging out with other people who had been doing similar sorts of things: climbing on Polaris nuclear submarines, participating in peace walks to Moscow, and all kinds of romantic peace movement stuff. I knew people who were in prison in World War II as pacifists because they thought that war was really fighting for the rich and for the power of these countries to rule all over the world. Whether you believe it or not, I was a pacifist," he says.

As an Episcopalian teenager who was introduced to the Quakers' pacifist ways in high school, he was actively engaged in both the peace and draft resistance movements in his hometown of Pittsburgh. The eldest son of Kennedy speechwriter William H. Rodd, seventeen-year-old Tom had felt the charged air of liberal politics at home. His father, long involved in Democratic politics in western Pennsylvania, went to work at the White House after Kennedy was elected, returning on weekends to his wife and children in Pittsburgh. Tom recalls,

I got involved in draft resistance and I saw the draft as part of that militarizing America. Vietnam wasn't even on the national radar screen when I turned eighteen. It wasn't on mine, but I refused publicly to register for the draft. I sat in at the U.S. attorney's office and insisted that he arrest me as a protest against military conscription. So, I got arrested. For sort of a middle-class kid to have all this happen was crazy, but my parents were very supportive.

He pled guilty and received a five-year prison sentence. However, after he spent the summer of 1964 in jail in Pittsburgh and two months at the federal correctional institution in Ashland, Kentucky, they offered him a deal. "They said they would put me on probation if I would agree to work for a social service agency like a conscientious objector. Then they said, 'Would you register for the draft?' And I said, 'No, I won't.' But they let me out anyhow on probation."

Tom moved to Philadelphia to work for a Quaker social service organization, packing clothes to go to refugees overseas until the Vietnam War began to heat up. In April 1965, one month after the United States sent the first combat troops to Vietnam, the SDS staged its first demonstration. At this orderly event, sixteen thousand people picketed the White House and marched on the Capitol. Later that year, thirty-one-year-old Quaker Norman Morrison committed suicide by self-immolation in front of Secretary of Defense Robert McNamara's Pentagon office to protest the U.S. involvement in Vietnam.[10] Tom Rodd was paying attention.

As the war escalated, so did the number and vehemence of the protesters. Tom read about these demonstrations and others, about people burning their draft cards, and monks burning themselves in the streets of Saigon. "At that point I just said, 'Man, I think I'm on the wrong track here. I need to get back to where I was.' It was even more important now for people to try to speak out powerfully by doing civil disobedience against the Vietnam War. I told the probation officer I was going on a demonstration, which was forbidden," Tom continues. Nevertheless, he did demonstrate and was arrested in Philadelphia at a plant that made helicopters for use in Vietnam. Amid lots of hometown publicity, he was brought back to Pittsburgh, tried, and sentenced to a four-year prison term. Tom is very clear about the reasons for his protests. He says, "The first time it was sort of general pacifism, war draft resistance, and the second time it was a specific Vietnam protest."

Tom's youthful demonstrations foreshadowed the larger national antiwar movement. Few protested when the United States quietly sent advisors to South Vietnam and established the first U.S. military council in 1962.[11] But five years later, a massive March on the Pentagon, the culmination of five days of nationwide anti-draft protests organized by the National Mobilization Committee to End the War in Vietnam, brought more than one hundred thousand to Washington on October 21, 1967, for their march and subsequent rally at the Lincoln Memorial.[12] Tom wasn't able to participate, however. He was in prison. While he was there, dozens of campus uprisings erupted in the two years following the Columbia University protests.[13]

Tom wasn't at the Democratic National Convention when it became center stage for antiwar protesters, either. It was August 1968. The protestors were hell-bent on forcing the party to adopt a plank calling for an unconditional end to all bombing of North Vietnam. Absent adoption of their demands, they planned on disrupting the Chicago gathering. Alerted, Chicago mayor Richard Daley ordered barbed wire and chain-link fencing erected to surround the International Amphitheater, site of the convention. Daley had his entire police force of more than 11,000 scheduled on rotating twelve-hour shifts, along with over 5,000 Illinois National Guardsmen at the ready. Another 7,500 army troops were placed on standby in anticipation of the trouble Mayor Daley believed would result from the influx of an estimated 100,000 protestors.

Neither did Tom see the shooting and death of the seventeen-year-old in hippie garb in nearby Lincoln Park, though he heard about it. Like the rest of America, he listened to news reports that a curfew was to clear the park each evening, even though peaceful demonstrations by the protestors were still allowed. He knew jeeps with barbed wire on the bumpers were being mobilized and sent to hot spots where protesters were shouting anti-war slogans and waving banners. On Sunday, the chant turned to the now famous, "Hey, hey, LBJ! How many kids did you kill today?" That night about a thousand protestors refused to clear the park until they were met with an estimated five hundred policemen with busy nightsticks. And the convention had not yet begun. Clashes between the protestors and the police continued for the next two evenings as the crowd became increasingly unwilling to obey the curfew. Tear gas attacks, injuries, and arrests followed.

By Wednesday, when the convention was scheduled to vote on the platform, an estimated fifteen thousand had moved into Grant Park, across from the Conrad Hilton Hotel, for a rally. When a shirtless, long-haired young man lowered an American flag, something snapped in the ranks of the tense police and they charged into the crowd, swinging clubs wildly. Demonstrators were clubbed to the ground and arrested. Undaunted, protestors began marching toward the hotel chanting, "The whole world is watching!" The police fired tear gas then charged the crowd, clubbing anyone they encountered. The rest is history, captured by television cameras and broadcast into millions of homes across America. For the next half hour—from eight to eight thirty in the evening—America witnessed the breakdown of law and order in Chicago. Over 100 people were injured and more than 175 were arrested.[14]

This was one protest Tom Rodd sat out. After serving eighteen months in the Petersburg Federal Reformatory in Virginia, he had been released on parole. "Many of our war-resisting friends spent that summer of 1968 protesting," he says, "but I was burned out at the ripe age of twenty-two and looking for a calmer and more risk-free existence. So I worked for the summer at a pickle farm in New Jersey until it was time to return to college."

When a Quaker friend who taught at Berea College in Berea, Kentucky, invited him to come speak about his experiences, he declined, but said he *was* interested in attending college. She then invited him to apply there, and with the assistance of Berea's president, Willis B. Weatherford, also a Quaker, he was accepted as one of the non-Appalachian students in 1968.

It was there Tom became a potter. Berea College is known for requiring all students to work during their college career, instead of paying tuition. He began his student labor stint slinging a mop, but when Berea's student pottery industry opened, he jumped at the chance to learn to throw pots. His major, industrial arts and agriculture, satisfied a desire to learn how the world worked. He was through, he thought, with intellectual things. Although he didn't think of himself as artistically inclined, he did have an interest in mastering a craft. Pottery was his opportunity to do just that.

After three years, however, Tom was tired and really didn't want to complete his college degree. While hiking part of the Appalachian Trail on their honeymoon in 1968, he and his wife, Judy, had visited an electricity-free log cabin built by a back-to-the-lander. In retrospect, he concedes the experience sowed the seeds for their future interest in the homesteading life. When he finally dropped out of college in 1970, they moved into an old log building on the Hampshire County, West Virginia, farm her family had owned since the 1890s, with plans to homestead and live on his income as a potter.

With no electricity, Tom threw pots on a kick wheel for about seven years, selling them in the lucrative Washington, D.C., market. He didn't take orders; instead, he would drive to D.C., unpack at each store, and sell

Tom Rodd firing raku pottery, 1973, Hampshire County.

what he had. "By the time I was done unpacking four or five stores, the newspaper was pretty crumpled up," he says, laughing. For a while, he fired his pots in wood kilns, then switched to propane. In 1975 the family—now with three children—moved to Greenbrier County, where they bought a piece of land and then dismantled, moved, and rebuilt an old log cabin to live in. There, a midwife delivered their fourth child at the Rodd's home. Tom makes a strong connection between their lifestyle and the idea of the peace movement. To him, warfare is related to greed and over-consumption. By living a different way, he hoped he could change things. But after two years in Greenbrier County, the distance from their families in Pittsburgh proved to be too much, so they pulled up stakes and left in 1978. By then he also had decided to abandon pottery as a career; it was making only a subsistence living and the challenge had gone out of it. "I was really doing it to prove to myself that I could make some stuff that was okay, but it wasn't really what I wanted to do," he recalls. "After covering expenses I probably would make five hundred bucks a month, but we were able to get food stamps because we had kids. And we had some help from our families, no question about that. That allowed us to exist." By then he was more interested in making the world better by changing society, rather than by just living differently.

While in Greenbrier County, where old-time string band music was prevalent, Tom—also a banjo-playing folk musician who grew up under the influence of Pete Seeger—produced two series of music programs called *Back Porch Music Time.* "We had a little program on the radio station in White Sulphur Springs, me and a couple other guys. A mandolin player, a bass player, and I organized it. I think we called ourselves the Back Porch String Band and we just had a fifteen-minute program. We were sponsored by the True Value Hardware Store. It was fun," Tom recalls. He then took a tape recorder into the homes of traditional musicians and recorded their music. "I just knew these musicians, or I'd hear about musicians like Mose Kaufman, Jimmy Costa and Karen Mackay, Frank George, Russell Fluharty,

Tom and Judy Rodd on their front porch near Slanesville, Hampshire County, circa 1972.

Doug Irvin, and the Currance family from Elkins. I've still got the tapes. It was a good program."

After leaving Greenbrier County, they settled in Preston County, where Tom decided to complete his college degree. He enrolled in the state's Regents' degree program at Fairmont State College and was pleased to discover that much of his pottery experience would translate into college credits. After taking just a few classes, he had more than enough credits to graduate. Next, he took the Graduate Record Exam and the West Virginia University College of Law admission test, passing both. He had a problem, however: his felony conviction for draft resistance. Told that with enough letters of support he could be admitted provisionally, Tom scrambled for recommendations and was admitted. One was from Larry Starcher, who had told him he'd never get in law school when the two met in Morgantown a few years earlier. He then said, "But if you do, I'll give you a job."

The first day of law school, Tom went to work for Starcher on a work-study program. To support his family during law school, he also continued to make and sell pottery to supplement his income from student loans, worked odd jobs, and received a grant from the National Endowment for the Humanities to produce radio programs for West Virginia Public Radio. The couple tried living in Morgantown while Tom attended law school, but they didn't like it. Fortunately, their nearby Preston County farm hadn't sold, so they went back to it. When he graduated in 1982 with his coveted presidential pardon in hand, Tom was admitted to the bar. The pardon didn't wipe out his conviction, but it did allow him to practice law.

Following several years when Tom worked for a federal judge in Charleston, for the Legal Aid Society in Morgantown, and for a Morgantown prosecutor, he hung up his shingle with Larry Harless, whom Tom describes as a wonderful, maverick lawyer. This began what would become a decade-long career practicing mostly environmental law, winning some high profile cases, and receiving the West Virginia Environmental Council's "Mother Jones Award" for environmental litigation. By 1994, he'd made enough money to get out of debt. "I had paid off my mortgage on our farm, paid off all of my student loans, settled a few big cases, and just didn't want to get back into the rat race of having to work seven days a week, twelve hours a day, fighting, fighting, fighting," he says. The stress of running his own practice was getting to him as well, so he went to work for West Virginia's then-attorney general, Darrell McGraw, heading the Consumer Protection Division of that office. Because it was a three-hour drive to Charleston from their home in Preston County, Tom was home only on weekends.

When Larry Starcher was elected to the West Virginia Supreme Court in 1996, he finally made good on the promise he'd made to Tom some years earlier: he hired him as his senior law clerk. When we met, Tom had been in that position for ten years. Eventually, he persuaded Judy to move to Charleston, but they kept the farm, planning to retire there some day. On weekends, they return to the forty acres and the old farmhouse they've been restoring for almost thirty years. Judy developed a deep personal commitment to a campaign to save the twenty-five-hundred-acre Blackwater Canyon from development. They've had some real success, saving over six hundred acres so far, Tom says.

Political activism still runs hot in Tom's blood as well. In 2003, with the upcoming anniversary of the 1954 Brown vs. the Board of Education Supreme Court ruling, he wrote a play reenacting the first ruling in the United States to hold that racial discrimination in school terms and teacher pay was illegal. The lawyer, J.R. Clifford, was a black attorney in West Virginia who successfully defended Carrie Williams, an African American teacher from Tucker County. After the county board of education reduced the school term of African American schools from eight months to five months to save money, she sued the West Virginia Board of Education for her additional pay and won.[15] Since its inaugural performance, it has been replayed in various locations across the state. Subsequently, the J.R. Clifford Project has expanded to include other educational projects on slavery and the creation of West Virginia.

In 2008, when Larry Starcher's West Virginia State Supreme Court term ended, Tom went back into private practice with The Calwell Practice in Charleston, working mostly on toxic torts. In 2010, he returned to the attorney general's office in the appellate division, handling criminal appeals. While his legal career is a long way from his potter beginnings, it's not so far removed from his early desire to change society. For over forty years, he's been tilting at windmills and knocking down more than a few. But now Tom's mellowing out a bit, spending more time with his family, which includes several grandchildren, and enjoying the land he always wanted to live on. His impact on West Virginia, however, will be felt for years to come in the environmental arena, in the fight for citizens' rights, and in civil rights education. Not bad for an impetuous young boy who wanted to change the world.

John Wesley Williams – Furniture Maker

As the Vietnam War heated up, protesting wasn't enough for some young men. While Tom Rodd found himself on the wrong side of the law when he sat down and refused to register for the draft, others simply left the country. Furniture maker John Wesley Williams decided to take that route. The drive to the top of Butler Mountain in Greenbrier County, where he now lives and works, is not for the faint of heart. As you drive up the narrow, sometimes one-lane blacktop road that winds around the side of this mountain, the drop offs are sharp, the turns, switchbacks. If you dare take your eyes off the road, what you see in the distance are trees, more trees, more mountains, and every once in a while, a clearing where a farmstead has been hewn out of the side of the hill.

This mountaintop is John's oasis of peace, the retreat where he landed at the end of a circuitous route that took him to Canada, Florida, and Maine. Now a renowned West Virginia furniture maker, John was born to an officer on the naval base at Norfolk, Virginia, and was sent to a military prep school in Tennessee, where he rebelled. According to John, he and the school authorities didn't get along. "I had a gross non-military attitude and went all the way from officer to private," he recalls. In college at Tulane University in New Orleans, his protests against the Vietnam War—disrupting an ROTC event on the quadrangle—got him expelled for a year. He appealed and was reinstated. After graduating in 1970 with a math degree, John applied for and received a military deferment as a conscientious objector. Although he suggested several types of alternative service that he'd like to do, he was turned down repeatedly. Finally, because the duties they did assign him made him feel as if he was still supporting the war, he turned in his deferment and left for Canada, as did an estimated fifty thousand to ninety thousand others of draft age.[16]

While John says he had good parents, they weren't environmentalists. John always knew he didn't want to replicate their life. It wasn't that he resented the way his parents lived; he simply wanted to make as small a footprint on the earth as possible. "In college, besides the antiwar activities and going to class, I got really involved in the whole concept of moving back, an alternative lifestyle, and things like that. It was almost like the perfect opportunity," he says of his escape to Canada and a homesteader's life.

He landed near a town called Bancroft, about three hours northeast of Toronto, where he bought 150 acres for only sixty dollars an acre. He returned to the States briefly, convinced some friends to join him, and returned to Canada. "There were eight of us that went up in a 1952 school bus, arriving in Canada in February with five feet of snow and pretty unprepared for anything," John says. Coincidentally, on his first trip to town he discovered that Bancroft had attracted lots of folks like him. Although he says they called themselves "happies" rather than "hippies," the lifestyle was the same. "We wintered out in the school bus, and then the crew who came with me decided it was a bit much," he says. Because they were not avoiding the draft like John, they could return at will. Despite their misgivings, they stayed until spring before returning to the States.

John stayed behind, built a small log cabin, and started farming in earnest. After a couple of years on the property, the bigger city of Toronto beckoned in 1973. He had planned to spend a year there and had secured a job at a Glidden paint factory that he says he was not qualified to perform, but a case of mononucleosis put an end to his plan. "I was living on Jarvis Street—a great haunt for most Americans in Canada—right next to the Canadian unemployment office," he says. While recovering, he went into the office and saw a poster about a furniture design program offered by the Rochester Institute of Technology at Humber College. He applied immediately. Upon learning he'd built a log cabin and a few pieces of rudimentary furniture—one of which he built in the bus, then discovered it was too

big to go through the doors—the college accepted him. After two years of study and an apprenticeship, he saw the way he could live on the land and make a living without ever leaving it. His career path was set.

He returned to Bancroft, built a three-story octagonal log structure to house his shop and living quarters, and began making wooden toys that he sold at Canadian craft shows. The homestead experience blossomed. He bought a cow and a horse, felled and dragged the logs with which he built his workshop and barn, and put out an acre garden. Orders to build kitchen cabinets and some furniture came along, which subsidized his homesteading efforts, and he thought he was set. In 1974, after the Vietnam War ended, President Gerald Ford offered a conditional amnesty program for draft dodgers that required two years of alternative service. Few took him up on it. Then in 1977, President Jimmy Carter expanded the order in the

(Above) John Williams's shop in Bancroft, Ontario, northeast of Toronto.

form of an unconditional pardon, allowing all remaining draft evaders to return to the United States.[17] John was notified that he was free to come home. "Weirdly, I got this letter saying I could come back, but I loved Canada and had no intentions of coming back," he says. "Then my mom got sick." His father had died while he was unable to come home, but now he decided he needed to return. It was 1979.

John went to Florida—his family's last military assignment—and although his mother improved, he felt the need to be closer than in Canada. He sold his Bancroft property and joined a woodworking cooperative in Portland, Maine. After a year, his mother's health deteriorated again, and he returned to Florida, where he met his first wife, Jørn. There he got work making furniture for the 1982 opening of Disney's EPCOT Center. Although he could have continued working there, after a year, he wanted to be on his own. When a friend offered him space in a warehouse where he sold architectural antiques, John opened up a shop and began traveling to shows to sell his own work.

For several years, he made furniture and traveled the East Coast and Midwest to sell it. However, the couple hated Florida and wanted a place that would be central to the shows they were attending, yet give them a rural setting where they could again become self-sufficient. After a show in New York at Columbia University, they rented a cabin at Deep Spring Lake in Maryland for a vacation. While there, they noticed in a real estate brochure the prices of cheap land in West Virginia. Jørn had a good feeling about going there, so she called someone in Lewisburg who suggested they come give it a look. That's all it took, John says, calling Lewisburg "magic." In 1989, they found an ideal place in Clintonville with a farmhouse, a shop for John, and, once again, a group of like-minded homesteaders. He continued doing about six shows a year and in between he could still do the things that were important to him, like gardening and canning.

Following the farmhouse in Clintonville, John had a shop in Ronceverte until a flood inundated it and destroyed some of his work. It was a big setback financially and he decided not to let it happen again. When he found his current five acres in 2006, he said, "Okay, I'm going to get up on top of that mountain and I'm never going to experience this again in my life." He cleared the land, aligned the building north and south to maximize the sunlight, and put in a garden. Outside, the structure looks like a new tobacco barn, but inside, the equipment and trappings of his craft—sanders, saws, drills, piles of lumber, and partially completed work—fill the high-ceilinged space. John, who still sports a ponytail, lives in the second-floor loft above. It's a perfect setting. "I love the trees. I like getting up in the morning and being able to walk out on that porch and touch a tree," he says. "I've just always been amazed at them. And then of course I have a business that requires cutting them down, but I make a point of planting more trees than I use."

In the early days, John sold a cross section of furniture to demonstrate his capabilities over a range of styles. Then for a year he did just sculpture. Suddenly, he knew the direction he wanted for his furniture. About eight years ago, he started carving on the furniture, causing one viewer to dub it Gaudi-like. John's response was that he'd been trying to copy the nature-inspired organic style of the Spanish architect for years. Following a trip to Spain to see Antoni Gaudi's work, John began to put more and more carving into his pieces. "Furniture is very tactile. You can't walk into my booth without touching the wood, so I thought, 'I need to come up with a way of texturing it that still keeps all the beauty of the wood, but then just gives it this extra dimension.'" Now his work is a combination of graceful curves, silky-smooth surfaces, and carved detail, usually built from cherry, oak, maple, and bubinga or African rosewood. He produces only about sixteen pieces a year, working painstakingly on one until it starts to wind down, then beginning another. Although he does take commissions for his sideboards, tables, desks, and armoires, he prefers to sell directly from the show.

And although he travels across the country for many of his shows, in a perfect world, John would never leave his mountaintop. Truth to tell, he's a bit of a loner. His mountaintop retreat provides him most of what he needs. Since he grows most of his own food, his trips into town are few. It's not that he wants to be a hermit, he just loves working and homesteading. All else interferes. Yet in West Virginia, he's found a bond with other artists in the work that he does, rather than with others who homesteaded.

Many of those artists, he says, now have blended into the community as a whole. Not John. His artistry stands out among his fellow woodworkers, and his work has been recognized repeatedly for its excellence. He's received awards from the Philadelphia Museum of Art Craft Show, several West Virginia Juried Exhibition Governor's Awards, and best of show awards from the American Craft Council.

John's website states his creed well. "As a craftsman, I want my work to make a bold and assertive search for an identity. Once my work becomes more of an exploration than an exercise, then every aspect is exciting. Even the most tedious functions are riveted to a realm of possibilities. Each piece I build must be important to demand from me the highest level of craftsmanship. Work this excellent demands a design equally enduring."

After many years, John Wesley Williams may say that he fell into the perfect life, but it was a long path to get there. Now he wakes up excited each day and walks twenty feet to his studio just to see what might happen.

4

Hell No!
We Won't Go Either

Ric MacDowell – Photographer and Community Activist

A lthough they were prepared to do so, not all young men of draft age resisted as vigorously as Chasnoff, Rodd, or Williams. Many others, including Ric MacDowell, chose alternative service—the Peace Corps, Volunteers in Service to America (VISTA), or Appalachian Volunteers— rather than fight a war in which they didn't believe. VISTA was created by President John F. Kennedy and modeled after the Peace Corps. However, the legislation authorizing the program was not passed until after Kennedy's death, signed into law by President Lyndon B. Johnson. The news media loved the concept and reported regularly about the new program.

Ric's interest was piqued when he read the reports. He, like other idealistic youth, wanted to effect changes in the system and was intrigued by this grassroots approach. VISTA was "designed to place individuals at nonprofit organizations and public agencies that are fighting illiteracy, improving health services, reducing unemployment, increasing housing opportunities, reducing recidivism, and expanding access to technology for those living in rural and urban areas of poverty across America."[1]

Once he'd come to West Virginia, Ric fully understood President Johnson's words when he greeted the first twenty VISTA trainees at the White House: "Your pay will be low; the conditions of your labor often will be difficult. But you will have the satisfaction of leading a great national effort, and you will have the ultimate reward which comes to those who serve

their fellow man." These first volunteers were assigned to yearlong place-
ments in the eastern Kentucky hollows, migrant camps in California, and
the slums in Hartford, Connecticut.[2]

One of the most recognizable early volunteers to land in West Virginia
was Senator John D. "Jay" Rockefeller, who arrived in the state in 1964 after
spending six years in Japan, Indonesia, and the Philippines with the State
Department and the Peace Corps. According to his website, his VISTA experiences in rural Emmons, West Virginia, "shaped his public service career and led to his lifelong commitment to improving the lives of West
Virginians and all Americans."[3] Spurred by a renewed interest in traditional crafts that the back-to-the-land movement may have helped spark, his
wife, Sharon Percy Rockefeller, was one of the young women who formed
the nonprofit cooperative Mountain Artisans in 1968.

While Tom Rodd was preparing to enter college in Kentucky and Joe
Chasnoff was worrying about the breakdown of law and order at Columbia University, another soon-to-be-transplanted artisan was graduating
from Grinnell College in Iowa. In May 1968, Ric MacDowell was the proud
recipient of a BA in English from the small liberal arts school, but he had
no clear idea of what he wanted to do with it. What he *did* know with
certainty was that he was vehemently opposed to the war in Vietnam and
didn't want to be drafted to serve there. "I got the *Des Moines Register* every
day, and there was a front page story that said 'VISTA Volunteers Uncover
Vote Fraud in Mingo County, West Virginia.' I thought, 'Wow, that would
be a neat thing to do,' so I applied to be a VISTA volunteer in West Virginia," he says, recounting what brought him over forty years ago to the house
on Harvey's Creek in Lincoln County that he still calls home.

Harvey's Creek is much like hundreds of other hollows in rural West
Virginia. Its two-lane road snakes through the hills for about two miles
after branching away from the state highway that runs through the county's rich tobacco bottomland. A gravel parking area just off the hard road
marks the last spot to leave a car and begin the quarter-mile trek to the
head of the hollow, now posted as a wildlife habitat, where Ric MacDowell
has lived virtually all his adult life. On good days, the sun peeks through
the thicket of saplings and undergrowth that lines the creek and dapples

the grassy path beside it. In harsher weather, the going is more difficult and crossing the plank footbridge across Harvey's Creek can be treacherous. On the far side of the creek the hollow opens to a meadow—sometimes planted in tobacco, today mowed clean—and beyond to a frame building that once was a schoolhouse, now weathered silver and gradually going back to nature. Only the chirping birds and the rustle of leaves break the solitude. The late summer air holds a hint of clover—sweet, clean, and free of city smells.

Against the far hillside sits the one and one-half story frame house, looking much as it did when Ric MacDowell first moved in with the Young family as a VISTA volunteer in 1968. On the welcoming front porch, strewn with tools and a few camp chairs, two dogs sleep in a patch of sunlight. They rouse only to dutifully bark at a scurrying squirrel, or me. Dried wreaths, bleached-white animal skulls, and a Pennsylvania Dutch hex sign decorate the unpainted plank siding.

Upon my arrival, Ric steps from inside, quiets the dogs, and welcomes me with a shout that echoes down the small valley. This is not my first visit to his home, for we served together on the board of directors of the Mountain State Art & Craft Fair (MSACF) in the late 1970s. Again, I am fascinated with the beauty he has fashioned in the simple house without running water or indoor plumbing. Once inside, my eyes dance across the eclectic artwork hanging in comfortable juxtaposition to the rough-hewn log walls. A photograph of a hissing snake, a poster promoting "Honest, Able and Fearless! Al Smith for President," an Andrew Wyeth print, an ancient marriage certificate, and a piece of Hmong fabric art share the available space over a plain wooden desk. Clearly, this home holds the soul of an artist.

We wander into the kitchen, where the open window, topped with a panel of stained glass, frames brilliant red zinnias in the yard below. Across the yard sits Ric's outhouse, recently moved for the ninth time since he took up residence on Harvey's Creek. Birdsong and noisy bees mingle in lazy harmony. Ric sets a heavy kettle on the old gas stove, turns the enamel knobs, and heats water for tea as we catch up on each other's lives and I restate the reason for this visit.

Now, settled on his couch, he continues his story. "I had just graduated and I got a thing from the draft board saying, 'Report.' But I had already applied to be a VISTA volunteer in West Virginia and was lucky enough to end up coming here," he says. Although service in VISTA would not have kept him out of the draft, the West Virginian in charge of the local program helped Ric delay the induction process. Moving initially necessitated his reassignment to a West Virginia draft board, thereby prolonging his reporting date. When that date arrived, Ric had left the family on Harvey's Creek where he stayed during his VISTA orientation period and was living on Sugar Camp Creek near Winfield. This caused further delay until enough area recruits were amassed to hold a group physical. Ultimately, Ric did not pass his physical. Perhaps a sympathetic nurse heard his voiced dread of needles and arranged to draw blood *before* they took his blood pressure, or perhaps he was simply too nervous. In any case, he failed the exam because of high blood pressure and was free to complete his VISTA service.

Ric was placed with a Community Action Program in Winfield to figure out what was needed in the poor, isolated little community of Sugar Camp Creek, but the assignment had no structure at all. Without a specific mission, he became an individual person's advocate, helping the often under-educated, rural poor penetrate the bureaucratic veil on all sorts of issues, from why the elderly folks' social security checks had been cut to how parents could get the school bus to go another mile up the road so their kids didn't have to walk through the mud.

When his proscribed VISTA year ended, Ric returned to Grinnell to serve as the assistant dean of students for two years, during which time the antiwar sentiment continued to mount. Following the United States secret bombing of Cambodia in March 1969, four students were killed in May 1970 by National Guard troops stationed at Kent State University to quell the antiwar protests there. Because of the potential that violence also might erupt at Grinnell, administrators there decided to close early that year and sent the students home.

Throughout this period, the reason he originally had come to West Virginia continued to drive him. Next to me, Ric shifts his position, resting his

elbows on his knees. He strokes his close-cut beard and frowns. "I went as a VISTA because I thought I could change the social structure and make things better, but it wasn't quite as easy as I thought it was going to be. But it did seem like one of the ways to change things was to work with the younger generation. I thought that teaching might be a way to effect social change. That sort of drove me into getting a teaching degree," he says, and his usual grin returns as he relaxes into the cushions once more.

Immediately after completing his master's degree, Ric returned to West Virginia, Lincoln County, Harvey's Creek, and the home where he had first lived in 1968, to teach all subjects to thirty-five students in a combined seventh- and eighth-grade class at a four-room school in Lincoln County. "When I came back into the area in 1972, the family had moved out of the

(Above) Ric MacDowell at the Mountain State Art & Craft Fair, 1974. (Photo by Ben Schneider)

house and it was vacant. I convinced the lady who owned it that it wouldn't hurt her a bit to let me move in and she wouldn't have to do anything to the house. I'd take care of the upkeep. I moved in, and I've been here since," he says with a smile of deep satisfaction.

Although he grew up in the second-largest city in Illinois, moving to Harvey's Creek wasn't the first time Ric had been exposed to a rural setting. Born in Chester, Pennsylvania, he had spent his earliest years hiking around the woods and playing in a creek on the five-acre tract of land where his father had built a house. He says, "I really liked it. Going back to West Virginia sort of rekindled all that." He brought more than a love of nature with him. He brought a Mamiya Sekor 35mm camera, a gift he received at his Grinnell graduation. "I asked for a camera because as a college student I would see other students who were doing photography, and so there were exhibits. I was really interested, especially in people's pictures of other people and what they were able to capture," Ric remembers. "West Virginia is a great place to take pictures, and I took a lot, but really didn't do very much with them."

But when he went back to Grinnell, he sometimes showed his slides to friends who were either students or fellow administrators. One really liked a certain picture, so Ric had a print made and framed it as a Christmas gift. Before he could present it, a fellow administrator came by and wanted to buy a copy of the photograph. That made Ric think that maybe he could do something with his pictures. Before he left Grinnell, he had sold several more. A funky, shoestring gallery in his hometown of Aurora, Illinois, then took his work on consignment while he was at Northern Illinois University for his master's program. Encouragingly, most of the pieces sold.

Knowing that when he returned to West Virginia he'd need to supplement his teacher's salary, Ric contacted the MSACF about exhibiting there. Although he had to convince the jurors that showing how he made his frames met an exhibitor requirement to demonstrate periodically, he was accepted. Ric reflects on that opportunity: "It opened up a whole new world and potential for selling my pictures and sort of spurred me into thinking about doing more photography, doing exhibits in different places, going to other little arts and crafts fairs, and actually developing a career as a photographer. I'm not sure I would have become a photographer if I had gone someplace else. I think the fact that I got my camera, came to West Virginia, and started taking pictures, I sort of learned how to see the world through a camera."

After his initial two-year teaching stint, Ric returned to Putnam County, where he taught middle school, but found the situation there too chaotic. Lured by the idea of a fulltime career as a photographer, he quit teaching after a year. He found, however, that making his sole living that way was very, very difficult. Seems he preferred taking photographs to peddling them. The following year he began to substitute teach in order to support his photographer's habit. He was living very frugally, and raising a big garden helped too.

A sense of community often was the make-or-break factor for many artisans who were able to carve out the life they had longed for. The arts and crafts community had a profound affect on Ric as a photographer.

I was this teaching principal for a year at Kentuk, which is in Jackson County. Barb Brostko, who was married to the potter Michael Brostko, taught there. V.C. and Damienne Dibble also lived there, and Mike had apprenticed for them. During that time and earlier, I had been close to the Dibbles. We would get together and talk about our art and what we were trying to do. Learning about pottery and glazes impacted my photography because I became a little more aware of forms and colors as well as the relationship of shapes.

When Ric discovered the West Virginia Art & Craft Guild, which had formed in 1963 to help artisans find ways to make money apart from the large Mountain State Art & Craft Fair, he joined and eventually became the guild's representative to that fair's board. His community organizing skills surfaced in the 1970s when he became part of the Lincoln School of Design.

There was Marion Hogan, who was a weaver; Lynn Ernest, who was doing batik; Greg Harmon, who did leather; Ann Contois, who did glass; and me. We did that because we were all going to these same little dinky arts and crafts fairs, and it occurred to us that maybe we could just send one of us and they could take everybody's stuff so we didn't have to do all these fairs, and we did. It wasn't real successful, though, because I think one of the things about arts and crafts fairs was that the public wanted to see the artist. But one of the things that sort of helped me grow as a photographer was that we would get together maybe once a month or something. Everybody brought the newest thing they were working on and something to eat, and we would sort of talk about, "Okay, what do you think about this picture? I sort of like it, but I'm not really sure." So, people gave you some constructive feedback and criticism. It was a real nice kind of thing.

Ric's earliest photographs often featured the bucolic scenery of West Virginia rather than the stereotypical run-down shack or the abandoned coal tipple. In fact, he dubbed himself a "nature photographer" back then, eschewing shots with any kind of structure in them. He says that was the way he saw West Virginia in those days, and also that it simply was more like that back then. An assignment from the Benedum Foundation forced him to take more of those bleak pictures, however. That in turn took him back to why he joined VISTA and came to West Virginia—to change the system so it supported people more—and gave him more motivation to solve the problems he felt they depicted.

For nearly twenty years, Ric successfully juggled teaching, community activism, and photography. While most of his work featured the landscapes or wildlife of West Virginia, trips to Nicaragua in 1986 and 1987 at the height of the contra civil war inspired him to create a multimedia slide show on that country and the impact of the war. A similar traveling exhibition of large framed photographs and words grew out of a 1989 trip to the Ituri Rainforest in Zaire. It showed how the Ituri environment and people were being affected by incursion from the developed world.

Initially, he also refused to sell photographs of people, feeling that it was wrong to profit from someone else's image. But the trips to Nicaragua and Africa once again enticed him to capture the images of people. There, he says, they were simply interested in having their picture taken, not in how they looked for the photograph. Both dictums have now been abandoned,

---

(Overleaf) Ric MacDowell, nature photographer. (Photo courtesy of Ric MacDowell)

but he does find that photographing the beauty of the state is a good anti-dote for the wrongs he works daily to overcome.

For ten years, Ric was an extension agent and a faculty member at West Virginia University, where he worked with at-risk youth and directed a wastewater project that managed to put wastewater systems into forty homes in one of the poorest rural areas of Lincoln County. Ironically, it's the same area where he began teaching in 1972. During this time, he also tackled dropout prevention and counseled kids at summer 4-H camps. Working to change the court system so it is more open to having advo-cates in court to assist the disenfranchised is another of Ric's success sto-ries. Now, as the Lincoln County extension agent, he continues the push to bring wastewater systems to additional homes. The reason he joined VISTA—to make changes in society—still drives him. And yet, along the way, he's given the world a view of West Virginia that says these things are possible; there is beauty in this state.

Maybe my photography sort of saved me from getting burnt out by always hav-ing to deal with this terrible kind of thing. The beauty is out there even now. This morning I made a conscious decision I was going to go in a half hour later than I usually do to the office, and I went out and walked around in the fog and the woods as the sun was rising, and it was just great. It was just wonderful, you know, and I couldn't . . . it's interesting because I couldn't . . . it was too dark to take pic-tures, but the kind of structures that I was seeing and the relationships that I was seeing and forms and things. Even though I couldn't take pictures, I saw myself thinking in terms of photographic images that I know sometime later, when I look at something, it's going to come back up and get used again.

And it does. Ric often refers to himself as a nature photographer, but he's much, much more. Although he can capture the exquisite joy of a frog in mid-leap, he's just as adept at showing his audience the enveloping solitude of a foggy morning or the nostalgia of an aging barn. His vision of West Virginia reflects the state in all its glory, through all its seasons, and through the life etched on the faces of its residents. Ric continues to exhibit his work at the gallery at Tamarack and at other regional galleries and shows.

Coming to West Virginia and being a photographer also taught him the importance of stopping: "You can't tell yourself, 'I'll come back later and take that picture, because that picture is there then. It's not going to be there again.' Through interacting with the environment and with the people, West Virginia has taught me that you've got to take the time to do those kinds of things. If you don't take that moment, it's going to pass. Understanding how clearly that applies to photography has also made me understand that it applies to your whole life as well."

James Thibeault and Colleen Anderson – Cabin Creek Quilts

Imagine the culture shock James Thibeault must have felt when he landed in Cabin Creek, West Virginia, in 1970 as a VISTA volunteer. Once, Cabin Creek was a busy coal camp town about forty miles east of Ric Mac-Dowell's Harvey's Creek hollow. In Kanawha County, it lies across the river from the state's largest city and capital, Charleston. In stark contrast to Charleston's cityscape, the rest of Kanawha County has its share of hollows. Rural poverty is a scant ten miles from the stately, gold-domed seat of government. In fact, tiny, unincorporated communities with names more picturesque than the lifestyle in them—Chelyan, Cedar Grove, Belle, Dupont, Cabin Creek, and Eskdale—make up more of the county's geography than does Charleston.

Boston-bred Jamie, as he was called back then, had dark hair worn in an overgrown Princeton that touched his collar, with bangs that fell over his eyes when he moved. His jeans, turtleneck shirts, and Earth Shoes gave him the look of a Beatles sidekick rather than that of a boy who had summered at the Kennedy compound. And indeed, his accent, with its misplaced *r*'s (*Haahvad*, not *Harvard* and *Asiar*, not *Asia*) sounded like the late President Kennedy.

Therefore, James's discovery that most roads in his new home state were primitive, unimproved, or simply gravel-treated must have been a shock. He found television programming consisted of three or four channels at best, with the reception quality dependent on the position of unwieldy aluminum antennae perched precariously on rooftops or hillsides. Telephone

service was not guaranteed. Burger joints primarily were of the drive-up mom-and-pop variety. The now ubiquitous golden arches were nowhere to be seen in West Virginia, but the Burger Boy Food-O-Rama chain, with its spinning satellite sign, was beginning to appear.

Born in Nabnassett, MA, a small town thirty-five miles northeast of Boston, Jamie grew up next door to a family who invited him to their summer home in Hyannis Port for several years during the Kennedy era. Although it was after the president had been assassinated, according to James, it still was Camelot with Jackie, Robert, Ethel, Rose, and the ambassador arriving often. "It was an extremely exciting place to be as a young person, but that also influenced me in terms of my future. I didn't want to become a lawyer or a banker and have a house in Hyannis Port and live in Wellesley Hills or something like that. I was looking for something different. I knew that," he says. "I didn't know what it was. I didn't know what I was looking for, but it wasn't that. I saw real holes in that kind of lifestyle, so VISTA came along and I went to Washington." James had protested the Vietnam War and considered going to Canada or applying for conscientious objector status. But in the end he chose VISTA because it offered him a much-desired draft deferment and kept him out of the dreaded camouflage. Upon reflection, he jokes that the choice saved him. "It kept me from making two tremendous fashion mistakes in the 70s— 'camo' and disco," he says.

James thought the name Cabin Creek sounded romantic. The mountains of West Virginia are breathtaking in autumn with foliage that rivals that of New England, but in the winter, the best that can be said for the rural hollows nestled below those glorious peaks is that they are bleak. Blackened tree branches stripped of their leaves weave a spider's web of shadows on sparse, coal-blackened snow or soggy, bare earth from late November until late April. In poor coal mining communities, or those that used to thrive like Cabin Creek and Eskdale, shotgun houses—long, narrow, modest structures featuring doors at either end of the center hall—sit diminished and forlorn on both sides of the railroad tracks, an

Cabin Creek, West Virginia, 1960s.

ever present reminder of what once was king in these parts. Towns like these became President Johnson's poster children for poverty when he declared war on it. These images, along with a healthy dose of anti-Vietnam war sentiment, prompted many to join VISTA in the late 1960s and early 1970s. No doubt VISTA targeted West Virginia because in 1960 some counties had poverty rates of over 50 percent. In Clay County, the rate was almost 64 percent.[4] Of the thousands who joined, James Thibeault was the only one in his group assigned to a rural clean water study project in Cabin Creek.

The mop-top look is gone now and his hair is beginning to thin, but James still sounds quite Bostonian as he recalls that his first impression of Cabin Creek was a far cry from what he expected. "It was a very grim kind of place. It was absolutely 180 degrees from Hyannis Port, a place of great

(Above) Jamie Thibeault and Tripper.

privilege and comfort. The leaves weren't out, water was rushing off the mountains, and the rhododendrons had yet to bloom. It was an ugly hollow with toilet paper, milk jugs, and everything else up in the trees. It took me a while to figure out how it got there; then I realized it was the high water mark."

At first he lived with a black family, the only folks who would take him, he was told. His quarters consisted of an upper bunk in a tinderbox-dry room overheated by an open flame stove. The family's water supply came from a garden hose stuck through a back window. After a month, he found other housing. With a waterbed and an Irish setter named Tripper, he moved to an apartment above the post office, where he lived for several more months. His assignment: interview the residents to determine the quality of their water. But that wasn't what the ladies of Cabin Creek needed. James says, "I'm asking questions about their dirty water and they're saying, 'Sell my quilts, sell my quilts.' So I went back to my VISTA supervisor who responded, 'We're not going to start another cooperative. There are cooperatives around and they don't necessarily work.'" But these were determined women. They had marched behind Mother Jones in 1912 and 1922. He packed a suitcase and headed back to Boston.

Mother Jones looms large in Cabin Creek's history. After organizing children's marches in 1912 to highlight the issue of child labor in the local coal mines, this firebrand Irish union organizer was charged with conspiring to commit murder and placed under house arrest near Cabin Creek during the violent 1913 Paint Creek/Cabin Creek coal mine strikes.[5] James soon realized these ladies were those very children and they were not to be deterred. "It was very clear to them that a single VISTA volunteer with long hair would not put in a sewage system and water treatment plants," he says. "They told me right out, 'You're not going to do it. Sell our quilts. We need money now.'"

Cabin Creek Quilts developed almost overnight. James invited another volunteer, an art student, to look at the quilts because he wasn't at all familiar with the tradition. According to James, "She was very effusive; she gushed and raved and went crazy about these things, particularly because these were the primitives. She was very excited. That confirmed that this

really was special. That gave them the energy to pack the suitcase for me." He headed back to Boston and the Cape. "I found a shop and sent some notes, one to Jackie Kennedy Onassis. She came into the shop in Oster and bought one and ordered two." With the paparazzi following her, the quilts became big news. "Next, Filene's Department Store in Boston asked if we would supply them and come up and bring some of the quilts to be on the *Today* show, so it happened very quickly." Now James had his work cut out for him. They had no formal organization yet, but orders were coming in and needed to be filled.

Little did he know, but help was on the way. In 1969, Colleen Anderson, now a noted West Virginia singer-songwriter and poet, was a discontented sophomore at Western Michigan University. Despite doing well in the school's honors program, she too had begun to sense the mounting unrest

(Above) Shack in Cabin Creek, 1960s.

in the country. Gradually school seemed boring and irrelevant. Then, she says, "I heard an ad on the radio for VISTA and possibly the Peace Corp. Anyway, it had that Eldridge Cleaver line, 'If you're not a part of the solution, you're part of the problem,' which for some reason really hooked me. I did not want to be a part of the problem." Wanting to be a part of the solution, this gal from Bay City, Michigan, sent away for the papers, filled them out, and forgot about VISTA until a plane ticket to Philadelphia arrived in the mail.

The daughter of a self-employed radio repairman who also installed two-way radios for police cars and fire trucks, Colleen was the first person in her family to go to college. Understandably, when she announced that she was dropping out of school to join VISTA, her parents were very disappointed, but she was undeterred. Colleen left her somewhat rigid, sheltered Lutheran community and flew to Philadelphia, where she trained for two weeks before coming to West Virginia. When she arrived, shortly after James took up residence above the post office, it was winter and snow blanketed the grimy earth. Placed in a household where everybody slept in the same bed except her, where twenty-eight chickens stayed in the kitchen, and where she had to go across the hard road to use an outhouse that was next to the train tracks, she describes it as "an amazing, exotic experience." She will admit, however, that during her first month in Cabin Creek, she frequently asked her VISTA trainer, Vernon Roth, to let her out.

According to Colleen, Roth was from Philadelphia's inner city. He received visitors wearing a blue silk kimono while sitting in his bed at the Daniel Boone Hotel in Charleston. He told her, "Oh, just stay for another day. You're going to be one of my best volunteers." She recalled that this went on for a month. He'd agree to get the papers ready, but he never did.

After a month or so, the house with two beds and twenty-eight chickens burned with everything she owned inside. She moved in with fellow VISTA volunteer James Thibeault and caused their joint eviction from his apartment over the post office. It might have been postmistress Hope Stanley's healthy fear that the waterbed would leak, but according to Colleen, "The notion of unmarried VISTA volunteers living together was probably a more convincing argument for eviction." James described their next house as "even shackier," but it elevated their status among the locals. "As a VISTA volunteer, the more rugged you could live, the more status you had," he says. The bigger house had an electric stove with one burner permanently stuck on "On." They had to chase out the mice and the rats every day.

Assigned to the same water and sewage project as James, Colleen didn't like going out at night to collect samples under the noses of the disapproving coal company bosses. Therefore, when James began the quilt project, she jumped at the opportunity to help. First she wrote product descriptions and made little catalogs. She recalls the first catalog was printed on brown paper and folded up like a map.

At James's urging, they borrowed a rusted-out Boone County Head Start bus, packed it full of quilts, and drove to New York, hoping to show them to buyers of the major department stores. Colleen created handmade invitations, which they sent to Bonwit Teller & Co., Lord & Taylor, and other high-end stores, asking them to come to the hotel in which they were staying. Nobody came. The pair sat there for two days. Now James laughs at his brashness. "We stripped the quilts off the walls and put them on the bus," he says. They drove slowly down Fifth Avenue from Lord & Taylor to Bonwit Teller to Saks Fifth Avenue. "The plan was I'd be out front with the bus. Colleen would go up and get the buyer or someone who would look at these," says James. Although she was terrified, somehow Colleen found the home furnishings buyer and got her to look out the window at the bus. By then the quilt-covered bus had created a huge traffic jam and the police had arrived. Nevertheless, the Saks buyer came down, looked at their wares, and ordered about five thousand dollars worth of quilts, wall hangings, and pillows. ABC also arrived to do a story for the nightly news, followed by a New York Times reporter. The Claude Worthington Benedum Foundation soon provided a new bus that enabled them to travel to retail gift shows in the best suburbs around the country. They formed a cooperative modeled on legal structures the VISTA lawyers provided, got a half dozen of the women to be the incorporators, and elected quilter Lena Hawkins as Cabin Creek Quilts' first president.

James believes their youthful energy and non-traditional approaches caused the cooperative to take off. Certainly his knowledge of the market outside of West Virginia helped as well. For almost twenty years, they sold their handcrafted quilts across the country—often to celebrities—and in West Virginia. While relying on the traditional quilt patterns the women knew well, James sometimes suggested color combinations that would be likely to sell well in contemporary markets. The women's expert needle skills—close, tiny stitches and sturdy seams—made the pieces highly desirable. Although sales took off, Cabin Creek Quilts also relied modestly on grants and was paying only meager salaries to its staff. Most of the money was funneled to the seamstresses. "If there wasn't any money, the director was the first one to do without," he says. And he should know; he was the director for most of its existence. Yet he admits that in bad times the women didn't have the depth of business experience to know how to solve a problem. In fact, he came back twice to work with them when they encountered business difficulties.

The Cabin Creek project also proved to be a perfect fit for Colleen Anderson. "Everything about that VISTA project was perfectly suited for my interests," she says, "and I really enjoyed it. I was able to travel a lot, going out to see old ladies who told stories. What could be better? I felt like I was doing something important. After a year, I signed up again for another three months. I ended up spending fifteen months in VISTA." During that period she moved thirteen times, living in practically every house in Eskdale; at least, she says it felt that way. Although the two VISTAs were looked at with a wary eye for the first six months, and at least one church circulated a petition to get rid of them, they were eventually accepted. One woman, Stella Monk, was like a mother to Colleen. "Stella used to call me her adopted daughter, and I felt about her the same way," she says. Colleen also attributes part of the local women's ultimate acceptance of these young "hippies" to the mere fact that they *did* stay, that they didn't give up and leave the hollow. James agrees, saying he felt protected

(Overleaf, left to right) David Bausman, Sandy Zimmer, Colleen Anderson, Carol Hendrickson, and Jamie Thibeault.

73

by these women. "It could have been trouble for me with long hair in the Vietnam era because their grandsons were being killed or their sons were there or some family member, but I was productive, so in that respect I was doing something for their mothers or their grandmas. I was protected material."

In 1991, Cabin Creek Quilts moved across the Kanawha River to Malden, and in 1994 restored two nineteenth-century houses—one of which was the oldest house in town—to serve as the headquarters and retail store for the cooperative. This effort set James upon an historic preservation effort to restore the home place of Booker T. Washington in Malden. First Jamie worked to create a park at the ramshackle ruins of one Malden home and turned it into The Women's Park, across from what was then Cabin Creek Quilts' retail home. In 1981, two lifelong Malden residents, Martha Cole and her sister Llewellyn, started the Malden Historic Society with Jamie's help. Then in 1998, he had Cabin Creek Quilts construct a prototype salt village, which included a reconstruction of Washington's cabin and school behind the African Zion Baptist Church. For his efforts, he's been called the "Father of Historic Preservation and Tourism Development in West Virginia."[6]

Upon reflection, James sees that real change followed his efforts in Cabin Creek. It's not just the income the cooperative was able to provide the quilters during those twenty years, but a change in attitudes.

If I look at the space of time for Cabin Creek, there are a couple of things that I've seen happen. The women who helped pack that pasteboard suitcase, who had walked behind Mother Jones, lived in tents as girls, and saw blacks being brought in from the south to break their strike and take their jobs . . . I saw thirty years later the next generation of their co-op supporting their next door neighbor in Malden, Booker T. Washington, and his legacy. In a place not far away on Campbell's Creek, where there had been lynchings in the last fifty years, the mentality and spirit had so evolved that there was never objection to my efforts for Booker T. Washington. They saved his church. They rebuilt his cabin. They created a school there behind it. It's a whole compound. You see the sign on the turnpike, and it's probably the most visible African American destination in West Virginia. Then what did they do? They turned around and gave it to West Virginia State University. They gave it to them.

He pauses and shakes his head slowly as his grin lights up his face. "Their mentality had evolved to accept something that would have been totally unacceptable thirty-five years earlier," he says.

James believes being in Cabin Creek taught him as much as he taught the women. "What I learned in Cabin Creek is to identify a product and find a market for it," he says. Since those Cabin Creek days, he's worked to show people in Slovakia how to market their crafts and has traveled to Kenya to do a similar project. There, people sick with AIDS and their caregivers now weave the dead leaves of banana plants into boxes that James sells in the United States.

Following her VISTA assignment, Colleen worked for the West Virginia Commission on Aging before completing her college degree at West Virginia University, to the delight of her parents. Then in 1995 she joined forces with a former college roommate who had moved to West Virginia, Pat Cahape, to form a graphic design business. Although her friend is no longer with the business, Colleen has been doing graphic design and writing ever since.

When she'd lived in the state for twenty years, she became a bit restless and considered moving to the Southwest, an area she had visited often. Before finalizing her choice, she decided to visit parts of West Virginia she hadn't seen previously. She spent six or eight months traveling to state parks all over the state and decided to stay. She says she just fell in love all over again. Now, as a freelance travel writer for the state's official travel guides and their electronic travel magazine, traveling the state is also part of her job. Through her creative shop, Mother Wit Writing and Design, Colleen teaches writing workshops, writes short stories and essays that have been published in leading literary magazines, and has produced two albums of original songs. She currently lives in Charleston. More than thirty years after landing in Eskdale, Colleen claims in her song of the same name, "West Virginia chose me." It was a good decision for both the woman and the state.

Dick and Vivian Pranulis – Wolf Creek Printery

Before there was VISTA, there was the Appalachian Volunteers, formed in the early 1960s by the Council on the Southern Mountains to help fight Johnson's War on Poverty. At its peak in the summers of 1966 and 1967, Appalachian Volunteers was receiving large amounts of federal funding and had over 500 volunteer workers in the field, most notably in southern Appalachia.[7] Although Dick Pranulis was not one of them, he credits that organization with his move to West Virginia. Now co-owner of Wolf Creek Printery, known for its calendars and note-cards since 1971, Dick seems destined to have settled there.

Born in a small Connecticut factory town of seventeen thousand, Dick graduated from Rensselaer Polytechnic Institute in Troy, New York, with an architecture degree. His first misgivings about the Vietnam War came in his senior year after listening to questions raised by a Chinese professor. After graduation, rather than enter the military, Dick chose alternative service and applied to the Peace Corps. When he didn't hear from them right away, he accepted a two-year commission with the U.S. Public Health Service, the equivalent of a lieutenant junior grade in the navy, sans uniform and combat duty. From 1964 to 1966 he worked on hospital designs and prototypes of intensive care units, emergency rooms, and operating rooms for several university medical schools.

His service commitment complete, Dick joined an architectural firm in Washington, D.C., and was on the fast track to making partner—jetting to New York, London, and Milan—when he decided to change directions. "I remember being in this office building in Washington, you know. It was like the tenth floor or something, looking down from this sealed building. You couldn't open the windows. There was a park below. I think it was Lafayette Park. I could see people sitting down there on the grass, reading, and I thought, 'My God, I'm trapped. Those people are having fun. Something's wrong here.'"

As we sip coffee at their dining room table in Alderson, West Virginia, Dick relates how he quit his job, traveled around the country delivering cars, and came on a lark to Charleston, which he thought was beautiful, with his friend David Biesemeyer. David was with a group of Appalachian Volunteers who had settled in West Virginia following several summers of volunteer work there. They were initiating Head Start programs with the help of government grants while David was forming a company called Designs for Rural Action (DRA.) The following winter, on Dick's second trip to the state, he met his wife-to-be, Vivian, and decided to stay. Originally trained as a nurse, Vivian had decided she wanted a career as an artist, so she had quit her job as well. When Dick got a commission to design elderly housing in Clay County, David gave him a place to work. After a while, other DRA projects gave Dick more commissions and enough money for the couple to buy their first piece of West Virginia land. Ultimately, Vivian says, "He was very interested in art too, and he's a wonderful artist, so we decided we would try to make our living with art."

Dick recalls, "That first commission gave us a couple thousand dollars to make a down payment on a farm and have some money to spend for a while. We bought a little place in Summers County for $4,900—seventy acres with a three-room shack—almost at the top of Keeney Mountain, a little place named Hix. My mom described it as a path to the outhouse and a barn and a chicken coop. But the people were very generous in sharing their knowledge." Vivian chimes in to describe an old couple they met when they moved there. "They took us in with open arms. They were so accepting," she says. Dick agrees, "That's how we made it through the winters."

And although Dick grew up on a little farm having to feed chickens and milk a cow, his parents didn't farm for a living; both worked in a factory. Vivian says he's a very good gardener, however. She, too, had some experience with country living outside of Charleston before moving to Hix, but *Mother Earth News* figured prominently in their day-to-day life. In fact, they still have some early copies of the magazine. Dick admits they made plenty of farming mistakes, despite their desire to live on the land, and got by mostly with the help of their neighbors at Hix. "We did that for two or three years before we moved to Alderson," he says. "We were just living hand to mouth; it was a struggle. We had a fifty-dollar-a-month mortgage payment, and it was pretty dicey sometimes coming up with that fifty bucks. Of course, that's 1971 or 1972." To make the payment, the couple started producing and selling batik and silk-screened wall hangings and T-shirts. Vivian was an accomplished artist who had worked for the Job Corps before making the break to develop her painting career.

During one of their first stints at the MSACF in Ripley, West Virginia, the T-shirts, which they had borrowed one hundred dollars to buy at a local store and dyed in a kettle in their front yard, flew off the shelves. Batik turned to silk-screening, and kettle-dyed T-shirts became calendars and note cards featuring scenes of rural West Virginia. Soon the Hix Mountain Trading Company, as their company was called then, was in business. They pedaled their first batch of three hundred calendars on the streets of Charleston. When the owner of the May Shoe Company bought a dozen—at two dollars each—they had their first big sale and their first wholesale account. Once they decided they never wanted to work for someone else again, but to make their living from their combined talents, failure was never an option. Dick says it wasn't that they were any more creative or talented than some who didn't last; it was that they stuck it out. After two and a half years on the hardscrabble farm at Hix, the couple bought a much larger farm in Monroe County.

For years, the MSACF and others events like it, including the Mountain Heritage Arts & Crafts Festival and Mountaineer Week in Morgantown, provided the bulk of their sales, but it was hard work. "Just getting ready, packing it all up in the truck, finding a place to camp, bad showers . . ." Vivian says, frowning. And for quite a few years, they spent most of the year creating the twelve designs for each calendar and hand printing a few hundred of them. Although Vivian had learned silk-screen printing from noted Charleston artist Robin Hammer, she says they were still basically pretty clueless and taught themselves by reading or trial and error. At first they did all the printing in a chicken coop in Hurricane, then in another one in Hix. When they moved to Alderson, they set up in the basement of the farmhouse, a large step up from the chicken coops.

Until 1992, the couple did all the printing by hand. It was such a time-consuming process that it required six months to accumulate enough work to meet the demand. "It took two of us because one person would print and then hand the paper to the other person to put on the drying racks," Vivian recalls. Even after they upgraded to a small press, it took two people to create their annual inventory, and it was tough work physically. When they found a commercial printer who could do all the printing in a day and a half, it freed Vivian to spend more time on the original artwork and Dick to handle the business end of things.

Each calendar or note card is a work of art beyond its functionality. The now iconic calendars feature one large print per month of a painting created by Vivian—scenes of rural West Virginia, spots she's seen and remembered, or the birds and creatures of the state. The blank note cards feature similar designs. Either hanging from a simple piece of twine or punched to hang on pegs, the heavy brown paper calendars are often collected and framed. Because the year appears only on the cover, they can also be saved and reused through the years as a perpetual calendar.

Eventually the couple decided they wanted out of the craft show circuit. With the large list of names collected over the years from their festival customers, they embarked on the mail order business that sustains them today. First they put out a small catalog, and then decided to try operating their own shops. When Town Center Mall opened in Charleston, they were there. When The Greenbrier resort at White Sulphur Springs offered them the tiny building near the tennis courts that Appalachian Craftsmen had vacated for an inside spot, they jumped at the chance. Next they opened a shop in Lewisburg in the old Hardware Gallery, which they eventually sold to their store managers, who moved it to a new location. "The '90s were incredibly busy because we were still doing the calendar and the mail order business, and we were running three shops," Vivian says. "Finally we realized we just couldn't do it all. Our calendar was our true love, so it worked out great."

Dick credits Vivian with pushing them into the world of Internet marketing. "I was really reluctant, but Vivian said 'We've got to do this,'" he says. "The first year we broke even, and every year it's gotten better. Now it's a good chunk of our income." Not surprisingly, many of their out of state customers are former West Virginians who love seeing images of their home state.

It's been forty years since Dick and Vivian printed calendars in the chicken coop at Hix, but their love of West Virginia and its beauty hasn't waned. Now Vivian does most of the paintings for the calendar at their home in Alderson while Dick spends a good bit of time traveling the state looking for scenes to photograph that will inspire his wife. "I don't think this would have happened if we hadn't come here. The mountains and the whole setting inspired our work then and it still does today," she says. "With the calendar, I wouldn't call it a mission, but I just want to portray the beauty of what we've got here."

Adrienne Belafonte Biesemeyer – Weaver, Social Activist, Dancer

The theory of "six degrees of separation" poses that through a chain of friends and their friends you'll find that any two strangers are only six steps away, by introduction, from each other. Adrienne Biesemeyer might agree. She's married to Dick Pranulis's best friend.

Sitting in her office in downtown Lewisburg, she flashes a broad grin when asked how she, Harry Belafonte's eldest daughter, landed in West Virginia. It's then you notice her father's features: the thousand-watt smile, the dancing black eyes, the hint of a widow's peak, and even the touches of gray creeping around the edges of the close-cropped hair. She's a fascinating mix of talents and interests, some, not surprisingly, nurtured by the activism of her famous father. Now she too is a social activist, the Executive Director of the Anir Project, a non-profit organization she founded with her daughter Rachel Blue that works primarily in South Africa, Zambia, Swaziland, Lesotho, Madagascar, and Malawi. The organization does a broad range of things: from taking interns to southern Africa to provide HIV-AIDS education or build houses with Habitat for Humanity, to helping preserve the cultural heritage of a region; from working with kids in the arts, to offering history courses for the universities. Presently, she is a licensed professional counselor and the coordinator for the West Virginia School of Osteopathic Medicine's Center for International Medicine and

Adrienne Biesemeyer. (Photo by Ric MacDowell)

Cultural Concerns. But, in the past, she was a weaver, a dance company organizer, and a dabbler in the arts.

In retrospect, it seems what brought her to West Virginia was her adventurous nature. After graduating in 1967 from a progressive Massachusetts high school, she tramped around Europe for a while and studied textiles in Holland until her parents decided their wandering child needed to settle down. When her uncle Charles Byrd—then a media professor at West Virginia State College—encouraged her to come there, Adrienne agreed, although she intended to stay only one semester and then go back east to pursue her love of art. Instead, after arriving in January 1968, she stayed; it turned out to be a fortuitous decision.

Born in Washington, D.C., but raised for the first thirteen years in New York City and Long Island, Adrienne was exposed to art from an early age. Fine art filled her home; her stepmother, Julie Robinson, was a dancer; and museums were her urban playgrounds. While dance was Adrienne's first love, she studied weaving in high school and then broadened her interests in college, receiving a BA in fine arts from West Virginia State College.

One day, two strangers visited a class Adrienne was taking in which their friend John Nickerson—then a noted glass blower at Blenko Glass in Milton, West Virginia—was demonstrating pottery. The two were David Biesemeyer and his buddy, Dick Pranulis. Although David was supervising a group of Appalachian Volunteers working on a Head Start project and Dick was designing housing for the elderly, both also wanted to learn about pottery. "I just flipped out over him," she recalls, speaking of David, now her husband of forty years. Adrienne says their politics and values were similar—David was a former Peace Corps volunteer who headed the first group to work in the Cameroons—and they just clicked. Born in Missouri and raised in Iowa, David had graduated from the University of Wisconsin with a law degree before coming to West Virginia as an Appalachian Volunteer. Now he is an administrator for the United Mine Workers Health and Retirement Fund, which focuses on health care and pensions for coal miners. And although he's white and she's black, Adrienne says she's never run into any overt discrimination in West Virginia. It's one of the things she loves about the state.

After completing her degree at West Virginia State College, Adrienne attended graduate school in Puebla, Mexico, at the Universitad de las Americas, where she studied art, archeology, and textiles. She turned to dance to support herself, working in the dance studio at the university. David's initial glow didn't fade while Adrienne was away, however, and the couple was married in Mexico while she worked on her degree.

When discussing where to live, the newlyweds decided to return to West Virginia because they loved its beauty and because it was cheaper than New England, which both also loved. At first they lived at Pliny in Mason County, where David was a rural mail carrier and Adrienne broadcast the weekend weather for WCHS-TV in Charleston. Together the pair made about $2,000 a year and subsisted on their small farm. After one stop in Whitesville, they rented a tiny cabin in White Oak. They had just started building a home in Alderson, in Monroe County when Adrienne got pregnant. "The house was under roof and just about finished, but not all the rooms were in. I told my husband that I was not going to bring this baby home to the little cabin we were staying in. As a good back-to-the-lander, I wanted to be in my own house. He went off to work in the morning, and I had our friends come over and pack the house. When he got home in the afternoon, he went, 'Whoa, wait a minute.' I was moving and so was he."

Once settled in their new home with baby Rachel in tow, Adrienne began weaving full time. She bought a counterbalanced, four-harness loom for $250, which seemed like $2,000 because their income was so meager at the time. But David insisted she buy it. At first she specialized in home accessories like pillows and rugs, using 100 percent natural fibers: cotton, wool, and goat hair. Designing the work was the part she loved best. Initially she used lots of whites and beiges in her weaving, forming rich, intricate patterns.

During this period, she sold at craft fairs, including the MSACF, for two years. However, when a child with a dripping chocolate ice cream cone began touching her nice fuzzy work, Adrienne began to rethink that avenue. Soon her work morphed into art wearables that she sold through

(Overleaf) Adrienne Biesemeyer working in her studio. (Photo by Ric MacDowell)

trunk shows at tony West Virginia women's shops like Schwabe-May in Charleston. She also sold her alpaca and mohair shawls through word of mouth, taking special orders from those who saw another woman wearing Adrienne's work. "David used to do all the knotting at the end unless I was doing something really intricate," she recalls. "If I put beads on them, that was my job. But if it was just a regular knot, like a little macramé finish, he would do that, finish the knots." The Shop at the Cultural Center—a precursor to Tamarack—also carried Adrienne's weaving.

In the early 1980s, wanting to do something different, she stopped weaving—just got tired of it, she says—and earned a master's degree in counseling from West Virginia Graduate College at Marshall University. But despite the space her large loom takes in their home, it still stands, dressed and ready to use. "Once you take them down you can never get them back together again because they warp in shape," she says. "But you know, hey, maybe when I'm about seventy-five I may go back to hand-weaving." Until 2009 she had a private counseling practice in Lewisburg focusing on children and their families. In addition to the international studies program, she is also a learning specialist at the West Virginia School of Osteopathic Medicine in Lewisburg, but when the "I can't sit still" gene kicked in again, along with her daughter Rachel Blue, she formed the project she now heads.

The Biesemeyers live on a forty-nine-acre piece of property that Adrienne loves returning to after each far-flung trip. Her dad calls it Shangri-la. Even though he visits regularly, "It's too Shangri-la for him," she says. "He is really cosmopolitan. He loves to visit, but he's gotta get back to New York City." Not so for Adrienne. Now the East Coast gal wonders how people live in those urban areas she used to roam. When friends back east suggest to her that she's isolated, she reminds them that we are now blessed with computers and cell phones, and that airports are close enough to accommodate travel to most anywhere. She tells them, "The difference is, you have forty-two locks and a security program on your house, and I don't. If I get out of the car and forget my keys in Lewisburg, I don't panic and have to go running back to the car. I realize 'Oh, they're in the car, it's OK.'"

Admittedly, her life would have been vastly different had she never heeded her parents' admonition to settle down, but her philosophy doesn't include that kind of speculation:

We make choices in life and that was an option I didn't take, so it's nothing that I think about. My philosophy in life is that there's always a plethora of choices, but once you've made that choice you go to the next set of choices that follow within that path. The only thing that conjures up something is, what if I'd decided to dance, as opposed to being a weaver, or a teacher instead of a counselor or something like that? But again, I don't even dwell on that. I believe we come to wherever we're supposed to be. I absolutely *love* the place where I live and feel great warmth from my friends here and, you know, it's the life.

Adrienne and David are now grandparents by their son Brian, who has a daughter Bella and a son Gab. Brian's wife is also named Rachel. "It's an enriching experience being a grandparent," Adrienne says.

And West Virginia's life has been enriched by her presence, although she demurs at that thought. Adrienne will tell you that her biggest gift to the state, however, had very little to do with weaving. Sure, she taught a few workshops at the Cedar Lakes Conference Center, where she hopes she inspired a budding weaver or two. But from 1988 until 2005 she headed the Alderson Dance Ensemble, which gave 150 kids, junior high age and up, the opportunity to learn to dance and perform at no charge. The troupe performed in North Carolina and all over West Virginia. Even today she has kids come tell her that the dance company was the best thing that ever happened to them. While she's justifiably proud of that, perhaps the best thing to ever happen to her hasn't yet. Even if her life takes another turn, she says she'll always be a West Virginian. Her eyes soften as she talks. "On the back of the *Greenbrier Valley Quarterly* that they have out there's a picture, a foggy picture of the Greenbrier and all these trees . . . and it says, 'There really is an enchanted forest.' I thought that was a great thing, but as a whole it is wild and it is wonderful. I'm glad to be in West Virginia."

Norm Sartorius – Spoonmaker, Sculptor

Spoonmaker Norm Sartorius and his wife Diane live in a lovely home in an unassuming neighborhood in Parkersburg. Driving by, you might admire the paneled front door with its leaded glass insert, but you'd never suspect it's the home of an award-winning artist whose taste reaches far beyond his medium of choice. Leaded glass fills many of the interior doors; contemporary art pottery, including several crocks, sits on shelves, the floor, the mantle, and the top of a corner hutch. Diane's antique regional pottery collection covers the top of the stereo cabinet. The decor centers around the eclectic assortment of handcrafted items collected during Norm's life on the craft fair circuit. But nestled behind the house, at the end of a tree-canopied path, sits the studio where his true passion lives. It's also where his extensive collection of work of other spoonmakers rests.

There among the saws, clamps, grinders, and hand tools sits a silver-bearded and bespeckled Norm, looking like Pinocchio's Mr. Geppetto and surrounded by half-finished spoons, his current work in progress, and hundreds of wood blocks, boards, and burls of native and exotic woods. A huge tree stump sits on top of the now cold wood stove. More wood is carefully stacked on shelves, and longer boards—both planed and rough with bark—lean against the walls, but a few pieces are close at hand. Norm likes to look at a piece or two until the unique shape or grain speaks to him. Then he lifts it purposefully and begins to rough out a shape, coaxing what he saw within to reveal itself. It may be a weathered spot in the wood he wants to highlight or the color contrast in the grain that suggests the shape. In either case, after hours of roughing, carving, sanding, and rubbing on the finish, Norm will have created another nonfunctional but uniquely formed spoon. It may look more like a human figure, a heart suspended on the end of a sectional handle. Or double ebony bowls branching from the handle body may resemble a bee. Some spoons rest on their sides; others have only a hint of a bowl hidden in the crook of a rough burl. One looks more like a letter opener than an eating utensil.

Norm Sartorius, winter 1975.

His trip to that studio, however, took a route much more circuitous than the path through his gardened yard. In 1968, Norm was starting his senior year at Western Maryland College, now McDaniel College. Although the man from the Maryland shore now realizes he was evolving into a hippie and a back-to-the-lander, at the time young Norm had little awareness of the coming changes. Because the draft was still the law of the land, he followed the advice of his father—a country doctor in Salisbury, Maryland—and naively enlisted after his college's mandatory first two years in ROTC. "Dad said I'd be much better off as an officer than I would be as an enlisted man, so why didn't I go ahead and sign up? That was as simple as it was; I committed myself at the end of my sophomore year to time in the military," Norm recalls. Signing up for two more years of ROTC was the same as enlisting.

But by the time he graduated in 1969, he was thoroughly disillusioned by the events of the past two years, including the buildup of troops following the Tet Offensive and Nixon's secret bombing of Cambodia. Now

(Above) Norm Sartorius, circa 1981.

opposed to the war, he was struck by the wrongheadedness of his youthful decision, but his commitment was irreversible. He reported to active duty at Fort Knox, Kentucky, then refused to cooperate and applied immediately for a conscientious objector's discharge. In his application, Norm had to prove his views had changed as a result of his association with the military. It wasn't hard, and after three and a half months, he was released from military duty.

Following his discharge, Norm returned to Baltimore, participated in antiwar marches on Washington, and worked with the American Friends Service Committee, a Quaker group, counseling GIs who were in the same situation he had encountered but didn't know what to do. Some were AWOL; some felt their circumstance in the military was grim. They were in trouble and needed legal and practical advice to keep from getting into so much trouble they would be in jeopardy of imprisonment. Norm provided it: the names of sympathetic lawyers, the locations of safe houses, whatever it took. In his day job, however, Norm worked as a psychiatric social worker in a state hospital, a field he says he fell into more by default than passion. Although he had a psychology degree, he hadn't really found his place in life. It's no surprise, then, that he didn't last long. He simply quit, dropped out, took the money from his mandatory state retirement fund, and went across country with his girlfriend, Wendy Cronin.

During college, many of Norm's friends had been part of the Study Opportunity Services, a sort of mini-Peace Corps, which sent volunteers to remote villages in Puerto Rico, impoverished Indian reservations, or Appalachia to work on various community projects like establishing trash collection systems and building libraries. Although Norm had never been to West Virginia, upon returning from volunteer stints there, his friends spoke of the beauty of the area and its wonderful people, but also of its poverty and the negative impact of coal mining on the land. After two of their friends married and went to do welfare rights work in the tiny community of Panther in McDowell County, Norm and Wendy headed there. "My girlfriend and I would go visit this couple and got to know a couple of their neighbors," he recalls and then smiles. "It was just spectacular—three-thousand-feet panoramic views of the mountain. I like cold weather and it was colder because of the altitude, a lot of snow. It was wonderful. I liked the privacy and the peace and quiet and the forests."

During one visit, Birdie, a neighbor's wife, broke her leg and the young couple helped get her out and to an ambulance. It was no small feat because the old couple lived at the end of a road passable only by a four-wheeler in dry weather; at other times, walking was the only way. Around 1973, Wendy made a solo visit to the friends in Panther and went again to see Birdie's husband, a retired coalminer and moonshiner. He confided that he might sell his land—his only possession—to prevent his children from fighting over it when he died. Instead, he reasoned, they'd have the money to divide. Wendy told the old guy to let her know if he became serious about it. A year later, she received a letter saying if they wanted a good deal to come on down. They bought his twenty-five acres immediately and moved there in 1974.

The tarpaper shack had electricity, but no running water or phone. Norm says they added on and upgraded from the old man's lifestyle, but not by much. During the five years Norm and Wendy lived there, they did build a new outhouse and got a phone. They also put in a large garden and tried to raise as much of their own food as possible. On the only two acres flat enough to plow, they also had a large orchard with cherry, apple, and peach trees that provided them fruit to freeze and can.

It was there in McDowell County, high on the ridgetop, that Norm started making and selling his woodwork, a skill he had learned by chance. During their cross-country trip, the beauty of some stunning but primitive redwood slab tables he saw in a craft shop in Santa Cruz, New Mexico, caught Norm's eye. He remembers thinking how lucky someone was to get to work with that wood all the time. After returning to Baltimore, he met silversmith Phil Jorous, who owned a craft shop in Towson, near Baltimore. Jorous knew a lot about woodworking as well and was looking for an apprentice he could teach the craft and who would eventually produce work for sale in his shop. The deal was this: Norm would work for Jorous for six hundred hours; Jorous would teach him everything he knew; and Norm's work (if it was good enough) would be sold in the shop with the money going to Jorous. It took Norm about six months to work off the commitment. His apprenticeship ended just as the offer to buy the land arrived, so he packed his band saw and his few basic tools and the couple took off.

Once settled, he heard about the MSACF, applied, and was accepted with some functional, simple pieces he'd made in Baltimore. "Didn't have a booth for the show," he says, laughing. "Didn't have a clue what I was doing. Didn't know. But it looked like fun, and it was what I wanted to do." His smile warms as he recounts those woodworkers at the fair who helped him: Bert Lustig, Bill Reed, and Dick Schnacke.

He's also quick to credit the support the state of West Virginia provided him and hordes of other artisans in those days. "I can't tell you how many people I have told that I was in a state that really supports arts and crafts people. Grants got me to workshops that Tim Pyles provided [at the Cedar Lakes Conference Center in Ripley], got me my very first computer, and helped me buy a lathe for my shop," he says. Rebecca Stelling, who at the time headed the craft shop at the Cultural Center in the state capitol complex, took his work to the Union Carbide Gallery in New York City and showcased it in a booth of West Virginia artisans at the American Craft Council show in Baltimore. He still participates in that show. He also credits the biennial West Virginia Juried Exhibitions with providing him and others with national exposure. "Michael Monroe, the curator of the [Smithsonian's] Renwick Gallery, gave me an award at the juried exhibition in 1982, 1983, or 1984, which led to me applying to the Smithsonian show, which led to them buying work from me for the museum. All that came from state funding for the juried exhibition."

But in 1980, life on the ridgetop ended. Wendy left, and Norm found it just too hard to go it alone. Again, coincidence led him down a new path. At WinterFair, in Columbus, Ohio, Norm met woodworker Bobby Falwell from western Kentucky, who saw Norm's potential and encouraged him to get off that hardscrabble hilltop and come work for him before he went crazy living alone. Falwell was making very sculptural furniture and offered Norm a work-study situation that he couldn't pass up. "I had

---

(Overleaf) Norm Sartorius carving. (Photo by Ric MacDowell)

95

somebody come and live in my house . . . and I never looked at it as permanently leaving," Norm says. "I was just sort of trying to straighten myself out and learn something. I worked for him all day, but at night I had free use of his shop to make my same old stuff." He lived in Murray, Kentucky, working for Falwell for eighteen months until he met glass artist Diane Bosley at the MSACF in 1981.

After a short, long-distance courtship, they married and Norm returned to West Virginia. Although Diane loved working with glass, she also had a regular job in Parkersburg, which she didn't plan to leave for subsistence living. Norm admits to missing the privacy and the quiet of his ridgetop, but knows that as he ages, it's easier and more practical to be in town. It's been a good marriage for both; Norm's had the stability of knowing the bills could be paid despite the prospect of a bad show. After their son Andrew was born in 1987, he was the stay-at-home father. He says it's an opportunity most dads don't have, and that the two are much closer than they would have been otherwise. Having that stable income also freed him to experiment without having to make products for the market. Instead he could concentrate on the unusual and the extraordinary. It has paid off.

Over the ten to twelve years he participated in the MSACF, his work evolved from practical, functional, lower-priced work to the more sculptural, nonfunctional pieces for which he's now famous. Like many other artisans who sold at the MSACF in those early years, Norm's work became increasingly sophisticated, until it was more properly classified as an art object than a craft item. Although the show was fantastic for him at that particular time, as his prices rose, he outgrew the fair.

Initially he sold to Tamarack, but that venue doesn't work for him now. Although he thinks the center is great for the state's artisans, he doesn't like repeating his styles, and that's not conducive to shop sales. Now he sells only to private collectors, at American Craft Council shows, the Smithsonian Craft Fair, and the Philadelphia Museum of Art show, which attract well-heeled customers and collectors. There he can connect with his customers, some of whom have been collecting his work for years and have visited his home. He loves the show life with his friends, who he likens to a bunch of gypsies who gather each year and root for each other to succeed. It's like the old days on the fair circuit, which he sometimes misses. Still, although virtually all Norm's sales are now to out-of-state buyers, he is quick to give the state of West Virginia much of the credit for his national success. By its help in the 1970s through the West Virginia Division of Culture and History, where Rebecca Stelling worked; the craft workshops at Cedar Lakes, organized and promoted by Tim Pyles; Governor Gaston Caperton's Tamarack vision in the 1990s; and the juried exhibitions, the state has been consistent in supporting artisans, he says.

As we've talked, Norm has wandered around his shop, lovingly touching the wood: a piece of afzelia lay from Laos, Madagascar rosewood, black locust from West Virginia. "The wood has stories, you know," he says. "Yes," I say, thinking of the stories Norm's spoons tell of him.

5

A Safe Place to Live

The Putnam County Pickers

"From PRI, Public Radio International, welcome to another performance of *Mountain Stage*, live performance radio from the Mountain State of West Virginia, with your host, Larry Groce." Each week, after this short opening announcement to an enthusiastic live audience, Larry launches into song: "There's a spring in the mountain and it flows down to the town..." He's joined by the sweet voice of Julie Adams: "There's a song in my heart, just a simple little tune..."[1] And behind them the music of the house band—Bob Thompson, Ron Sowell, Ammed Solomon, Steve Hill, and Michael Lipton—swells to fill the West Virginia Culture Center auditorium. Launched in 1983, *Mountain Stage* is the longest-running performance show on public radio and is now enjoyed by an international audience on both radio and television. Moreover, its home base has always been Charleston, West Virginia, yet not a person on the stage is a native of the state.

Originator, artistic director, and host, Larry Groce came to West Virginia in 1973 thanks to an artist-in-residence grant from the National Endowment for the Arts. The Dallas, Texas, native was already a force in the pop music world with his top ten hit, "Junk Food Junkie," and other recordings. Singer-songwriter Julie Adams grew up in Frostburg, Maryland, and was a guest on the first regular *Mountain Stage* broadcast in 1983. House pianist Bob Thompson, who hails from Jamaica, New York, arrived at West Virginia State College as a music major in the 1960s and over the years has become a jazz icon in the state. His trio, the Bob Thompson Unit, has recorded nationally and toured Europe, Africa, and South America. Guitarist, songwriter, and journalist Michael Lipton grew up in Miami, Florida, but moved to a West Virginia farm in 1973.

Andy Ridenour, *Mountain Stage*'s other originator and its executive producer until 2011, grew up in the heart of the nation's capital and came to Athens, West Virginia, in 1968 to attend Concord College. There, he was disturbed to find the college campus still segregated. One of the first students he met was also from D.C.: a basketball recruit who was not allowed to live on campus because he was black. In protest, Andy began an underground campus newspaper, *Speaking Freely*, for which his new friend wrote a column called "From a Black Eye." Through their efforts, federal agents were called in to help integrate Concord's campus the following year. Although he does not call himself a back-to-the-lander, he volunteered alongside friends who were VISTA workers, and from 1968 to 1970, he hung out periodically at the Isle of the Red Hood commune, where he recalls laying a stone walkway from the driveway to the house.

Each of these cast members came independently, but for the rest of the house band—Ron Sowell, Ammed Solomon, Steve Hill, and former member Bob Webb—it's another story. The four were early members of The Putnam County Pickers, the wildly popular, eclectic string band of the 1970s and 1980s, but they also had connections in their former lives. Though their arrival in West Virginia was not simultaneous, it was not coincidental, either. Their migration to The Farm at Coon Creek, near Hurricane in Putnam County, began because a young Greg Carroll (a retired historian with West Virginia Archives and History) spent summers there with his grandparents and fell in love with the land. He had gone to grade school and high school in Fort Worth, Texas, with a fellow named Mike Ivey; in turn, Mike Ivey had gone to Austin College, in Sherman, Texas, north of Dallas, with Bob Webb. When a friend of Greg Carroll's grandfather died in the late 1960s, Greg came to West Virginia, bought the man's ninety-eight-acre ridgetop farm for three thousand dollars, and invited Mike Ivey to join him, which he did. Soon Mike was writing to Bob and another college buddy, Billy Jack Gregg, telling them they should venture north as well. Once there, the new arrivals began inviting others, and by 1973, the Texas migration had begun.

Since I'd been a Pickers fan from the moment I first heard them sing "Vegetable Garden Blues" at the Mountain State Art & Craft Fair (MSACF), and had hired them on more than one occasion, it was like a reunion when I visited Bob, Ron, and Steve to gather the threads of their tightly-knit story. While the original members' stories intersect, over the years the Pickers evolved into several iterations of the original band. Therefore, keeping track of all the members is sometimes difficult. Surrounded by the trappings of his trade—a mandolin, dulcimers, guitars, recording equipment, and his cello—in the sun porch/recording studio at his then-Charleston, West Virginia, home, Bob Webb tells the story from his end.

I grew up in Washington, D.C., and for me that's where West Virginia originally got its mystique. When I was a kid, I would go with a friend's parents on fishing trips to Pocahontas County or around Elkins, and I just fell in love with it. A friend of mine from high school became a VISTA volunteer in the Hinton area. I was real proud of her and thought maybe I should do that, too, but I never got around to it. When we had the chance to buy land, I was sort of at the end of my rope in terms of living in the city. I had taken my social psychology degree and gone to work in mental hospitals in Atlanta and New Orleans, but I was ready to go somewhere else and start all over again. When I'd been living in Atlanta for four years, I finally decided that I wanted to try music again.

Bob left Atlanta with his wife and two kids and headed to New Orleans. He had tried to make it in the music world several times before he was successful. As the guitar player in the New Orleans-based bluegrass band Swamp Grass, he met Steve Hill, the band's bass player. Along with banjo artist "Tabby" Crabb and female singer Sandy Dimon, the band was booked on a 1972 USO tour to Vietnam. Although Bob was a pacifist, he says he was not against the soldiers. "I justified being in the band by saying that we were going to go over and relate to the soldiers. We went to Vietnam and on into Thailand. It was a defining moment in my life. It's one thing to live in this country and read headlines about our soldiers doing this and our soldiers doing that, but when you're there on the front line, seeing how American foreign policy looks when you take off the velvet gloves and just use the fist, it's another."

He reminds me that 1972 was a defining year for the war, as well. Although in January President Nixon had begun to pull troops out of Vietnam, he also had launched a massive bombing attack along the Laos/South Vietnam border in February; suspended the Paris peace talks in March; authorized massive bombings of the North Vietnamese troops who were invading South Vietnam in April; and bombed Hanoi and Haiphong Harbor, sparking a new wave of student protests back home.

Throughout the spring and summer, while Swamp Grass was planning their tour, the peace talks were on-again-off-again. In July, Jane Fonda made her now-infamous visit to North Vietnam denouncing the war effort and earning the nickname "Hanoi Jane." Resentment against her was equaled by the growing antiwar sentiment that followed the publication of Vietnamese photographer Nick Ut's graphic image of five children crying in terror as they ran down a road near Trang Bang, where their village had just been bombed with napalm. One girl was completely naked. She had torn off her clothing because it was on fire. U.S. soldiers appeared to be casually walking down the road behind them. When the photo appeared, many Americans began to wonder how their government could do such a thing.

Although Steve Hill was busy in graduate school, no doubt he heard the news of troubles with the peace negotiations that fall. By October a peace treaty had been proposed, but the North Vietnamese refused to agree to it. The elections in November gave Nixon the largest margin of victory in history to date and the resolve to threaten severe retaliation against North Vietnam if their government did not abide by the peace proposal. When talks again broke down, Nixon responded with a massive bombing campaign that did not end until December 29. Although Nixon's decision was roundly denounced around the world,[2] one hundred thousand bombs were dropped over an eleven-day period on Hanoi and Haiphong, and the campaign was soon dubbed "The Christmas Bombings."

As the bombs dropped in the north, Bob Webb, Steve Hill, and the rest of the bluegrass band were landing about four hundred miles south in Hue—the old French provincial capital of Vietnam—on Christmas eve,

1972. It proved to be the last USO tour to entertain in Vietnam. "We played Christmas eve in Hue for two hundred marines," Steve Hill says. "There wasn't a dry eye in the house. They were short-timers, the last Americans in Hue, and they were just trying not to be killed. Everybody had pulled out, and the place was surrounded. We were brought in on a helicopter, we played, and they took us out on a helicopter," he says. "It was remarkable, just a remarkable experience. I'm really glad I got to go, to see what it was like. It was unbelievable. Not good!"

Back in West Virginia, finding The Farm is a daunting task even now. Steve described its location as "at the slap end of Benedict Road, north of Hurricane about two to three miles." I'll say. It took thirty minutes and four phone calls from the road to find it. Steve's two-story, octagonal house sits on the highest point in Putnam County and is at the end of a steep, gravel road. Wooden plank siding covers the top floor of the frame house, which is cantilevered over the stucco ground floor. The upper level, reached by climbing a two-story set of stairs, holds the living area and offers a spectacular view on a clear day. The massive timbers and rough barn wood interior give it a lodge-like feeling, and it's no surprise that his musical instruments seem part of the furniture.

As I sit there with Steve, his expression grows somber as he continues the tale. Recalling the first draft lottery drawing, he says, "I was doing my laundry at school in Auburn. It was eight o'clock at night and everything stopped. All these guys were just sitting there with the car doors open, listening to the numbers. It was a death sentence. If you got a low number you were going, and you weren't coming back, most likely." Steve's number was 131. In Opelika, Alabama, the tiny mill town where he was raised, those with numbers below 200 were being taken. As an engineering student at Auburn University, he had joined ROTC hoping to go in as a lieutenant, although he now realizes that that, too, would have been a mistake. Fortunately, neither happened.

While in college, Steve had been diagnosed with Hodgkin's disease. Although he was subsequently cured with radiation treatment, it gave him

Steve Hill building his octagonal home.

a 4F classification and a new perspective on life. "When you're twenty-one and realize that you may have six months to live, that does a lot to you. I kind of went on a different turn at that point." Free from any military obligation, he turned to his music. Like many young wannabe rock stars, Steve had started a band in high school. Without a trace of irony, it was called The Penetrations. But unlike most teenage rockers, Steve didn't see music as a passing phase; he played his way through college. At Auburn, fraternity gigs easily paid the seven-hundred-dollar quarterly tuition. After graduation, he took off for New Orleans on a graduate school scholarship to Tulane and continued playing. At The Wrong Place Saloon, where "you'd pass a little orange pitcher and people would put in money or dope or whatever," Steve met fellow musician Ron Sowell between their late night sets.

Steve had joined Swamp Grass between his first and second years of graduate school at Tulane but was in his final year when the band embarked on its trip to Vietnam. The following spring the lanky bass player finished his MBA at Tulane and headed down his own path. Although he'd heard about the charms of West Virginia from Bob and others and thought it might be the place to go, he wasn't quite ready. And although he had a degree in business, he wasn't ready to head to Wall Street either. He decided to stick to music instead.

Meanwhile, Bob Webb was back in New Orleans following the USO tour when the letters from Mike Ivey began to arrive. Now, thirty-some years later, Bob is balding, but his smile is like that of a kid with a new toy as he talks about his move to West Virginia in 1973. For those who came, it was a big change, he says; they had been city dwellers, and this was just the opposite. "What we called the Coon Creek Community was almost an intentional community. I think that the intention was that everybody would be a vegetarian, but we weren't that well defined. We were all interested in maintaining a lifestyle that didn't take away too much from the environment. Somehow we thought that by moving there, it was like a fresh start." Bob, whose sensibilities were formed by the stories of his Dust Bowl-survivor father teaching farmers ways to preserve the land, was among the first to arrive.

"There were five of us; we each pitched in a little over five hundred dollars and bought twenty-six acres for about twenty-five hundred dollars. I think Mike Ivey was the only one who had seen the land at all. We bought it on his word with no regrets," says Bob. The five were Bob Webb and his wife, Soleil, Michael Ivey, Billy Jack Gregg, and a potter from Austin. "The thing that prompted the owner, Mose Sovine, to sell us the land was that he felt maybe we were going to renew and bring things back," says Bob. "During the 1920s and through the beginning of the Depression, the ridge was very populated. The ridgetops were all cleared off and pastured, but there were houses right and left, all up and down. Mose used to show me where the foundations were for these houses." But by the time Bob and the original settlers bought the land adjoining Greg Carroll's ninety acres, no homes remained. The big city boys had a lot of work to do.

Steve Hill spent Thanksgiving 1973 at The Farm, but didn't stay. By now he was in Louisville with his girlfriend, Bobbi—who later became his wife—and was still trying to make it as a professional musician. Following the USO tour, Steve had been turned off by the idea of war:

I thought that plowing ahead with what seemed to be a pointless war, slaughtering all the people I went to high school with, was not a good idea. I thought we were headed down the wrong track and I wanted out of that. One way to get out was to disengage from the normal societal track. I was really concerned that if things really went to hell in a handbag, I wouldn't know what to do. I'd really thought this back-to-the-land idea made a whole lot of sense. And I was sort of looking for a place to be . . . a place that I could call home . . . call my own if things got weird . . . a place really to be. When I came here I said, "Well, this is kind of cool. It's pretty primitive, but I like it. It's real."

For him, West Virginia was unique—not the South, but not northern, either. He sensed a level of acceptance for who you were, and not—unlike the South—who your daddy was. He also felt the vibe of a very strong socialist ideal, left over from the days of Mother Jones.

Later, as I bid Steve good-bye, a veil of fog shrouds the driveway. But through the gathering March drizzle I can still see the glow of redbud and dogwood—the welcome harbingers of spring in these hills. Where the gravel is thin, the roadbed is slick and driving my low-slung car down the hill is nerve-wracking. As I wind my way to the hard road below, I wonder how on earth Ron and Sandy Sowell ever found the rest of the Texas transplants when they arrived.

Bob said he had wondered the same thing. "Lord knows how they found us because they had to park down on this road off Hurricane Creek. They started asking people and they just sort of kept pointing up the hill," he says. In 1974, Ron and Sandy were living in Cincinnati while Ron traveled the college coffeehouse circuit as a folk singer. They'd gotten letters from Bob touting the cheap land in West Virginia, so that summer, after a Wheeling Jesuit College gig, they decided to visit Ron's old buddy from the New Orleans days.

Although Ron had spent only a year in New Orleans, it was a fortuitous one. Born in Rotan, Texas, he'd grown up in Roswell, New Mexico, and was slated to study law after graduation from Eastern New Mexico University in Portales. But at the last moment, he came to his senses and realized he wanted to be a musician. "In one way it was a very impractical, unpractical thing to do, but I must have been tuned in to some deeper wisdom because once I let myself do that, I never looked back," he says thirty-some years later. That realization took him on the road—sometimes living in his car—and eventually to New Orleans. There he was, working four or five gigs, playing on street corners, and living in an apartment on Bourbon Street with his wife, Sandy, when he met Bob and Steve. According to them, he was the "cat's meow"—the most popular folk singer in the city.

Nevertheless, after a year, the New Orleans scene ended for the three friends. Bob came to West Virginia, Steve joined a rock and roll band that headed for Kentucky, and Ron went on the college circuit. But the bonds of music and friendship had been forged. When Ron came to visit that summer, he did not intend to stay either, but in his words, "It was just so strange how beautiful it was and just something about the vibration of the land or just the feeling I got from it, the feeling of peace; I just instantly felt connected."

Bob and Soliel were living on the ridgetop in a farmhouse previously used for tobacco storage. They'd moved from one of Gregg Carroll's houses, where three others were living, because she was pregnant and wanted some privacy. When Ron and Sandy decided to stay, Bob found them a house on The Farm just below their own. Bob describes his second home as better than a lean-to or a teepee, but still primitive. Ron and Sandy's was little better; it had no running water, just a well.

At the end of that summer, Steve and Bobbi returned. After graduation, Bobbi, who had made close friends among the West Virginia transplants, decided she wanted to make The Farm her home. So Steve helped her move, but he hadn't planned to do the same. Like Ron and Sandy, however, he didn't leave either. The musicians were together again. For five hundred dollars, Steve bought an unfinished A-frame—four poles and a platform—which another guy had started to build on the highest point of the ridge. Although he didn't know carpentry then, Steve managed to throw together a ramshackle building and lived in it for a while before loaning it to friends when he and Ron went on tour. While they were gone, it burned, and Steve lost all his possessions, including an upright piano several guys had wrestled up the hill.

During the winter of 1974–1975, some of the guys pitched in to build what is now the community center, an odd shoehorn-shaped building with a hexagonal tower on one end. As a group, they lived there and in the old farmhouse for a couple of years while each family built a home of their own. Although the living wasn't intentionally communal, it evolved into that arrangement, at least at the beginning. Steve says this unstructured, loosey-goosey confederation probably ensured the community's success. Three of the residents—Billy Jack Gregg, teacher Pat Dawson, and Steve—who had jobs off the land, made the rest an offer. "We agreed to throw our money together and support everybody if the rest of the folks on the farm would go and tear down old houses to get wood so we could build our houses," Steve recalls. "All that summer [1975] the rest of the folks on the farm—we bought an old dump truck for eight or nine hundred dollars—went out and tore down an old piece of a warehouse in Winfield, a house over on the west side of Charleston, and several houses in Institute. We had a barn down here and we cataloged all the houses, all the lumber, and put it in the racks in the barn. Then we divvied it up five different ways and made five different houses out of it." One of those, Steve's octagonal home on top of the ridge, contains pre-Civil War timbers and was built with only a handsaw and hammer, for there was no electricity at that time.

Because Steve had a business degree, he suggested they form a land-holding corporation, Amalgamated Coon, Inc., with each person owning equal shares. "I went to the secretary of state's office and, for forty dollars, we incorporated. Although we had really long hair and were completely covered with mud, Jack Wilson, who was then vice-president of the Putnam County Bank, loaned us eleven thousand dollars to buy the fifty-eight acres. We paid it off thirty dollars apiece a month over five years. Over the years, other people have added on to it. The Farm totals around four or five hundred acres now." Despite the name, almost no one farmed, even in the early days. Steve recalls a few fields of barley or wheat and one big garden that soon morphed into individual gardens, but he says you couldn't really call it farming.

Sandy Sowell refers fondly to those years as "the era of the stupidest pioneers." The college boys and girls had their *Mother Earth News* and their *Foxfire* books, but Steve agrees, "They didn't know jack." Fortunately, the winter was mild, or they all would have frozen to death. They cut saplings with a handsaw, put them in the fire, and, in vain, waited for them to burn. Ron's chimney threatened to collapse until a neighbor showed him how to mix concrete and rebuild it. Furthermore, Bob's car broke down, forcing him to walk everywhere. "The road was a boggy mess from November to March," says Steve. "We had to walk from the valley floor with backpacks of milk, water, groceries, and laundry. We used to backpack our laundry into town, wash it, fold it up, put it back in the backpack, and bring it up here. Every day I went to work, I hiked down the hill and crossed the creek." Steve and his family continued to live without electricity until about 1981 or 1982. The electricity was there; he just didn't want it. He wanted to know that if the worst should happen—he thought it could under President Nixon—they could survive.

Even hard work didn't keep the musicians from playing, of course. It wasn't long before the three, along with Mike Ivey and a friend of Ron's who lived on The Farm the first year, began to gather at one another's houses to pick and jam as they had in New Orleans. Guitar players all, they called themselves "pickers" and soon were entertaining the gathered families. Ron remembers it this way: "We'd get together for social functions three or four times a week. We'd all make something and get together and have a party in the evening and socialize and make music." It wasn't long before a real repertoire of songs developed.

Their first gig off the mountain was at the Mountaineer Dinner Theater near Hurricane, where one of the residents of The Farm worked as a cook. Owner and Huntington entrepreneur Walter Lewis invited them to play between acts for a special group he was hosting. The musicians simply sat in a circle on the center stage and, although they weren't very well rehearsed, played. And according to Bob, the response to the group with no name was great.

Their official name, The Putnam County Pickers, was decided after their next appearance. Steve's wife, Bobbi, worked at the time for the Yesteryear Toy Company, whose stock-in-trade was a contemporized and often satirical version of the old-fashioned folk toy known as a stomper doll. Terry Barron, the company's owner, was headed to the 1975 MSACF to ply his wares with taped music that he used to demonstrate the dancing dolls when Bobbie proposed he try live music instead. Bobbi suggested that if he could get all her musician friends into the fair, they would camp and play in front of his tent. "We spent three or four days there playing music," Ron recalls. "Virtually every time we would play, the other exhibitors would get irritated at Terry because we were drawing a huge crowd. We walked away from the fair with all these engagements, these gigs, and we didn't even have an official name. When somebody looked at the Putnam County Bank calendar and said, 'How about Putnam County Pickers?' we all said, 'That'll do.'"

Ron and Steve went back on the road in the fall to finish Ron's college circuit engagements. When they returned, the Pickers came to the attention of Jim Andrews, the director of arts at the West Virginia Division of Culture and History. The department was about to hold its first artist

(Overleaf) Putnam County Pickers practice at the Sowells' home. Left to right: Bobbi Hill, David Ziems, Ron Sowell, Steve Hill, Sandy Sowell, Michael Ivey, and Bob Webb.

showcase to identify musical talent within the state, and he was recruiting people for that showcase. "He'd heard about us, so he called, but nobody had a phone. When people wanted to get hold of us they had to call the post office in Culloden and tell the postmaster the next time one of us came in to call this number." Ron laughs at the memory. "A week or so went by and finally somebody's message got to us and we called him. Jim said, 'I would like to come out and hear you. Where are you playing?'"

When Ron told him they didn't have any upcoming performances but were practicing regularly, Andrews said he'd come hear them practice. "Well, you have to understand, this was at my little four-room house on the side of this hill. To get there he had to come down this gravel road, park his car, walk over a rickety, swinging-rope bridge, through a big meadow, and up the side of this hill," Ron continues. "He auditioned us in our living room. When we finished playing he said, 'Oh, this is great. You have to be on the showcase.'" They said yes and participated in the Clarksburg showcase in August. That first group consisted of Ron, Sandy, Steve Hill, Bob Webb, Mike Ivey, and a friend of Ron's, David Ziems, from New Mexico. David and Mike soon left, reducing the group to four. Bob also dropped out because he needed to work full time to support his family. After Rusty Wells replaced him on bass and they added Gregg Harmon on drums, the group's makeup remained stable for a few years. Eventually, Sandy also left the group and now has a solo entertainment career.

Looking back, Ron says:

We were doing this as kind of a wild, little, new age string band that was mostly do-ing original material. We were enamored with the music we heard. I wasn't aware there was a difference between old-time music and bluegrass, but I discovered they have common ancestry. We were trying to learn, pay attention to the traditional music and the country music and bluegrass music and everything that was hap-pening in West Virginia. We respected it and let it affect us as we blended it into our original music. We asked Jim Andrews, "Why are you considering us cultured?" He said, "The symphony and a fiddle player and an opera singer and a traditional

Pickers, including John Kessler and Ammed Solomon.

singer and somebody from an old coal mining tradition—it's all culture." They considered it all valid. We ended up getting about twenty or thirty offers from it.

Following that showcase, the group enjoyed the continued support of the West Virginia Division of Culture and History, played and gave workshops in schools, and was the first group to play on the stage of the Culture Center when it opened in 1976. Soon everyone wanted to hire The Putnam County Pickers, including one of the owners of a Charleston Chevrolet dealership. The Pickers' original song, "No Better Feeling," became part of one of dealer Tag Galyean's commercials.

In retrospect, the seven years the band toured, gave school workshops, and recorded several albums were the halcyon days of The Putnam County Pickers, although Ron Sowell says in band years that was like twenty-one. Traveling together in a retrofitted bread truck, playing gigs all over the country, and catching sleep when they could became their

(Above) Rusty Wells, Bob Webb, Steve Hill, and Ron Sowell—early Pickers.

way of life off The Farm. Nevertheless, Ron credits support from the West Virginia Division of Culture and History with much of their success. The state agency often paid half of their performance fee, enabling communities and organizations to afford their concerts. Furthermore, through the state's funding, the band gave innumerable workshops and concerts to school kids in virtually every West Virginia county, in which they set up their lights and sound systems before playing to show them just what it took to be a professional musician. That gave them invaluable statewide exposure. Ron hopes they left a positive mark on those kids as well. The band's days ended in 1981 when Ron felt the itch to do something different. He took a year off to just listen to music, write, and think about what he wanted to do next.

After an intermediate group called Rhino Moon—a trio of Steve Hill, John Kessler, and Ammed Solomon—folded, Ron reassembled some of the Pickers into a new group. "I started another concept, which included Ammed as the drummer and John as the bass player. They were in the last version of the Pickers," Ron recalls. "I drug Bob Webb out of his living room when I found that he played cello because I always wanted to do something with a cello. Then I met Julie Adams and Deni Bonet, and we became Stark Raven." The two girls had been playing as the Fabulous Twister Sisters in Morgantown, where they were in school. The new band premiered in 1982 to more rave reviews and another nine-year stint on the road.

In March 1981, when the Pickers were still together, they appeared as guests on the pilot broadcast of *Mountain Stage*, along with Bob Thompson's Jazz Trio. The show didn't become a regularly scheduled program until December 1983, and by then the band had reconfigured itself into Stark Raven. Some Stark Raven members—Ammed and John Kessler—were an early part of the *Mountain Stage* house band, and the Twister Sisters, Julie and Deni, were regular guests; Ron Sowell didn't join until later. Bob Webb played a few shows and then was pulled in a different direction and dropped out. When Larry Groce needed a harmonica player, Ron stepped up and was hired. Next he began playing background as Larry sang, and soon he was a regular as well. Now he leads the band, and Bob Thompson is the band's pianist. When John Kessler moved to Seattle, Steve Hill took his place on bass.

Despite all the changes in the band, The Farm family remained close. Although they don't all live on that land now, thirty years later, the family feeling is still as strong as if they were blood kin. Ron waxes nostalgic as he talks about the phenomenon. "I think we not only found West Virginia, this culture, and the natural beauty, but we found each other too," he says. He also agrees that the remarkable support from the people who lived here was immeasurable. "Finding the support amongst the people who lived here—the traditional craftsmen and musicians, especially the oldies—was just incredible. I think it's a real tradition here in West Virginia for the elderly people to take people in and apprentice them by bringing somebody into your workshop and having them stand there while you show them how to do it," he says.

Additionally, all The Farm family musicians hold the Division of Culture and History in high regard. "People don't really appreciate how big that is, how important the support of West Virginia maintaining the artists was for me," Ron says. "That's why I was able to stay here. Otherwise I would have had to travel more and maybe end up going back to New Mexico." The solitude that life in West Virginia afforded him was also incredibly important, Ron says. "It's necessary for an artist or musician to get in a creative state of mind and stay there. I think that's one of the attractions to West Virginia for artists. I think we impacted the culture and were impacted by it. I brought the skills of knowing how to function in a recording studio, and Andy and Larry brought the skills to create this radio show. *Mountain Stage* is just an absolute incredible feather in West Virginia's cap. There's just no question about it. It's beyond even the dream Larry and Andy had when it first began. It is really something that it is absolutely the most cutting edge, impressive, risk-taking music show in the United States, and where's it coming from? West Virginia. Who'd have thunk it, you know?" Ron laughs, but it's a laugh full of pride, as it should be. In 2013, *Mountain Stage* celebrated thirty years of continuous radio broadcasts.

This Land is Cheap Land

While the hills of West Virginia became home to antiwar refugees, protestors, and peaceniks looking for a safe place to live, it also drew folks because of its sheer beauty, or for the opportunity to live a slow-paced, rural life. Admittedly, they did share that desire to leave the city behind to stake out a new, alternative lifestyle, but they weren't draft-dodgers; they hadn't protested; and they weren't necessarily avid devotees of Helen and Scott Nearing's back-to-the-land philosophy. For many, the decision grew out of multiple factors. Some admit the state's cheap land was the primary draw in making the choice about where to raise their families in a rural setting. For others, West Virginia already was a beloved vacation spot or a new treasure they had recently discovered. Still others came after friends who'd previously migrated there invited them to follow.

The verses of Colleen Anderson's song, "West Virginia Chose Me," echo the state's out-migration of the 1960s and 1970s, but joyously, the chorus speaks of those who came during the back-to-the-land migration. She understands; she was part of it. Although many young natives were finding greener economic pastures elsewhere, those who came to West Virginia found a receptiveness in the hills that rooted them instantly. Most bought land within weeks, if not days, of arriving. Many are still on that land today and they express a love for their adopted state as deep as any whose family roots go back several generations. If they could form a chorus, they'd join Colleen in singing:

Someone's always leaving here, it's just that kind of place
It's just that kind of world today, you learn to live with loss.
The grass is always greener there, just on the other side
The air is always clearer there; the sky is twice as wide
I'm not the type to argue, I won't say it isn't true
It's just that kind of place for passing through.

Chorus:

But a few of us are staying and it's not a point of choice

It's not we who do the choosing, we are chosen by the place.

And West Virginia chose me, sure as my own mother knows me.

If I leave you West Virginia, it don't matter where I roam

I don't know where I'm going, but I know I'm coming home.[3]

Cheap land drew two husband-and-wife teams of potters: V. C. and Damienne Dibble, and Ren and Pam Parziale. The Dibbles moved to the state in 1972 after a stint at the University of South Carolina. When V. C. taught periodic workshops with Charles Counts at his Rising Fawn pottery in Georgia, he met West Virginia potters Scottie Weist and Susan Maslowski. They talked glowingly of the opportunities for craft sales in West Virginia, notably at the MSACF.

Damienne says they came in July 1971 specifically to check out the fair. They liked what they saw and stayed afterward to look for land because her sister—a practicing realtor—told them land was cheap there as well. They went first to Roane County near Spencer and then to Jackson County, where they bought twenty-five acres and five usable buildings—including what had been a general store in the 1920s—for $6,500. They returned the following August, immediately set up their pottery shop, and went to work making their house habitable.

As Scottie and Susan had predicted, sales opportunities came quickly. While Damienne and V. C. both worked in the pottery, their styles were very different. His work was functional, ranging from huge platters to traditional bowls and jars. Damienne, on the other hand, loved sculptural work that often included whimsical, if not otherworldly-looking, creatures. In any case, Kilnridge Pottery had many loyal customers, from avid individual collectors to retail shops in nine states.

V. C. and Damienne passed down their considerable skills through workshops at their pottery studio, by serving as mentors in the MSACF apprentice program, and by teaching a few weekend workshops at Cedar Lakes. In addition, they had four long-term resident apprentices, including Mike Brotsko, who arrived from Buffalo, New York, in 1975. He worked with them for a year before setting up his own studio where, according to Damienne, he specialized in magnificent pit-fired vases and bowls.

While the town of Kentuck, where the Dibbles' home and pottery studio were located, is certainly rural, the couple didn't farm and didn't call themselves back-to-the-landers. Damienne laughs as she recalls her only attempt to grow beans. When they bloomed, she discovered they were morning glories.

Although Damienne worked in the pottery business in the early days, her first love was publishing. As a young woman, she had worked on the production side of the industry in New York City. After moving to South Carolina, she was the production manager for the university's press. Therefore, when someone suggested there was a need for a West Virginia arts newsletter, Damienne took up the challenge. Gradually drifting away from the clay, she produced *West Virginia Arts News* for several years.

After almost twelve years, the couple closed Kilnridge in 1985. Although V. C. died in 2003, Damienne is still active in the arts and just took up a new discipline: jewelry. Her apartment now serves as her studio. There, in one corner of the living room, she arranges gemstones, glass beads, found objects, and various metals on her jeweler's bench until she's pleased with the design.

Damienne is of Scottish lineage but, interestingly, never focused on her heritage until she came to the state. When she did, she says she understood their fierce bond to their adopted land. "Somehow the mountains and I absorbed, and I felt connected in a way that no other mountains would probably have [made me feel]," she says with a wistful smile. Now, however, the gal who lived in New York City has rediscovered her urban roots in Charleston. She's lived there since 1990, she says, "courting the muse that West Virginia allowed me to nurture back in the day."

About the same time the Dibbles landed in Jackson County, another pair of potters, Pam and Ren Parziale, moved from metropolitan Washington D.C. to West Virginia's eastern panhandle. Back then, land was still relatively cheap there. In the home the couple bought in 1971, the sun

(Overleaf) V. C. and Damienne Dibble on the porch.

streams through the stained glass dining room window behind Pam as she tells me their story. Beside her, ready to add to her running monologue, Ren smiles. Both are gray now, but, after thirty-five years, still energetically producing pots.

While Pam had grown up in Caribou, Maine, and Ren's childhood home was in the Bronx, both were living in Washington, D.C., when they met. Each had been married previously and had two children. In addition to his position as a potter for the Smithsonian's Anacostia Museum, Ren, a political science graduate of New York's Iona College, was building a kiln for Pam's pottery instructor. Pam says the temperamental teacher never forgave her for running off with the kiln builder.

Although a National Park Service's offer to hire Ren to set up a pottery studio in Harper's Ferry never materialized, the couple came to nearby Kearneysville to look for land. At a friend's urging, they also looked in Maryland, but, in the end, couldn't beat West Virginia prices. Both were ignorant and arrogant, Pam says, in deciding to set up their own studio and commit to making pots as a career. "We had quit our jobs with steady incomes to live a dream that was vague on details, but full of romance: to work the land, raise our children with food from our garden, and make pots the way our biblical ancestors did—on the potter's wheel," she said in her 2005 acceptance speech of the Governor's Distinguished Arts Award for lifetime achievement.

Like the Dibbles, the Parziales were quickly juried into the two large, statewide craft shows: the Mountain Heritage Arts & Crafts Festival in Harper's Ferry and the Mountain State Art & Craft Fair (MSACF) at Ripley. There, she says, they made lifetime friends who contributed to her understanding of what it meant to be a West Virginian.

Not only did I learn to drink bourbon, I tasted "shine" for the first time. They told stories of our state's history, Chief Logan, the mine wars, the fight to preserve Blackwater Falls. The story of West Virginia was spun out, night after night, a web

V. C. Dibble demonstrates at the Mountain State Art & Craft Fair. (Photo by Ric MacDowell) (Overleaf) Dibbles clear land at Kilnridge, 1972.

that enchanted us all with possibilities. We all shared one thing in common: a commitment to our work and our love of the land. We all aspired to the same goal: to make a living wage from our craft so we could continue to work and support our families. These friendships endure and define for me the West Virginia artist: articulate, educated, gritty, and loyal.

Ironically, with one or two exceptions, those she mentions were fellow transplants as well. Like others, the Parziales say this community of artisans became their family, in lieu of the blood relatives they'd left behind.

In the beginning, Pam taught first grade, but in 1978, she quit to work full time in the pottery business. Now, for the Parziales, it's a short walk to work each day. Two kilns flank the entrance to Sycamore Pottery, nestled at the edge of their property against a backdrop of towering pines. The building's wooden siding has weathered to silver over the years. However, a large arched window gives an air of dignity to what otherwise might be mistaken for a large storage shed.

Inside, we meander through the workroom, the kiln room, and the small salesroom. Ren picks up a platter to point out why it's obvious that Pam should always decorate the work while he does the throwing and the firing. Like the Dibbles, Pam and Ren divide the production tasks. Her stylized brushwork graces Ren's work, and he revels in firing the twenty-six-year-old gas kiln that he built. Specializing in stoneware and redware pottery, Pam often adds clever or touching phrases to the line of dishes, serving pieces, and cookware she decorates with fruit or vegetables.

For the Parziales, as for many others, support from the state was essential in the early days. She praises Tim Pyles for being there when needed and Don Page for helping them set up their business. For several years the couple continued to participate in the two statewide fairs and sold to retail shops. However, they stopped when they realized their proximity to Washington, D.C., was their best marketing advantage. After seeing pots the couple made for a Shepherdstown Historical Society fundraiser, folks began to come to the pottery to buy directly from the Parziales. When the

Pam and Ren Parziale at home, 1971. (Photo by Charlie Galis)

trickle of visitors grew to a steady stream, they were able to sell all their work directly to the public. In 1984, they joined other area artisans to create the Over The Mountain Studio Tour, now a popular pre-Christmas event that lures Washington-area residents and visitors to meet artisans, tour their studios, and purchase art.

Today Pam says with pride that West Virginia has been good to her and Ren. They were able to raise their family here, make deep and long-lasting friendships, succeed in their business, and have a sense of purpose in their lives. "I could not ask for more," she says.

Going Up The Country

"Going Up the Country," the quintessential Woodstock theme song by Canned Heat, aptly describes the vibe circulating in 1969: "I'm going up the country, babe, don't you wanna go? . . . I'm gonna leave this city, got to get away . . ."[4] Like the lead singer, photographer Chuck Wyrostok was looking for the country experience in 1975 when he bought his place in the Clover Ridge community of Roane County, near Spencer. He didn't move there from New York until 1977, however. Chuck was over thirty, the single father of two, and the owner of a photography business when he decided he wanted a change from that Long Island existence. With five employees and high-demand clients like Newsday, United Press International, and the New York Daily News, he was spending less time with his children than his parents were. Fed up, he started thinking of moving to the country. First he looked at Vermont and New Hampshire, but he kept running into people who were moving to West Virginia. He had no concept of the state and wasn't even sure where it was.

After a chance meeting with Dell Denny, a West Virginia back-to-the-lander, Chuck began to meet others, including former New York neighbors of Steve and Gail Balcourt, who had already made their move to the mountains. Finally he decided to go see what everyone was raving about. "I

Chuck Wyrostok in his booth at the Mountain State Art & Craft Fair, 1981. (Photo by Jennifer Wyrostok)

took a trip down here and looked around and I was just floored," he recalls. "All the people here were great. They were all accustomed to the idea that people were going to be moving down here. Those who had already landed here were taking newcomers around to show them the different homesteads that people had set up." Although he'd already picked out a place in New Hampshire, Chuck says there was no comparison. Down here, the extrication from New York felt freeing.

In 1975, he put money down on forty acres with a trailer on it and reluctantly returned to New York to earn the $16,500 to pay for it, tie up the loose ends of his business, and learn how to garden and cook. Although he didn't have a clear plan on how he would earn his living, he knew, after working for himself for years that he would be able to make it. In preparation, for two summers he turned his entire suburban backyard into a garden, took cooking lessons from his mom, and studied *Mother Earth News* to gain the pioneering skills he knew he would need.

Echoing the remarks of many other homesteaders, Chuck says he was lucky. "I was very fortunate in having landed in a place where people were generous and friendly," he says. While some of the locals looked askance at his long hair, they gradually began to accept him. He recounts folks who fed his kids when he was away at craft shows and helped when he was stuck in the mud, his gas line broke, or his electricity went out. "They just did it," he says with a touch of wonder in his voice. "And to them it wasn't anything out of the way. It was what you did. That was what community was all about. After I realized the quality of that, it was hard to think about moving. Because you feel safe, you feel secure, you feel appreciated, and your generosity opens up big time."

While Chuck grew close to many of the older locals, the other artisans became like family. Chuck says he had more of a cultural connection with those who moved here because they came from all over the United States. Additionally, many of them held work parties to do planned projects every few weeks. They would pool their food, tools, and skills to get the job at hand accomplished. The Growing Tree food co-op in Spencer was also a central gathering place for the newcomers, many of whom were fellow artisans.

This community of artisans showed him how to make a living too. Along with Steve Balcourt and Dell Denny, Chuck met potter Joe Lung. The three convinced Chuck he could support his family by selling photographs on the craft show circuit. He decided to try it, and sold successfully at craft shows in West Virginia, Ohio, and Pennsylvania from 1978 to 1983. When being on the road became too difficult, he quit and began to provide stock photography for business clients. Now his immersion in West Virginia is complete. As an outreach worker for the Sierra Club, he's actively working to ensure that Marcellus shale gas drilling is done responsibly and safely in his adopted home.

While moving to West Virginia was spurred by her husband's job offer, potter Kate Harward was ready to jump at the chance to live in a rural setting. A VISTA worker at nineteen in Buffalo, New York, she knocked on doors taking surveys before dropping out of the program to take up pottery. After courses at Federal City College in Washington, D.C., she set up her own studio, and by twenty-two she was supporting herself partially through her sales. This maker of extraordinarily large vessels has lived in Belington, overlooking the Tygart River, since she, her husband, and their six kids moved there in 1976. Kate and Tom, a physician's assistant, wanted to raise their children in a rural setting, instead of ten blocks from the National Zoo in the nation's capital, where they had been living. The prospect of Tom's new job in Elkins was the answer to their dreams—to live in the country, garden, and raise their children in a less urban environment. He accepted.

Like many others who came at about the same time, Kate recalls the first few winters as brutal. While they had fallen in love immediately with the heavily forested, seventeen-acre site they bought, she admits the house wasn't much of a structure. When winter came, they all slept on the living room floor around a small oil burner. While the couple is a bit older than many of the others that came, Kate and Tom did feel a connection to the back-to-the-land movement. They gardened and often relied on the advice of their elder neighbors to help them over the rough spots, especially in those early days. Caught with a book in her hand as she contemplated planting sweet corn, one neighbor chastised her, saying, "City farmer, you don't plant with a book." Then he showed her how. Kate says, "How else was I to learn? I didn't have a grandmother to teach me." In turn, Kate milked for him. They also helped look after a neighboring older couple until they both passed away.

While Kate didn't have to rely on sales for her livelihood, she did believe the pottery business had to pay for itself so it wouldn't be a drain on her family. Soon after they arrived, Kate began attending local craft fairs to sell her work. In the first two years, she participated in twenty-six local shows. When the travel and disruption to the family proved to be too much, she began to sell wholesale to shops. Although she continued to attend the MSACF until 2003, retail stores, including Tamarack and MountainMade, soon became her primary markets. She, too, was one of the first artists juried into both outlets. Kate considers herself a full-time potter; she works every day, many evenings, and some weekends. It's her art, her love. Selling the work to approximately fifty shops simply allows her to make more pots.

Dancer Carli Mareneck also came to West Virginia with her husband, but it wasn't her original plan. As a child in suburban Chicago, she developed a strong affinity for nature during family camping trips. She didn't intend to stay in Chicago or the suburbs after college, but living on a farm was the furthest thing from her mind. Nevertheless, when she met Peter Mareneck in college and he told her of his dream to carry on his family's farming tradition, she went along for the ride. They started looking for land when she was eighteen, and they married two years later, in 1974. Peter, an Indiana native, already had made two previous trips to West Virginia when they found their farm during a camping trip the same year. "We came over the mountain in Monroe County at Waitville and we all looked at that Peter's Mountain valley . . . and thought, this is it," she recalls.

When they bought the farm at Sweet Springs, there was a barn and some machinery sheds, but no house. After they finally moved in 1976, they lived first in a teepee and then in a cabin while building their house. As soon as it was warm, dry, and had running water, they moved in, even though it still had only subflooring. The land is beautiful, she admits, and although they never meant it as a true working farm, they've always had a large garden. "I'm still a homesteader," she says. "I never moved up into a suburban lifestyle."

While farming wasn't on young Carli's mind until she met Peter, dancing was. After she graduated a year early from high school, she went to New York City to study modern dance. She'd been captivated by the form in seventh grade and had taught creative movement and dance to young children while she was still in high school. After a few years in New York, she entered the University of Utah to major in dance and eventually received her degree in fine arts there. When she and Peter moved to rural West Virginia, she was determined to continue her career, although she admits it wasn't an easy task. Yet, as Carli puts it, she feels lucky. "I found the person I wanted to live with in my life young, found my vocation young, and I haven't really veered from it," she says.

In their search for land, the couple had traveled through Oregon, Washington, California, Colorado, and other parts of the Appalachian Mountains. In those locales, they felt a bit like Goldilocks; none quite suited them. Here, she says, they found an original, authentic culture. Moreover, the land was cheaper, and they could own their mineral and water rights. Carli says that West Virginia has provided a richness in her life that she doesn't believe she'd have had elsewhere.

Unlike many other homesteading couples, both Carli and Peter always worked off the land. In the early years, Peter taught high school English and she worked at The Greenbrier resort as a waitress and masseuse. Later he became a residential designer and builder and she returned to dance as a career. "I used to do my own dance work at the community center, which was then a wooden building that was attached to the library in White Sulphur Springs. Eventually I would put up my little flyers for classes that I was teaching—exercise and little children's classes," she recalls. When she noticed another woman's similar offerings, she was afraid there'd be competition. She didn't need to worry. When she met Beth White, they were instant friends and eventually partners. Together, they opened a studio in Lewisburg in 1982 and are still working together. "I feel like I've had two good marriages, really," Carli says of their relationship.

Both are members of Trillium Performing Arts Collective, which they founded along with Lorrie Monte and several other artists in 1982. Dance was essential to the trio, as was living rurally. Early troupe practices were held in what is now Carnegie Hall in Lewisburg or in the Greenbrier Valley Theatre's original space. Before long, the three began performing throughout Greenbrier and nearby counties. When they decided they wanted to choreograph dances as well, they started teaching others in order to have a full dance company. In classes for adults and children ages three to eight, they taught improvisation and modern dance techniques. Soon the students began performing at nursing homes and schools as a form of community outreach. In 1992, the collective gained nonprofit status and today has its home in Lewisburg's renovated Lewis Theater.

As with many of the back-to-the-landers, the couple's first friends were the older neighbors nearby in Sweet Springs. Although most have since died, the couple holds dear the friendships of those few who remain. Carli laughs as she remembers that, at first, they were the couple's only social contact. Unaware that others were moving to West Virginia, it was three years before they saw other young homesteaders. "We went to a little square dance down at the Gap Mills gymnasium and saw all these people that were like us. We started talking to them . . . Bob Zacher, Kate Hentchel, Joe Chasnoff, and Judy Azulay. It was three more years of knowing Kate and Zach before we realized we were married the same day, the same year, and we'd both found our farms the same summer." The Zachers and the Marenecks remained close friends, celebrating their anniversaries together each year until Peter's death in 2010. For fourteen years, Bob Zacher was in The Juice Band with the Marenecks; Carli sang and Peter played bass. That sense of community bonds them to the land and to those who came with much the same purpose. Not surprisingly, it echoes the sense of family and community that tied the early pioneer migrants to Appalachia.

Oh, The Hills . . . Beautiful Hills

By some geological reckonings, the Appalachian Mountains are the oldest in North America. Since West Virginia lies within that range, it's no surprise, therefore, that lyricists and poets have sung the praises of its hills for centuries. Even the state song champions them. Perhaps the young folks who came to the hills in the 1960s and 1970s had heard these songs, or at least John Denver's "Country Roads." In any case, before they arrived, many knew the state was a place of abundant natural beauty. As children they'd camped with parents on vacation retreats from suburbia, or hiked as adventurous teens, or ridden through on their own escape from urbanization before making the mountains their home.

Artist, musician, composer, and dulcimer maker Sam Rizzetta and his equally talented wife, Carrie, moved to West Virginia specifically for its beauty and isolation. Sam wasn't an antiwar protestor or a pacifist who served in another capacity; he was drafted and, ironically, that's how the midwestern couple learned of West Virginia. They first found solitude on a hard-to-reach Randolph County mountaintop farm where they could watch Cheat Mountain turn pink with the bloom, in turn, of azaleas, cranberries, mountain laurel, and rosebay rhododendron. Now their home near Inwood, in the eastern panhandle, is a bit easier to reach, but it's still a trek up their long, graveled lane.

It's nearly dusk when I arrive, so I remain in my car for a moment to relish the stillness of the impending night. As I sit peering into the woods, I recall fondly the hours I've listened to Sam play a hammered dulcimer, either at his MSACF booth or on one of the tapes recorded by Trapezoid, the dulcimer band he co-founded. For me, that sweet music epitomizes Appalachia, although I know it is older than its life in those mountains.

Greetings and hugs completed, we settle at the dining room table with the dense trees still beckoning through the expansive windows. These woods must be bliss for the couple, since both grew up in Chicago. Carrie says she worshiped the only tree on her inner-city street. Nestled on a ten-acre wooded knoll between two creeks, their home and adjoining workshop sit in virtual seclusion, if you don't count the deer, wild turkeys, bobcats, or bald eagles they often see from their screen porch overlooking a serene pond.

The two met in high school, attended the senior prom on their first date, and maintained a seven-year correspondence throughout college and

graduate school—Carrie at Illinois's Rosary College and the Art Institute of Chicago and Sam at Ripon College in Wisconsin and Western Michigan University—before marrying in 1966.

In 1967, Sam's military orders sent him to Brooke Army Medical Center in San Antonio. There, because of his background in biology and art, he served as a medical artist. After a year, he was assigned to the Pentagon, where he completed his army service in intelligence. Carrie, too, gained a working knowledge of the Vietnam War that year. As a librarian for the Joint Atomic Information Exchange Group, she catalogued classified documents dealing with neutron tubes and weapon systems. What she saw made her want to escape eventually to a remote setting, to leave that insanity. For her, that setting eventually became West Virginia.

After his discharge, they stayed in Washington, D.C., where Sam drew biology illustrations for the Smithsonian and Carrie catalogued books at the Library of Congress. To escape the big city, they began vacationing in West Virginia, where they found the solitude they both craved. The couple had begun their working life illustrating a college textbook, and Sam had put himself through school doing illustrations. But music also had been part of his life since early childhood. He recalls falling in love with music at age three when he heard an uncle play stringed instruments. Fascinated with the sound, he began experimenting with making stringed instruments before he was a teenager. Cooking pots became banjos and gourds became guitars or fiddles. Little by little, he was able to make some that actually could be played. While he did study the history of instrument making and of dulcimers, it was through trial and error, like the old-timers, that Sam eventually became adept at his craft.

In graduate school, he began repairing dulcimers and guitars, deconstructing and rebuilding them in the process. Soon he was building instruments from scratch, improving on the design, the bracing, or the style. At Carrie's urging, he turned his attention exclusively to dulcimers—both the plucked Appalachian or mountain dulcimer, which has frets, and the

Trapezoid, left to right: Pete Vigour, Paul Reisler, Sam Rizzetta, and Paul Yeaton.

hammered dulcimer, which does not. She said guitars were a dime a dozen, but dulcimers were unique. That turned out to be good advice. Because Sam was also a performer, he built them for himself until people started begging him to build them one just like it. When other performers, including the legendary John McCutcheon, wanted to buy a Sam Rizzetta dulcimer, the course of his life changed.

He'd been making instruments in his spare time since getting out of the army in 1969, but when his backlog of orders proved overwhelming, he left his job at the Smithsonian to perform and make dulcimers full time. It was 1973. "More and more people wanted these instruments that I built as an obsession," he says with a note of surprise in his voice, despite his successful forty-year career. While Sam was embarking on the new venture, Carrie continued to do research at the Library of Congress, where she had little interaction with people. "Sam would come home from playing music saying he'd met the most wonderful people. He loved his life," Carrie says. Envious, she longed to join him.

That year, the couple moved to Charlottesville, Virginia, where she took a job at the University of Virginia library, but it would be her last. There, Sam connected with another Virginia instrument builder and musician, Paul Reisler, whom he'd met while exhibiting at the Philadelphia Folk Festival. Paul introduced him to two others—Paul Yeaton and Pete Vigour—and in 1975 they formed the band Trapezoid, which played traditional, old-time mountain music. Sam designed a family of dulcimers, from bass to soprano, and they became known for their dulcimer quartet performances. Initially influenced by English, Scottish, Celtic, and European music, the band also took on the flavor of other sounds they heard in West Virginia—the blues, soul music, and accordion music played by miners, lumberjacks, and railroad hands. Trapezoid toured the state so often that all its members eventually relocated to West Virginia. Although Sam left the band in 1978 to write music and build instruments, Trapezoid performed extensively, produced many recordings, and toured with McCutcheon in 2004 and 2005, albeit with some recurring changes in personnel.

Finally, in 1977, Carrie decided to join Sam in making dulcimers. "I discovered if you could use a sewing machine, you could operate woodworking machines just the same," she says. By then, their love affair with West Virginia was in full bloom. Rather than stay in Virginia, they thought it would be fun to build a house and live in the mountains. They chose an old farmstead in Randolph County's tiny town of Valley Head, about forty miles south of Elkins. It fit their primary requirement: it was away from town and offered quiet and seclusion. It hadn't been farmed in years, but it had an orchard and a Christmas tree farm on one side, and the Monongahela National Forest on the other. The two of them built a house using green wood—a technique Carrie learned before leaving the University of Virginia—but it was small and rough. A pole building, it swayed in the strong winds that swept across the mountains, but in the winter, the sun beating through the south-facing wall of glass heated the house. Carrie says it was so small that if a guest arrived with a fiddle case, there was no room for it. They lived in the home, which was only twenty-five by thirty feet, for seven years.

While they didn't consider themselves back-to-the-landers, they did have a garden that supplemented the food they purchased. However, because of the remoteness of the house and adjacent shop, UPS couldn't reach them in the winter or during the heavy spring rains. This made operating the business very difficult. Eventually they decided to move closer to paved roads and larger transportation hubs so they could attend festivals with more ease.

They entered the MSACF as soon as they moved to West Virginia and continued to participate until the mid-1980s. Isolated on their mountaintop, Carrie and Sam built dulcimers half the year, then traveled to fairs and festivals to sell them during the summer and fall. As with other artisans, the friendships they made at those festivals have remained. Ren and Pam Parziale, who live nearby, are among their close friends. Carrie says, however, that the families near Valley Head, where they came as complete ignoramuses about farm living, adopted them as family. Yet the natives whose children were moving away to the big cities seeking a better life couldn't imagine why the Rizzettas quit well-paying jobs to live so frugally. Carrie told them, "We don't need jobs anymore. We build our instruments and we work."

As if to add an exclamation point to Carrie's declaration, Sam suggests a tour of his home studio and their workshop. As he talks, I realize he is the epitome of Joseph Campbell's notion of following your bliss. "Building instruments was not so much a job where I turned out instruments to sell them," he says, "as it was to build instruments to experiment, to learn to make them better, to design them better." As we walk through the room, dodging some dozen instruments, his sound equipment, and several amplifiers, he explains how many "Rizzetta" features, like the simple system of black-and-white bridge markers that Sam added to make it easier to learn the instrument, have become industry standards. The demand for his instruments increased to the point that even with Carrie working by his side, their backlog of orders often topped five years. The two could only make a dozen hammered dulcimers—his instrument of choice—each year.

However, in the mid-1970s, Sam and Carrie met Nicholas Blanton, a student at Davis and Elkins College in Elkins, West Virginia, when he enrolled in an instrument-building class the couple was teaching at the college's Augusta Heritage Center. He went on to build instruments of his own, but helped out the Rizzettas from time to time. The men maintain a collaborative relationship to this day. Periodically, the Rizzettas hired subcontractors, but when that proved contrary to their preferred work style, they stopped. By the late 1970s, Sam had licensed some of his designs to Dusty Strings, a highly respected instrument manufacturer in Seattle, Washington. That provided some relief from the overwhelming demand and gave him the freedom to work slowly—the pace he prefers. Those more affordable instruments are based on older Rizzetta models, for Sam makes changes, if ever so slight, with each one he builds. Using his math and science background to engineer his instruments, he's constantly searching for the perfect sound.

Until two frozen shoulders sent Carrie to the office to manage the business, she built the dulcimers and hand carved their hammers, which Sam calls little sculptural works of art. The dulcimers, too, are exquisite works of art that feature intricate wood mosaics inlaid with abalone or turquoise. The legs are often crafted from tree limbs, snaked with tightly clinging vines, or are of deftly turned and polished contrasting woods.

As a working musician, Sam also writes much of the music he plays. Approximately half the songs on his thirteen albums, tapes, and CDs, including those he recorded with Trapezoid, are his original compositions and include several tributes to Carrie. One, called "Carrie Under the Arbor," was inspired by an arbor Sam built at home near Charlottesville, where the couple played music and watched the sun set over the Blue Ridge Mountains. This spritely tune that makes you want to dance is the first one he wrote for her. Yet in the early days, he didn't write down any of his songs. Sam, like the old-timers, always played by ear until other musicians begged him for his music so they could learn to play it. Not only did he give in, he wrote a whole series of books for the Mel Bay Company—the publisher of the how-to books for many musical instruments—that contain his original sheet music. Although he spent many years on the road performing, taking orders for his instruments, and selling his music, now he plays strictly for pleasure. "The sound of music is what's magic to me," he says. "I've had in my mind the sound of an idealized music and idealized musical instruments. Through a lifetime of involvement with that instrument, I've been lucky enough to come closer and closer to that. At this stage in life, there are many moments of ecstasy in just hearing the musical instruments."

According to Sam and Carrie, West Virginia has given them those moments. In exchange, they willingly gave up high-paying jobs to have the isolation and quiet they craved. While knowing they could live cheaply in West Virginia partially influenced their decision, it was more than that, they say. Like a lot of West Virginians they knew, they believed one didn't need so much to be content. "I decided I would just keep adjusting my lifestyle to fit a West Virginia income," Carrie says. Sam agrees, "There's such a thing as enough," he says. "We have friends who have a lot, but whose lives we would not want." It all enticed them: the land, the beautiful woods, waters, and hills. However, the people charmed and held them. "Part of what drew me to West Virginia is the feeling that West Virginians were independent," Sam says. "Whether that's a stereotype or not, that's what we found. When I traveled and met so many independent and artistic people, craftspeople, and real folks who could learn to do anything and get by, I found a

A Safe Place to Live

real bond with those people." All in all, Carrie believes West Virginia is "the most spiritually satisfying place" the couple has lived.

The following evening, I accompanied Sam and Carrie to O'Hurley's General Store in Shepherdstown, West Virginia. Each Thursday night the owner transforms it into a community gathering, a jam session of old-time music. Displays are cleared away, chairs are assembled for the audience, which often numbers twenty to one hundred, and the musicians gather. It's a happening. Tonight at least fifteen musicians have arrived, and it's clear they know one another from many Thursday nights spent here. Sam says the proprietor, Jay Hurley, has a policy that allows everyone who comes, even if it's a child with an accordion, to take his turn playing. They go around the circle, each musician playing a tune of his or her choice. Carrie and I are in rocking chairs on the front row as music fills the large, timber-frame building. Sam's face radiates contentment. I glance at Carrie's and see his expression mirrored by hers. I remember the same look from earlier days at the fair when Carrie's long, brown hair wasn't streaked with gray, and when Sam's beard was black, not silver. I smile, too, content to bask in their bliss once again.

Leaning on Friends

It's human nature to crave companionship, to make friends, and to form bonds. Therefore, when the young men and women of the 1960s and 1970s severed or stretched their hometown bonds by leaving, it's not surprising that they sought to develop new ones among those they met in their adopted state. Most back-to-the-land artisans describe these new friends as "like family," whether they were the old-timers who "adopted" them, other back-to-the-landers, or their fellow artisans. For others, like Bob and Kate Zacher, Ann Contois, and Mark Soukup, the bond of an existing friendship drew them to West Virginia.

Bob Zacher grew up the oldest of nine children and studied art and music in college on a scholarship he earned by playing oboe in high school.

Bob Zacher making porcelain earrings. (Photo by Ric MacDowell)

145

From 1969 to 1970, he staged light and sound shows for big-name performers like Janis Joplin and Bob Dylan. However, he soon decided it was an ugly business full of people willing to do anything to get a bigger share of the money pot. He wasn't willing to compete like that, so he left the business and started making pottery.

Bob says from childhood he knew he wanted out of the city, to live in the country. As he matured, his resolve deepened. "The denser the urban environment, the more people look right past each other and the less regard they have for an individual unit," he now says. After leaving the business, Bob rode his motorcycle all over the Ozarks, out West, and even in Canada looking for a new home in a rural setting, but to him all those mountains looked too harsh.

Bob's motorcycle-riding buddy in his native St. Louis had been Jack Chasnoff, the father of Monroe County back-to-the-land furniture maker Joe Chasnoff. An attorney, Jack had been a Corsair pilot in the navy and now the two rode together on the weekends. Through him, Bob met Joe. Consequently, after Joe came to West Virginia in 1972, he told Bob about what he'd found, knowing Bob wanted to leave St. Louis. In 1976, Bob and his wife, Kate Hentchel, whom he'd married in 1974, followed the Chasnoffs and settled in Monroe County. Joe and his wife, Judy, had their eyes on a piece of land but couldn't afford the whole plot by themselves, so they approached the Zachers. Bob says they thought about it for a while, then decided to jump in. Bob says that while the land wasn't cheap—nineteen thousand dollars for their sixty acres—it was affordable. And as he puts it, they were loving mountains. "The people that were here at the time, the old-timers, I want to call them, were so generous and so inviting to all of us young people," he says. "Their children had to leave, but that had to feel like rejection of their lifestyle. Us coming as young people was reaffirming, and they just would do everything for you." Bob says he wouldn't trade that time for anything, repeating the common sentiment of many homesteaders.

After the Zachers settled into their house in Lindside, Bob began to throw pots, often working in the difficult clay body of porcelain. He moved

Ann Contois. (Photo by Ric MacDowell)

an old bus beside the house to create a glaze room. From 1976 to 1984, he produced and sold an amazing array of pots, some of which are in museums today. Unable to use a gas kiln, Bob worked to adapt glaze recipes meant for a gas kiln so they worked in an electric kiln. The resulting work distinguished Bob's from that of many other potters. Primarily, he sold to shops across the country, but he did sell at craft fairs as well. Additionally, for seventeen years he ran the arts and crafts building—which he also designed and built—during the West Virginia State Fair in Fairlea, near Lewisburg.

Although crippling arthritis cut Bob's career short in 1984, the glaze bus is still there. "I know it's a dream," he says, "but I honestly dream about making pots again." Whether or not he does, he's made his mark on the state. From 1990 to 1998, he successfully led some ninety petitioners in the fight to keep the world's largest high-voltage power line from crossing through Pipestem State Park, where it would have violated his beautiful, friendly mountains. While Bob no longer is active in the community of potters, his friendships from those days remain.

Stained glass artist Ann Contois came to West Virginia by a similar, but more circuitous, route. After spending half her childhood as a military brat in Japan, Germany, and Cambodia, Ann was living in the San Francisco Bay area when she decided to move again—to West Virginia. In 1968, the country's political upheaval only added to Ann's personal turmoil. Her father died of war-related injuries within three months of the assassinations of Bobby Kennedy and Martin Luther King Jr. Also disheartened by the earlier assassinations of President Kennedy and Malcolm X, she began to question society's established values and the country's future direction. Despite the military protocol and the strict religious training she'd been exposed to as a child, Ann now felt that neither the government nor big business was to be trusted, and that religion was not responsive to modern social problems.

Perhaps some of these beliefs grew out of her college years as she earned her degree in fine art at the University of California, Berkeley. There she also studied stained glass with master glass artisan Peter Mollica at his studio near campus. Following graduation in 1971, the single mother of two was driving her self-named "hippie truck" around the country when she met Bob and Stephanie Martin, who were doing the same in their Volkswagen van. She'd always loved the peace of country living and, concerned about raising two children in hectic California, she was looking for a safer, quieter place to settle. For two years, she and the Martins lived together on a Vermont farm, but in 1973 the Martins moved to a rural farm near Hamlin, West Virginia. They invited Ann to join them. She packed her children, two dogs, a cat, goldfish, and a philodendron plant taller than her kids, and drove to the Mountain State.

There she met other talented artisans who quickly became close friends. "Though not family," she says, "we are a close-knit group and have supported each other in many ways throughout the years." After several years, Ann met her current husband, Steve Reynolds, then a self-employed photographer. He had moved from outside Baltimore to West Virginia in 1976, also looking for a slower way of life with less traffic, less noise, and fewer people. The previous year, he and some friends had been to Taos, New Mexico, looking for land, but after he began subscribing to *United Farm Realty,* he realized West Virginia had lots of listings for cheap land. During one land-search trip, he was shown property in Tyler County, which he subsequently bought, along with a few friends. When he moved to Sistersville the following year, he knew no one. Undeterred, he opened a photography shop. Although he had specialized in wedding and portrait photography in Baltimore, he switched to landscapes after landing in West Virginia. With his photographs, Steve began attending art and craft shows in 1979.

The following year, Rebecca Stelling organized a craft show at the Cultural Center targeting shop buyers, gallery owners, and interior designers. Ann had a glass booth and Steve was displaying his landscape photography. They met and were married a year later in 1981, and Steve immediately began making stained glass alongside Ann. Now their work blends glass with modern materials to create a contemporary style of mirrors, stained-glass windows, suncatchers, and jewelry. Steve says rural living allowed them time to become master glass artisans, but also forced them to log many miles traveling to East Coast craft shows to sell their products in more urban areas. With the advent of the Internet, however, their business changed, and they could reach their client base without having to leave Lincoln County.

When Ann's health prevented her from continuing to work in the studio, she took on more of the computer work while Steve continued to produce glass. Since 1996, the couple has been developing digital art and websites, primarily for other artists. Their Juried OnLine Arts Festival and more recent Electronic Cottage Gallery have given artists nationwide a valuable online sales venue. Without the support of the state government, however, Ann and Steve might have had a tougher time making their dream a reality. Ann credits much of their success to the continued awards, grants, training, workshops, exhibits, and marketing help the state provided over the years. Now they are paying it forward by supporting other artists through their websites, by conducting workshops on web design, and by offering marketing advice. And it all started with the invitation of friends.

In the case of furniture maker Mark Soukup, friendship allowed him to settle in West Virginia as well. Originally from Cincinnati, Mark had been living in Washington state, where he taught mountaineering. He and his then-girlfriend missed their families back East, however. Mark, who had gotten interested in woodworking, also missed the hardwood forests in the East. Since trees were a needed resource for what he wanted to do, they decided to return to the Appalachian region where they had spent time previously. When a friend of Mark's, who was visiting his girlfriend at Mark's school, offered the couple his cabin near Gap Mills in Monroe County, they saw their chance to return East. Actually, the man was a marijuana farmer who was leaving for Jamaica and needed someone to harvest his crop. Mark refused to do that, but the couple did accept the cabin and lived there for the next year.

A man of multiple interests and skills, Mark worked at various jobs: house building, sheep raising, and sheep shearing. Although shearing sheep was a seasonal job, it connected Mark to the land and his interest in agriculture. Mark and Ann moved to a nearby farm and for seven years managed it and its flock of sheep. Here he began developing his woodworking skills. Although Mark quit college before receiving his degree, he had studied art while there. When he became interested in reproduction Windsor chairs, he picked up the books again, reading all he could about their history and design. As he read, he built, quickly becoming a self-taught expert craftsman of the distinctively styled chair.

Some have called Monroe County "God's Country," and as I drive to Mark's home, I can see why. Gap Mills is nestled in a lush, broad valley of rolling farmland that looks as if it should have been left in Virginia, only six miles away. In fact, it resembles the neighboring Blue Ridge valley more so than any of its West Virginia counterparts. What I also notice is how few homes there are. That remoteness first appealed to the Soukups, but after a few years the isolation began wearing on them. Gap Mills also is a Mennonite community and because the Soukups admired them and their sense of community, after several years they joined the Mennonite church. "They're not only Mennonites, but also they're Mennonites that came right out of the Amish tradition," Mark says. "They have a lot of very good aspects to their culture that are quite beautiful, yet are gone from American culture and probably have been for a hundred years. We admired those things from the outside, but we could never have been a part of them at all had we not become Christians." Non-believers when they arrived, the Soukups found, as they called it, "food for life" within that church. But the strict culture was difficult to accept. College-educated parents raised both Mark and Ann, and the old-order Mennonite belief in not sending children to school past eighth grade was unacceptable to them. They homeschooled all five of their children from eighth grade until graduation, and after fifteen years, left the church.

Being a Mennonite also affected the way Mark could market his work, for the church had strict rules against working on Sunday. This kept him off the craft show circuit, since most shows run throughout the weekend. Instead, when he first began, a friend in Lewisburg who sold factory reproduction eighteenth-century furniture admired his work and sold it for him. He also developed a clientele in his hometown of Cincinnati and began to take orders for sets of chairs as his reputation spread. The scent of wood, varnish, and furniture oil fills the air as we sit in his workshop, surrounded by Windsor chairs in various woods and designs. Mark continues to tell the story of his twenty-plus years of success. "At the 250th anniversary of Jefferson's birth, the folks at Monticello wanted to replace a number of chairs that were listed in Jefferson's inventory, but had completely disappeared," he recalls. "When they figured out what they wanted, they went looking for people that would do the work." Mark was chosen to make the chairs.

About ten years ago, after he and his wife left the church, Mark felt the need to get out into the marketplace. He wanted to get customer feedback and to experience representing his own work, which now includes chests, sideboards, and tables as well as his signature chairs. He also saw that as a way to expose his children to the larger world. He first went to the Roanoke, Virginia, farmers' market and sold some expensive pieces, which was encouraging, he says. Now he attends other shows and continues his commission work for individuals and museums like Poplar Forest and Monticello. He sells through a website as well.

Despite the growing number of reproduction furniture makers, Mark believes his high-quality work and his adherence to the standards of eighteenth-century craftsmen make his handcrafted work stand out. Often, Windsor chairs are painted and made of a variety of woods, with seats and arm boards of tulip poplar, spindles of hickory, and legs of sugar maple. Each wood has particular qualities that make it suited for a specific use, and Mark knows this. It's this research and attention to detail that make his chairs worth their $1,150 to $2,400 price tags. Now Mark's son has joined him in the business.

Granted, Mark and Ann had a romantic, idealized vision of what life in the mountains would hold. Although she once taught at the Pine Mountain Settlement School in Kentucky, Ann found reality here somewhat different. Fortunately, the friends they discovered in the Mennonite community enabled them to survive, and in some ways, to succeed. The Soukups' five children are almost grown, yet the family still struggles with how to live both apart from, and as part of, a community. "The initial thing we were looking for, we found, in a sense, through the Mennonite church here," he says. "I really believe that we had something for our whole family, for our children, for their peers, and for ourselves that I think many people probably want. Still, the biggest question in our lives is finding the solution to how to meet one's need for feeling like you're part of the world and not withdrawn from the world. It's something we still want, but in general, I think, it's very elusive."

While friendships played a slightly different role in the lives of each of these artisans, like those who came without knowing anyone in the state, the ties forged in those early years are a vital element in their lives. They speak fondly of their friends, old and new, citing favors given and received, marking their loyalty and support, claiming these relationships as an integral part of what keeps them in the state. Other artisans—Carli Mareneck, Ric MacDowell, Joe Chasnoff, Chuck Wyrostok, and Jim Probst—speak similarly of Zacher, Contois, Reynolds, and Soukup. They've fashioned a tight-knit family, despite the hills that separate them geographically.

6

Living the Good Life

Looking for the Good Life

While the seeds of the back-to-the-land movement may have blossomed in the antiwar unrest afoot in the late 1960s, civil disobedience and the desire to avoid what was perceived as an untenable war were not its only nourishment. To understand the deep roots of the largest urban-to-rural migration in our history you must think back at least three decades. After emerging from the painful Great Depression of the 1930s and enduring the sacrifices necessary to wage war on two fronts in the 1940s, weary parents vowed to make life easier for their children, who were ultimately dubbed "baby boomers." Thus, middle-class children of the 1950s were the beneficiaries of a largesse of material goods unprecedented in their parents' time and, for the most part, were raised to take their affluence for granted. That the back-to-the-landers were largely children of privilege was perhaps inevitable, according to Timothy Miller, chronicler of the hippie era. "Those who would reject middle-class comforts had to come from comfortable backgrounds; the have-nots of society had no material luxuries to rebel against," he writes.[1]

Although all classes of society did not share equally in the economic boom, in contrast to the past, most families *were* better off. Moreover, it was this comparison that mattered, not the comparison to others. Nonetheless, haunted by the memories of what they'd gone through, many now-comfortable parents feared it might not last forever. A child of that period, former student activist Todd Gitlin points out in his perceptive book about the 1960s that insecurity was lurking around the edges of all that affluence. Some feared that the Russians were coming, bringing communism to destroy their way of life. Others saw juvenile delinquency skulking on every street corner, and still other parents didn't know what a world full of rock and roll was coming to. This pervasive insecurity translated into movie bogeymen like alien invaders or body snatchers and thereby created a new generation of wary children.

In 1956, William H. Whyte's book, *The Organization Man*, described in great detail how man's driving ethos had shifted from the Protestant ethic of individualism to the pack mentality of the organization man. Belongingness and togetherness for the good of the company, or any organization, were now what mattered most.[2] Perhaps this conformity and its attendant belief that what was good for the organization was good for its members also provided the security adults were seeking. But the emerging "cocktail party" social model and the parent who was "bad to drink" may have been a result of underlying insecurity and unspoken fears, as well as the worry that the effort necessary to maintain the new reality might not be worth it after all. Therefore, it's perhaps not surprising that the number of psychiatrists in the United States multiplied almost sixfold between 1940 and 1964.[3]

For the most part, though, a generation overwhelmed with gratitude for their current wellbeing expected their children to be grateful as well. However, with what may have been simply the perversity of youth, rather than reveling in all that abundance, teenagers began to reject the material goods heaped on them and to rebel against their parents' way of life. In spite of themselves, the boomers' parents probably set the stage for that rebellion through their unwitting generosity. According to noted psychologist Abraham Maslow's *A Theory of Human Motivation*, individuals generally do not seek self-fulfilling goals until their basic needs for shelter, food, sleep, sex, and security have been met. Those middle-class kids who were twelve to eighteen when the civil rights sit-ins began and seventeen to twenty-three in 1965, when the US started bombing North Vietnam, had not been raised with a money-grubbing mindset. They already had it all. Instead, as they either headed to college or were about to gradu-ate, they began to look beyond the acquisition of things toward realizing Maslow's higher needs: finding solutions to the emerging world problems, looking for meaning in their lives, and working to become all that they could be.

Additionally, the boomers were the first generation raised with two un-avoidable realities that clearly shaped their young-adult worldview: "The Bomb" and television. At school, daily "duck and cover" drills presented children of the late 1950s with a new fear: the end of the world. The bomb not only undermined the future their parents blithely seemed to be plan-ning for them, but the basis for their affluent status as well. It already had been used twice; it could be again, this time on America. If the world was in such a mess, in whom and what could you trust? Meanwhile, the early days of television were filled with westerns—*Death Valley Days*, *The Lone Ranger*, *Wild, Wild West*, *Rawhide*, *Gunsmoke*, *Bonanza*, and *The Big Val-ley*—that re-ignited America's love for the rough-and-tumble western tra-dition, for individualism, and for the pioneer spirit. Despite the hardships endured between commercials, young watchers could easily dream at the happy ending of each television hour that a fresh start and better prospects were possible just over the next forested mountain range or across the roll-ing plains. No wonder they sought to return to the land.

Other segments of popular culture added to the youth's growing disaf-fection with the world around them as well. Because the adolescents of this generation had more time on their hands than ever before, they were also free to spend it indulging their teenage tastes, which often included drink-ing, smoking, making out, swearing, and staying out late—all of which were popularized by movies, literature, and music that made folk heroes of angry young men. Think of the rebellious students of *Blackboard Jungle*, Marlon Brando in *The Wild One*, and James Dean's Jim in *Rebel Without a Cause*. Literature's lost souls and embattled antiheroes Holden Caulfield, Willy Loman, and the characters of Beckett, Ionesco, and others suddenly became the new figures to emulate. Satirists Lenny Bruce and Mort Sahl became famous for pillorying every value ever held by the middle-class establishment. When *Mad* magazine first came on the scene in 1952, it considered itself a comic book. But in 1955, it began to parody everything from popular comic strips to television and reading. Understanding its satire was considered cool. Its overwhelming success among the youth came when it began poking sick-joke jabs at the trappings and mores of suburbia. In a 1962 poll, *Mad* ranked second only to *Life* as the magazine read most widely by high school students.[4]

The unmistakable beat beneath all the growing disaffection was rock 'n' roll. Across the country in cities where the Gallatin, Tennessee, fifty-thousand-watt station, WLAC, could be heard clearly after local stations went off the air, often-suggestive lyrics by black rhythm and blues artists Howlin' Wolf, Muddy Waters, Aretha Franklin, Otis Redding, or Hank Ballard and The Midnighters electrified 1950s teenage hormones. Double-entendre commercials for "White Rose Petroleum Jelly" or "Royal Crown Hair Dressing" kept Randy's Record Shop on the air at 1510 AM and taught white teens that the counterculture was the cool place to be. When Elvis swiveled his hips from Tupelo onto the national stage, teenagers were ready to sing, dance, and swing along. Rock 'n' roll became the music of choice for teenagers across America. Allen Freed's rock 'n' roll revues enticed white youth to defy parental rules and sneak into traditionally black events for a chance to hear "pure" rock instead of the sanitized versions by Pat Boone or Bill Haley. Overnight, music producers rushed to produce music full of longing, loneliness, parental misunderstanding, and defiance—staples of the emerging teen angst.

In some quarters, cool jazz flowed from 1950s coffee houses as freely as the espresso and as individualistic as the verse of the beat poets rejecting prevailing middle-class values and touting withdrawal and protest as the only sensible responses to what they saw as the hopelessness of life. Young rebels like Charlie Parker, Dizzy Gillespie, and Thelonious Monk had pushed the sound from big-band dance music to small-group music meant not for dancing, but rather for showcasing individual expression. In the 1950s, the hard beat of "bebop" had softened into "cool jazz," but by 1960, both had morphed into even more individualized styles.[5] This newly found freedom of expression and improvisation once caused comedian Sid Caesar to parody jazz musicians (although he was a Julliard-trained saxophonist) with a character called "Cool Cees" who, as Sid said, "improvised until he found the tune." Then rock and roll made its appearance, and the influence was a two-way street. Jazz groups made heavier use of the drums, like their fellow rockers, while rock bands such as Blood, Sweat & Tears and Chicago began to feature solo instrumental improvisation.[6] Individual expression was the jazz watchword of the time, perhaps further influencing the social scene to come.

On other airwaves, the folk music of the early '60s began to give way to protest music. The songs of Joan Baez, Arlo Guthrie, and Pete Seeger regularly held political messages, calls for social consciousness, and lyrics demanding activism. From there it was only a short riff to the harder rock music of the 1960s, full of demoralization, the destruction of the environment, and a sense of hopelessness, according to those who objected to the dire prophecies in the quintessential song of the decade, "Eve of Destruction." It marked a turning point in youthful expression. Although Bob Dylan's "Blowin' in the Wind" leveled allegorical warnings that the world of 1963 was no longer Camelot, in 1965, "Eve of Destruction" was a blunt and full-blown polemic against the world situation. When the Rolling Stones screamed, the same year, that they couldn't get any "Satisfaction," the personal and world agonies merged. Perceived resentment over mistreatment by everyone combined with the evil they believed was being inflicted upon the earth and set the stage for a youthful rebellion unlike any other.

By now, parents were completely mystified by their children. Unable to make their offspring understand the fears that lay beneath their when-I-was-your-age tales, they were shaken when their children ignored them. Parents didn't understand why kids weren't grateful for the abundance their generation had worked so hard to provide and were horrified when teens began to turn their collective backs on everything adults held sacred, including their fealty to "the organization." On the other hand, the youth were concerned with pollution, pesticides, preservatives, consumer waste, the destruction of nature, and the dangers inherent in city living. Most of these problems, they believed, were the result of the older generation's single-minded focus on materialism, and they often said so, to their parents' dismay. This was the crux of the generational divide.

Television in the 1960s brought more than entertainment into the living room; it brought the harsh realities of the Vietnam War, civil rights and antiwar protests, the killings at Kent State, and the murders of a president, a senator, and a civil rights leader. In the light of these black and white realities, intellectuals on college campuses broadly discussed the meaning of life. Budding existentialists—many of whom were the very children influenced by this new literature, music, and pop culture—believed that individual human beings, not a higher power, create the meaning and essence of their lives. In their view, it was up to them to create an ethos of personal responsibility outside of any brand-name belief system.

So, what to do? In 1965 the individualistic ethos of "Mr. Tambourine Man" and the communality of "Let's Get Together Now" suddenly merged. For some, the belief that the old world was coming to an end meant you might as well have it all. Par-tay! They dropped out to join the counterculture in a self-indulgent life of drugs, sex, and rock 'n' roll. For others, that wasn't necessary or even desirable. Individualism resurfaced. These young people believed they could drop out of the polluted, corrupt mainstream and live according to their own values. They believed they could do it right; they could build alternative institutions and families. For them, dropping out meant no longer participating in a world with which they didn't agree; instead, they believed they could build a better life, a utopian paradise. They could go back to the land.

According to Eleanor Agnew's personal chronicle of why the back-to-the-land movement failed, going to the country was also romanticized in poetry and song and the boomers flocked there despite the fact that they had never milked a cow or shoveled manure. Maybe it was the universal appeal of "amber waves of grain" or "purple mountains' majesty," but the idea of moving back to the land enticed thousands, if not a million, young, educated, and ill-equipped folks to find "the place where I belong." And perhaps it is not coincidental that many of them came to West Virginia, the state John Denver longed for so plaintively in 1971.

It is interesting to look at a map of the state and see the pockets of homesteaders who stayed in West Virginia. They gathered in the fertile foothills north of the Allegheny Mountains in Clay, Calhoun, Braxton, and

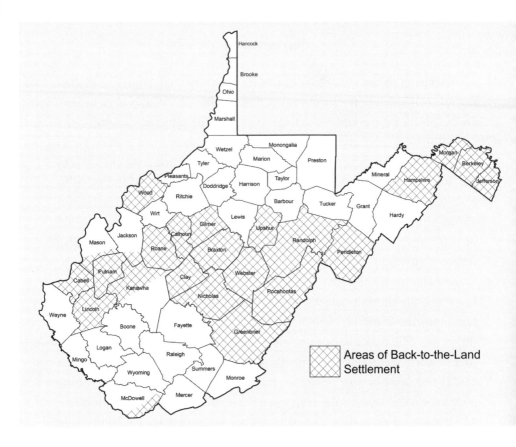

Areas of Back-to-the-Land Settlement

Roane counties; settled in the lush hills and valleys along the New River in southern Greenbrier, Monroe, and Summers counties; chose the Shenandoah Valley plateaus of Berkeley and Jefferson counties; and migrated to the farmlands of rural Lincoln and Kanawha counties. Predominate areas of coal mining were, in no case, the destination of choice. Perhaps it was chance that formed these enclaves, but more likely it was the word-of-mouth stories of others who had gone before and found a sense of place in the hills that enticed them.

To this day, several of the former back-to-the-landers still call Lincoln County home: Ric MacDowell and Jim Probst, who later brought his parents, artisans themselves. It's not the only pocket of homesteaders, however. North of I-79, rural Braxton, Calhoun, and Roane counties drew large numbers of would-be back-to-the-landers long before there *was* an

(Above) Areas of back-to-the-land settlement in West Virginia.

interstate highway. Although they may represent only a small handful of those who came initially, Jude Binder, Keith Lahti, Joe Lung, Chuck Wyrostok, Gail and Steve Balcourt, Bill Hopen, and Tom and Connie Mc-Colley are among some of the most successful artisans to arrive on the scene in the 1970s.

Because of the nature of that lifestyle, counting the exact number who went, those who left, and those who stayed is like trying to count the germination rate of dandelion seeds blown across the field by a child. Yet the national rush back to the land has been studied, documented, and parsed by sociologists, psychologists, historians, casual observers, novelists, and those who experienced it first hand. Timothy Miller, Jeffrey Jacob, Judson Jerome, and others spent considerable effort counting communes in both urban centers and rural regions of the country, but individual homesteads or farms often were difficult to find. Therefore, the estimates of all those social historians are vague at best, but it's worth repeating that the total number of those living on the land probably topped one million by the end of the 1970s.[7]

So, what of West Virginia? As noted, the population trend in the state shifted dramatically at about the same time as the peak of the movement. And the back-to-the-landers' arrival *did* help reverse the state's out-migration, but the following decade the population regained its downward slide. Are those who left the state in the 1980s like the folks Eleanor Agnew chronicles in her book, *Back From the Land,* as evidence that the movement was a failed utopian dream? She believes those who went back to the land in the 1960s and 1970s hoping to live an alternative lifestyle are now unnoticed, living middle-class lives because they were forced to abandon their dream as life grew too difficult. Granted, former potter Tom Rodd is now an attorney; nature photographer Ric MacDowell is a county agent; and weaver Adrienne Biesemeyer spends much of her time working with the youth in Africa. However, all remained in the rural setting they dreamed of when they first escaped their respective urban jungles or ranch houses in suburbia.

Nevertheless, the folks who stayed on the land in West Virginia may only represent 5 percent of the ones who came originally. The artisans

I know offer this estimate based on the number who once lived nearby. Basketmaker Connie McColley once held a "hippie" reunion of those who were originally on the land in their area of West Virginia, and she said it numbered more than 160 of their acquaintances. Furthermore, I've seen evidence that many others are still in the state but now hold jobs "off the land" as lawyers, hoteliers, restaurant owners, environmental activists, teachers, social workers, medical personnel, or dance instructors to allow them to survive in their chosen state.

It is difficult to argue with the researchers' numbers, however. Agnew quotes Simon Shaw, producer of the PBS series *Frontier House*, who estimated that the number of western homesteaders who succeeded was only 40 percent. She believes that the gap between the dream and the daily challenges, danger, and near impossible odds was too much for most back-to-the landers to bridge.[8] Jeffrey Jacob's extensive research on the national phenomenon—although he concentrated primarily on the 1980s version of homesteading—indicates that "only 3 percent of back-to-the-landers subsisted from a combination of cash crops, bartering, and resources on their own property; only 2 percent survived through intensive cultivation of cash crops; and 15 percent were able to generate a major source of income from entrepreneurships at home. On the other hand, 44 percent worked full time away from the homesteads; 18 percent had pensions and investments; and 17 percent survived on part-time or seasonal work."[9]

The issue then becomes not why they left, but how the few survived and succeeded. No one who reads their stories can question the naïveté displayed by these children of the middle class who headed for the woods with big dreams, few skills, and the back-to-the-landers' bible, Helen and Scott Nearing's *Living the Good Life*, tucked into their backpacks. Two such back-to-the-land wannabes—furniture maker Jim Probst and sculptor Bill Hopen—made it work for a while, but then they moved closer to civilization. And although Steve and Gail Balcourt now live in a cozy home with all the usual amenities, including two massive Newfoundland dogs and air conditioning, the couple and their two children lived out their dream on an isolated farm for over thirteen years. According to basketmaker Tom

McColley, marriages or relationships that fell apart sent some back to their original homes, while others left because of the struggle to make a living in often economically depressed areas. That's why, as his wife Connie points out, many of those who did survive were able to fulfill their dreams because of the cash a marketable craft provided. They worked hard at their trade, improved their skills, and were willing to stick it out to become successful. Tim Pyles presents another reason. He knows some who left in order to give their children a better education than they found in their counties. One Calhoun County basketmaker said she got tired of being poor and wanted more for her girls.

Jim Probst – Furniture Maker

Jim Probst sits behind his desk in the tiny office above his Lincoln County wood shop. Sketches of future furniture designs compete for wall space with photos of his family and posters from past craft shows. Unshaven and in shorts, a dusty T-shirt, and steel-toed shoes, Jim will return to the blond piece of curly maple below when we finish talking. For now the wood is secured between two vices as he waits for it to bend into just the right curve. Under the rim of his ball cap a pencil protrudes, hanging near his ear for easy access. His drooping mustache and collar-length blond hair are only slightly changed from the younger face captured in the dog-eared 1970s photo he shows me. In it, his hair is below his shoulders, starkly blond, and parted in the middle. Sitting on a porch swing, he plays a dulcimer.

Now deep creases bracket his easy smile as he recalls that time. Although college kept him out of the draft, he admits to being prepared to head to Canada if necessary. He explains his decision to move back to the land this way:

I read this book by Scott and Helen Nearing called *Living the Good Life* that really promoted the lifestyle. A lot of other people were doing the same thing. The times were part of it—the Vietnam War, dissatisfaction with society. My father worked very hard and ended up with ulcers so I sort of saw that as an example of that kind of lifestyle. I thought I was going to be a teacher, but there was a glut of

teachers at the time. I knew people who were graduating with teaching degrees and working in factories because they couldn't find teaching jobs. All of those sorts of things kind of combined to make me ask, "Why am I staying in college?" We were interested in buying rural property somewhere, in being part of the back-to-the-land thing.

After a friend who had spent the summer in Lincoln County working with the herbalist, "Catfish" Grey, came back and reported that there was property in West Virginia that the couple could afford, Jim and Glenda traveled to the state, purchased the property they still live on, went back to Indiana, and worked for two years to pay it off before they finally moved.

It was a big jump for a twenty-five-year-old, middle-class boy from north-central Indiana. When they bought their first piece of property for one hundred dollars an acre, people in the neighborhood were upset; they

(Above) Jim Probst, Glenda Probst, and daughter Emma.

said the couple ran up land prices. But the Probsts thought they got a bargain; land in Indiana was going for a thousand dollars an acre when they left in 1977. Jim admits that his motivations were rooted in idealism:

We never really succeeded in living that lifestyle. We thought we were going to come, grow all our own food, and raise animals and stuff. We bought a very remote piece of property that required a four-wheel drive to get to. We had a mile of private road to get to our property; about half of it was in a creek. About five or six years after we moved here we had our first kid. Kids just change everything. Especially when they start needing to go to school and getting in and out. My wife went to work as an accountant. She was having to dress up and drive out everyday. She was getting stuck in the mud and having to push the car out. It finally got to a point where we moved closer to civilization, built another house.

That didn't change Jim's underlying plans, however:

I didn't choose this as a place to have a business; I chose it as a place to live. There was a house on the property that I fixed up some. It was a pretty funky little three-room Jenny Lind house, [a modest house typical in Appalachia built on a foundation of stone, block, brick, or wooden post piers and marked by its lack of internal studs] but it had no insulation, a little coal fireplace. I studded it out from the inside and insulated it. We sort of bumped it out in a few places and stayed there until my oldest daughter was twelve. We lived there at least fifteen years. No indoor toilet. We had gravity feed running water from a spring I developed and we had electricity.

Soon Jim and Glenda discovered that other folks about their same age with similar interests had already moved to Lincoln County and had formed an organic food pantry. Suddenly there was a sense of community. But he still had to make a living. He turned to his hands instead of his college education. As a child, surrounded by the tools of his father, an amateur woodworker, Jim spent his days in his dad's shop, learning and perfecting his own woodworking skills. This, he thought, could be the means of support.

Now, as we enter his studio, the self-taught artist with about a month of formal workshop training under his belt points to a work in progress. "This is what I'd really rather do," he says. When he decided to end his formal schooling, Jim earned a living constructing farm buildings. As his cabinetry skills improved, he moved on to building houses before settling on furniture building as a career.

After fifteen years, the couple built a second house on property his parents had bought that adjoined Jim's original acreage. "We were getting ready to move into it. My wife and kids are cleaning the house of the construction mess, and my wife hands my youngest, who was seven at the time, a half-empty can of Coke and says, 'Here, go throw this in the toilet.' Glenda goes in there a little while later and it's in there, can and all. Our daughter didn't know any better," Jim laughs.

Now he considers the Mountain State home. "I don't have any regrets about coming here. We've been here twenty-eight years, longer than I've lived anywhere else. I love West Virginia. Some of the things I regret are that I'm just so busy that I don't get out and travel in West Virginia enough," he says.

In the sprawling workshop, jazz drifts from the very dusty CD player. Coats hang on pegs near the front door, each one progressively more sawdust-laden than the last. It's as if, instead of cleaning the first one, he simply donned another; when it too was unwearable, he chose yet another. Sawdust clouds swirl around our feet as we inspect several pieces in various stages of completion. Jim combines the style of the Arts and Crafts movement and the simplicity of Mission design to create furniture that has clean, beautiful lines.

His first line, named "Otto" for his German immigrant grandfather, has a lighter look with more curves than traditional Mission furniture and is usually made from cherry and walnut, rather than traditional white oak. It features curved arches in the chests, chair braces, and table bases, rather than the stark, straight lines associated with Mission furniture. "Dora," the second series, was influenced by Shaker, Arts and Crafts, and the Eastern aesthetic, which all come together to form an even softer, more feminine style with more open spaces than the "Otto" series.

Although he didn't always know where his inspirations originated and worried that he tried to force it, in the past few years he's simply opened himself up to it. He now believes creativity is simply contingent upon recognizing inspiration.

"Meander," the newest line, is a perfect example of his theory. It was inspired by a sculptural piece entitled "Blue Highway," and Jim says the idea simply wandered into his consciousness one day after he'd finished reading the book of the same name by teacher-traveler William Least Heat-Moon. The sculpture—wood sawn apart and then rejoined with an *s*-curve of blue glass between the halves—became the starting point for the "Meander" line. The work in all of Jim's lines is constructed of Appalachian hardwoods, including cherry, walnut, maple, and white oak.

Although modesty prevents him from listing his honors, his brochure states that he was featured in the 2001 biennial West Virginia Juried Exhibition and earned a merit award for one of his pieces. He also received a Tamarack Foundation Fellowship Award in 2006, an artist fellowship from the West Virginia Division of Culture and History and the West Virginia Commission on the Arts in 2004, and a "Best of Show" award in the Fine Furnishings Providence Show in 2004, adding to the prestige of owning a piece of his furniture.

Now a new generation of Jim's family is deeply rooted in the hills, homegrown from the neo-immigrant stock of the back-to-the-land movement. Emma, the daughter who blithely tossed the Coke can in the new toilet, is married to another furniture maker, Eddie Austin, who learned at her father's knee. Eddie has worked at Probst Furniture Makers since 2000 and recently developed his own distinct furniture line, after graduating first in his class with a degree in furniture making from the University of Rio Grande. Emma also helps in the office and with the company's marketing efforts, and Glenda keeps the accounting in order.

Walking away, I notice Jim's car. It still sports bumper stickers: "John Kerry for President," "If you aren't outraged, you aren't paying attention," and "Get Rid of Bush." Some things—the ideals of protestors—never change. As I leave Lincoln County, the goldenrod and dock are still in full bloom and fill the air with pollen. Roosters peck aimlessly by the road. I'm

dwarfed by the corn stalks towering over the fields. At the first house on the hard road, a piece of log is nailed on a stand, hollowed out, and used as a beehive. Fresh-mown grass scents the breeze and billows across the road as my car speeds through it. The leaves of three silver maples wink goodbye in the setting sun.

Bill Hopen – Sculptor

The trees are still bare, but spring is coming. You can see it in the weak March sun that warms the air even though the sky is cloudy. You can smell it in the earth coming to life around Bill Hopen's patio, high above Sutton, in Braxton County, where he gazes at the nearly deserted main street below. Bill is the artist whose ten-foot-tall bronze of Senator Robert Byrd stands sentinel under the state capitol dome and whose sculpture of the hands of artists graces the welcoming plaque at Tamarack.

Nestled between the Elk River on one side and the rising hills on the other, Sutton looks like a movie set from the nineteenth century, with a two-lane main street marking the center of the town. The vintage brick storefronts look frozen in time except for the incongruent and sometimes damaged metal awnings that were probably added in the 1950s. Along the sidewalk, a faded metal Sealtest Ice Cream sign marks a now-closed soda fountain. The defunct Sutton Theater wears a flaking Mail Pouch Tobacco logo on its brick exterior, while in contrast the stately courthouse stands in a raised block of neatly mown grass with well-tended flowerbeds flanking its sidewalks. In the hills, adventurous birds call from the protective trees that seem to hug the town, and Bill pauses. When he speaks again, his narrative has turned poetic. "Listening to this bird's song, watching your baby play with flowers. I don't need anything but this peace, and my art, and the time to make art and to concentrate on the soul of life and the true meaning of it," he says. That search for peace and quiet brought the now worldrenowned sculptor from New York City to the mountains of West Virginia.

Bill Hopen preparing a sculpture of U.S. Senator Robert C. Byrd for casting. (Photo by C. J. Brunt)

Robert C. Byrd
United States Senator

As we drive the short distance to his two studios, on separate hillside streets mere blocks from town, Bill keeps up a running monologue about his journey, his work, and his current life. One studio, a Victorian-looking church, appears abandoned, with its peeling paint and overgrown grounds. Its bright red mailbox is empty. We enter, and a skeleton standing sentinel in the corner of the sanctuary startles me. Bill laughs, saying he came with the place. Streams of light pour through the plain, arched windows, giving a warm glow to the litter of packing boxes, heaps of rope, drawing easels, and shelves of bubble-wrapped sculptures ready to ship. The skeleton seems to be watching over it all, including the mounted busts, a life-sized kneeling angel, and the dozens of graceful, bronze, female-figure sculptures that cover the tables, waiting in frozen poses for Bill to return to complete their patina. In the adjoining narthex, Bill points to a three-foot sculpture of three female figures jointly holding a bowl above their heads. As he opens the flame of his blowtorch, he explains the patina process of applying and then heating certain chemicals to achieve the desired color. When finished, the commissioned baptismal font will travel to its home in another church.

In Bill's second studio—a towering silo of a structure, set high in the hillside and reached only by a breath-robbing, steep set of steps—one large figure dominates the space. The original clay sculpture of Robert C. Byrd still stands intact, pointing authoritatively, surrounded by scaffolding, as if Bill had just climbed down after a long day's work. He ascends the framework and, standing beside an ear as large as his hand, talks about the modeling process and how this commission came about.

He was working at the Xcel-Premet foundry in Huntington when he received a call from Bill Drennen, then Commissioner of the West Virginia Division of Culture and History. Although he was surprised by the call, he shouldn't have been. By then Bill's reputation was firmly established with a bronze bust of fallen astronaut Christa McAuliffe at Sunrise Museum; the National Mother's Day shrine in Grafton, West Virginia; religious statues at

Finished statue of Robert Byrd in West Virginia State Capitol rotunda.
(Photo by Jergen Lorenzen)

several hospitals and churches around the state; and the statues of Booker T. Washington and a fallen soldier on the state capitol grounds. Drennen summoned him to a high-level meeting at the Cultural Center, giving him no details as to what would transpire.

"I went to Gabriel's, bought some decent slacks and a shirt to replace my wax-spattered foundry clothes, and made the meeting," he recalls. Among those assembled was West Virginia Supreme Court Chief Justice William Brotherton, who was working on a secret plan to honor Byrd with a sculpture in one of the niches of the rotunda and a celebration of his fiftieth anniversary in Congress. "They wanted to know if I could do it, how much/how soon, what should it look like, etc., etc.," he says. "I didn't get

(Above) Bill Hopen with Senator Robert C. Byrd at dedication of his statue.

it at first and then, incredulous, I asked straight out, 'So is this going to be my commission? Without a competition?' Brotherton said, 'We just asked Commissioner Drennen here, 'Who's the best?' He told us you, so we want you; will you do it?'"

A few days later, he presented plans, a first maquette (a miniature representation of the statue), and a budget to a larger group of decision makers. "I told them one hundred thousand dollars. They raised all that money by the next day and told me to proceed. Although they liked the maquette, they said they couldn't proceed until Byrd gave his approval." After a series of meetings with the senator and his staff, and seven trips to Washington for the maquette, the project was approved. "I suppose when you have been controlling your image in politics for fifty to sixty years you get kind of particular about how you are represented," Bill says, laughing. He then recalls the way in which Byrd gave his input on the sculpture:

I visited Senator Byrd in the Capitol and at his request sat in the visitors' gallery to observe him in person as he spoke. His gestures were his typical ones, but exaggerated for my benefit. He held poses a little longer for effect and profiled this way and that way, playing to me in the audience. Then Byrd met with me later and said, "That's what I want—a pose of action." He told me he had the speech filmed and would sent me a copy of the VCR tape to me. I was amazed, sitting there . . . here I was, a back-to-the-lander hippie, sitting in Congress, having one of the most powerful men in the world pose for me, look up from the floor of this great chamber of power and play to me, entrusting me to capture his image. Later, I took physical measurements of him, like a tailor, during a staff meeting while he discussed the situation in Bosnia and what our policy should be.

The sculpture was installed in one of the capitol rotunda's niches in 1998. Sadly, Brotherton died the previous year, before his dream became a reality.

As Bill talks, I watch his strong profile, his laughing eyes behind rimless glasses, his broad shoulders, and heavily muscled arms. He gestures strongly and speaks intently through his thick mustache, but around his smile is the hint of a little boy who's simply delighted to be playing the game he chose to play. He grew up on his grandmother's strawberry farm in Scappoose, Oregon, and knew early on that a rural setting would always be his natural habitat. Sadly, through twists of family fate he spent much of his adolescence in an apartment in Brooklyn, a setting he hated.

As a junior at Brooklyn Technical High School in New York City in 1968, he actually thought about volunteering for military service to "save the world from communism," but the wave of antiwar sentiment caught his attention, and he began to question his idealism. By the time he entered City University of New York two years later, he was fervently against the Vietnam War. He burned his draft card, allowed his hair to grow into the ponytail he still sports, attended peace marches, and as a member of SDS helped pull off campus takeover protests. "I remember blocking a door to the administration offices, telling the dean of my college to 'Go home. This campus is closed down,' sleeping on the terrazzo floors and living on Twinkies, cheese crackers, and Sprite while we occupied the buildings night and day to send a message to LBJ," he says.

By 1970, he had given up his student deferment to apply for conscientious objector status. "I went to my last appeal before the selective service board and I had my speech laid out. I was planning to say, 'You are either going to be able to seize me and put me in jail, or I will escape to Canada, but you are losing the opportunity for a good, hardworking, law-abiding citizen to work in some other work for the nation, for my national service. I'll scrub toilets in a hospital or whatever I have to do to do my part, but I will not let you put me in Vietnam where I napalm babies.'" His speech wasn't necessary. The offices were closed due to a congressional filibuster over a bill to fund the selective service. While the filibuster dragged on, Bill's lottery number was bypassed. After his college years, he fled the city that he hated.

Although West Virginia wasn't his original destination, a camping trip with a buddy who had been there once sold him. On that first trip in 1972, Bill found land in Webster Springs, but when he came to buy it, the property had been sold. The following year, another "urban refugee," as Bill called him, told him of a beautiful piece of land in Braxton County that he wanted but couldn't buy:

He asked the owner if we could just go and camp out there and see how we liked it and it was—pardon the cliché—almost heaven. It was just like Eden. It was early in the summer and everything was in flower and nothing but birdsong and sweet nature and total and utter freedom with nobody looking at you. You were just able to be whatever you wanted to be there. It was a hundred acres for thirty-three dollars an acre. That was a no-brainer because I had the money in my jeans. I thought, "Okay, I'll just buy it because it's land and it will always be worth something, but this could be my home of my lifetime." I was just in love with this piece of land that I could own. This is mine. There was just no need for a decision.

He bought the land, but then detoured to Warrensburg, Missouri, with his girlfriend, Olga Gioulis, who was seeking her master's degree at Missouri State University. The little college town of about ten thousand also held the kind of peace Bill had been seeking. He worked as a carpenter and tree trimmer—skills he picked up during college, albeit not in the classroom. There, although he was nominally listed as a pre-engineering major, he'd been goofing off making art and hanging around in the art department. He says that although he felt guilty then, he now realizes that all that "irresponsibly wasted time" was preparing him for his life's work.

In Missouri, he recalls, everyone knew everyone else and trust was a bankable commodity. It was a different world from New York. He and his girlfriend—later his first wife—stayed until she finished graduate school, then they returned to New York for a year to be closer to her family. Bill hated it more than before. "I just felt like I was in prison, so in the spring we packed up and . . . ," he says with a toss of his hands.

Upon their arrival in the West Virginia hills, they lived in a teepee, along with Olga's brother. Bill worked as a carpenter and, as he puts it, they "lived like a tribe of Indians." Although a rural lifestyle was still their choice, that summer cured them of wanting to continue living off the land. That fall, they rented an apartment in Sutton—temporarily, they thought. Bill shakes his head and recalls the transition:

I even went out there. I built a building. I started the foundation of another building. I had a garden going and I was trying to make a little bit of money as a carpenter and make a little bit of art and get somewhere. I was just defeated by the energy it all took. You beat down the weeds here and they grow up there and you think, "What's the use?" I had a romantic idea about living on a little farm and raising my own food. But now I was unwilling to sacrifice that time to an unexpected other thing that was happening: my art career was blossoming. When the house that we were renting came up for sale it made more sense to buy that, live in town, have electricity, and make sculpture all day instead of chopping down weeds with a chainsaw and reading by a kerosene light all night. It was a change of direction. One part of my life was blossoming, and the other was not as attractive as it once seemed.

Although Bill had begun to make art while living in Missouri, it was when he saw the readily available chunks of hardwood and sandstone in West Virginia that he began to work in earnest. As a carpenter and tree trimmer he had worked with various tools and materials, so in Sutton he began to attack the native materials, cutting, slicing, and carving the wood and stone to make sculpture. "I rented a whole house for eighty bucks, and it had a workshop in the bottom of it and land and backyard and I could make all the noise I wanted . . . wonderful," he says with a nostalgic twinkle in his eyes. "So I could do a little work on the side and begin to study my sculpture and carving and just make whatever I wanted to make."

To Bill's surprise, he quickly became somewhat of a town curiosity. Folks apparently had never seen anyone do what he was doing, and they wanted to learn how to carve wood. When they asked, Bill agreed and began teaching an adult education class that also supplemented his income. Within a year, he was convinced he wanted his life to be about art and that he could do that best right here in West Virginia.

Bill never received his college degree, but what art education he did have was more than enough for the West Virginia Division of Culture and History to give him an artist-in-residence position guest teaching in the public schools. Both of his parents had been teachers, so perhaps it was in his blood, but he found teaching extremely rewarding. A two-year residency in Harrison County gave him a thousand dollars a month, a budget for materials, and a place to work. With his basic skills in life drawing and oil painting and his knowledge of stained-glass techniques, sculpture, and ceramics, he could and did teach whatever was needed. He says that residency made him into a sculptor. "Those two years of teaching in Harrison County were so very formative to me. I began to really take on the life of an artist, making art all the time," he says.

With a body of work and two years' experience, he went to a symposium on carving stone where he met a man who, coincidentally, was a key decision maker for a large stone commission commemorating Mother's Day. He got the commission and some national press that landed him more commissions, which led to others. Looking back now, he can hardly believe he's been working full time as an artist for over thirty years and making a living at it. "I don't know any other place in the world where that could have happened," he says, looking over his valley from the patio to which we have returned. "This was fertile soil for that seed of a career to fall on and germinate."

Bill kept the land in Braxton County for years, although he never lived on it again. Later it was sold to help pay for his children's college tuition and to buy an old church in Sutton, which was turned into an art center. The Landmark Studio for the Arts lives on; today it houses an award-winning theater and a performing arts center. "I probably would have been wiser to invest that money in some kind of stock fund or something, but I invested in what I love, which is historic architecture and art and community. That's investing in your life and what you love and the meaning of your life. So a poor financial move was a wonderful investment in spiritual goods."

In the mid-1990s, Bill and his wife divorced, but his career continued to flourish with commissions and gallery sales. Now he began modeling his figurative sculptures in clay and casting them in bronze, sometimes in West Virginia. But soon Bill learned that casting in China was much more affordable, and he began spending about half the year there overseeing the progress of his pieces. He began selling some of his smaller work from his website—direct to customers—rather than through galleries. "I just thought it was great, and for West Virginia, it's such a new chapter in the history of this place," he says. "To live in this place that's just so quiet and calm and peaceful, and to have the Internet bringing the whole world to buy your goods, and you can import and export. It's amazing," he says.

The computer brought him more than customers, however. It brought him the connection to his second wife, Ai Qiu. One day a curious email from a sculptor who had read of Bill's work appeared. Bill says he was intrigued with the way the sender's English grammar was poetically fractured. It was a month before he discovered the writer was female. They began talking about art, life, and poetry, and soon were exchanging pictures. Their conversations became the most anticipated part of his day. "I would spend an hour or so answering her in poetry because to speak simply in these broad images that are like Chinese characters, it becomes a poem—just automatically does. Now we have a whole book of this poetry that was sailing back and forth on electronic media." Ten months later, after both had completed big projects, Bill went to China for a month, and the couple fell in love with each other's work, life, and philosophy. Bill invited her to come work in the United States, which she did. It didn't take long before they were married. Now in his midfifties, Bill's family numbers four young children, as well as his two grown ones, Gabe and Mya, from his first marriage.

Both Sutton and Bill Hopen have benefited from his move to the mountains. "In New York City you feel you could work just night and day and work your fingers to the bone and do all kinds of great things and no one would ever notice or appreciate," Bill says as he gestures over his shoulder to the town below. "In a community like this you can really see your imprint and how you change the history of this place, its nature, and its quality of life. Living here you really see your own actions make a difference," he says. Sutton did notice and does appreciate the artist in its midst. Not long after he began to gain success as a sculptor, he says, "people that I didn't really know would stop me on the street in Sutton and say, 'You're that artist fellow, aren't you?' They'd say, 'We're so proud that you came here to live with us.' I'm welling up right now." Bill removes his glasses, wipes his eyes, and then smiles. "That doesn't happen in a lot of places in the world, you know. It's a feeling of acceptance, that you're a part of the family. You're an adopted son, but you've made the grade. You're all right and you become a part of their community and people start bragging about you. I like that," he says. His soft laughter floats across the town below.

Gail and Steve Balcourt – Candlemakers

As I drive to the tiny Braxton County town of Exchange, West Virginia, to visit Gail and Steve Balcourt, my mind wanders and I'm back at the Mountain State Art & Craft Fair (MSACF) in 1978 or 1979, when I first met them. The stream of fair visitors has subsided in the late afternoon heat. Perhaps they've stopped to listen to the fiddler over the way, or to eat an ear of fresh-roasted corn as they rest under the dining tents. It doesn't matter, for I, too, am taking a longed-for break from selling the patchwork and quilted designs of Appalachian Craftsmen. Leaning on the counter of our lakeside tent, I watch Gail Balcourt cover the fairway in purposeful strides. She is what my mother would have called a raw-boned girl. She holds a baby hiked against one hip and grips a toddler with her other hand. In a long, flowing skirt, tied-dyed tank top, and bare feet, she looks sturdy and able to handle almost anything that comes her way. Her ash-blonde pigtails, thick as a cowboy's lasso, brush her breasts, loose under the knit top. She's headed back to the bright-topped tent beside the lake, where her wiry husband, Steve, stokes a fire to melt wax for the multi-armed candelabra sculptures that are his trademark.

He, too, has the hallmarks associated with the back-to-the-landers: a full beard and collar-length hair, which he brushes off his high forehead as the sweat beads gather in the July heat. He's leaning over a vat of molten wax, carefully dipping the braided cotton wicks up and down, up and down, until his candles are just the right diameter. A small crowd has gathered in front of the hot kettle to watch Steve's demonstration. Gail quickly puts their daughter, Ruthie, on a blanket at the rear of the tent and admonishes three-year-old Josh to sit still. She turns, smiles, and reaches across their rough, lumber counter to complete the sale of a pair of Steve's variegated, hand-dipped candles. This particular set fades from royal purple at the base to pale lavender at the tips. As she counts back the change, her accent belies her address. It signals New York, but their farm in Shock, West

Virginia, sits high on a ridgetop overlooking Calhoun, Gilmer, and Braxton counties.

Now, as I arrive at their home, I realize it's been thirty years since I've seen them, yet they greet me as if it has been only a few days. Gail's hair is collar-length with a few streaks of gray and Steve's beard is nearly white, his forehead higher. But they sound just the same, as though they arrived in West Virginia only a few days earlier. As we sit around their dining room table sipping coffee, they talk over each other as they relate their story.

Brooklyn boy Steve Balcourt learned to make candles while attending the Art Center School of Design near Los Angeles, then used his skill to pay for the film and chemicals needed for his major and life's passion: photography. He was slated to go back to New York to join his artist father's business, Balcourt Art Service, when his focus shifted. Edward Balcourt was a well-known painter of movie posters, paperback book covers, romance novels, and westerns. He wanted Steve to be his photographer so badly that when Steve's interests changed from commercial photography to fine art photography, the elder Balcourt thought his son had lost his mind. Greatly disappointed, he stopped supporting Steve's education. Undaunted, Steve returned to Long Island, set up a candle shop, and began to develop his own client base.

Meanwhile, Massapequa-born Gail was rebelling herself. Her parents were determined that their daughter attend the Catherine Gibbs Secretarial School, but she wanted to become a teacher. When they refused to pay her tuition, Gail moved out, got an apartment in the nearby ocean town of Long Beach, and took a job at a produce market to pay her community college expenses. Enter Steve Balcourt, who says Gail came to his door one day under the pretense of buying a candle. Gail laughs as Steve says, "The rest is history." It was a whirlwind courtship. Gail recalls, "You said, 'I'm moving to West Virginia. If you want to come with me, we better get married because they really frown upon people living together down there.' And I said, 'Oh, OK.' So the next day we went to Virginia and got married, and

Gail Balcourt shows off Steve's candles at the Harvest Moon Festival, 1979. (Photo courtesy Parkersburg Sentinel*)*

then came home and called our families." Gail was eighteen, and he was twenty-four when they married in March 1975.

Although Steve had never been to West Virginia, he *had* read an article in *Mother Earth News* that reported good things about the state, including its cheap land. He wanted to live in the country, raise kids, and make candles. It seemed to be the right spot. Shortly after visiting a friend's farm in Sissonville, near Charleston, Steve rented a house from him on nearby Coon Creek Road. A few months later, he bought his own homestead: twenty-five acres just down the road for fifteen hundred dollars. It was nothing but a rugged hillside with an old shack and a hand-dug well. He also bought a 1950 Dodge Power Wagon so he could navigate the road. It was a military truck—a three-quarter-ton weapons carrier with chains on all four wheels—necessary for reaching the house.

When the Balcourts arrived in April, the shack had no insulation, no electricity, and no windows. Gail was pregnant. Although appalled at the rats' nests and left-behind garbage, she realized this was to be her home, so she grabbed a broom and began sweeping. Steve went to work installing windows and insulation. They did without electricity, however, using instead a wood cookstove and candles in both the house and the shop he built for the candle business. Although neither of them had done more than a little backyard gardening, they soon learned what to do with the rich bottomland on their farm. Friends who owned a bookstore in Charleston traded them books for candles so they could learn the skills they lacked. Gail laughs as she describes their learning curve. "We have pictures of Steve butchering a pig with a book up on the windowsill. We'd go step by step, figuring out how to cut it," she says.

Following a harrowing night that culminated in the birth of their second child, the Balcourts moved to a farm in Gilmer County. Gail recounts that night:

I was pregnant with Ruth. My water broke, and we had to walk two miles out just to reach our truck. When we got in it, neighbors who were night custodians at Sissonville High School had borrowed the battery. We got in somebody else's van and just made it to Memorial Hospital in Charleston. We didn't know a single soul, and Josh is with us. He's only a year and a half. There was an elderly grandmother sitting in the waiting room, and Steve said, "Here, watch him. We're having a baby," and he comes running in with me. Ruthie was born just ten minutes after we got to the hospital.

By 1978, with two children under the age of two, they were on the ridgetop farm—a completely different experience from living up the hollow. As Steve and Gail's words tumble forth, you hear how much they loved it:

It was liberating. There was a lot of sun. It was warm. The sun would rise early. You could watch the storms come in and see the thunder and the lightning. We had four or five big gardens, and we built a big double-chamber root cellar out of cinder blocks. We had two freezers and a small orchard. We planted thirty-five apple trees and peach trees. We had a nice blueberry plantation. We hunted for deer. We raised rabbits, chickens, ducks, turkeys, and pigs, and had a dairy of ten or fifteen Saanan milk goats. We sold milk and cheese and made yogurt. We raised the pigs on excess milk and whey. It was great quality meat. We butchered everything ourselves, and we raised field corn to feed the livestock. There were no tractors. Just the two of us. We had a team of twelve-hundred-pound draft mules and a lot of Amish equipment. We had hillside plows, a buck rake, mowing machines, cultivators, and all that stuff. I built a big candle workshop over the root cellar. We taught Josh and Ruth at home until high school. What we loved about the farm was the twenty thousand acres of woodlands that adjoined it. It was uninhabited. I mean we were just in the middle of nowhere. There was no industry, no pollution—just us and the bears.

Although they didn't have much knowledge, they learned fast—by experience and with the help of their older neighbors. The neighbors had huge gardens and willingly shared their information about planting with the young couple. Interestingly, Gail said some of the children of the older couples seemed to resent the relationship their parents formed with these young transplants. "I don't know if it was because they had to move away to get jobs and they saw us almost like being the children with

their parents," she said. "But, the old folks would call Steve up and say, 'Could you come plow my garden?' and Steve would go over and plow the garden. We helped each other in that respect." The Balcourts showed an interest in what the old people thought and what they knew. In turn, the farmers told Gail and Steve about old-time remedies, introduced them to rhubarb, and showed them a plant they used to substitute for aspirin. One man dedicated a poem he wrote to their son, Josh.

While Gail now waxes nostalgic about life on the farm, it involved lots of hard work and sacrifice on their part, as well as on the part of their kids. Gail says Ruth and Josh remember eating sausage every day for lunch, and that Ruth says the thought of beet soup now makes her sick because her mother made it so often. Nevertheless, processing their own food made the family nearly self-sufficient. Gail even made their ketchup. They relied on the local Kroger only for sugar and paper products, racking up a bill of only twenty dollars on each infrequent visit.

If Steve could have had his way, he'd have spent more time gardening and less time pouring over vats of hot wax, but the candle business began to thrive. And these were no ordinary candles. Steve specialized in multicolored, contemporary-looking tapers—a style he developed on his own—that resembled a candelabra made from wax. The flat base supported six gracefully curved tapers, like arms reaching toward the sky. He used five different kinds of wax to ensure a dripless, smokeless product. While the wax was hot and pliable, he shaped and pieced them together until they formed the desired structure. Once built, each sculpture was re-dipped in different colors of wax to achieve the multicolored effect. Some were the hues of autumn, and others relied on subtle shadings of the same color: gold to pale yellow, crimson to pale pink, or deep indigo to baby blue.

When the Balcourts arrived, the West Virginia Art and Craft Guild was just being organized and The Shop at the Cultural Center in Charleston was only a dream. Therefore, Steve relied on the East Coast craft and gift

Steve and Gail Balcourt at their home near Sissonville, West Virginia. (Photo by David Vick, courtesy Charleston Gazette)

shows and a catalog to produce sales. Soon they began to net thousands of dollars, but the orders necessitated hand delivery to Boston and Baltimore because the unusual candles were too delicate to ship. Before the days of Tamarack, the West Virginia market consisted primarily of a few fairs. Some, like the Mountain State Art & Craft Fair, were large, but most were small local shows. Even attending these was difficult. Gail says, "There reached a time where we couldn't go as a family because we had goats to milk and other things like that. Steve usually would go and take one or both of the kids with him. The owners of the health food store at Glenville had a daughter, though, who would come out to our farm from time to time so I could go to the fair at Ripley."

Neighbors proved a literal lifesaver one winter when Steve and Gail needed some cash. Orville, one of their neighbors and an old logger, offered to teach Steve about felling timber to sell, despite his total ignorance of the process. Orville walked him through the steps, and Steve set out one morning to tackle the job. The tree fell the wrong way and pinned him. When a blizzard blew up and Steve didn't return, Orville went out to get him. When he found Steve, Orville cut the tree off his leg and then tied Steve to a bulldozer to pull him up. The Spencer hospital couldn't care for the leg, so Steve had to be transported to Charleston. Gail recalls that time vividly. "I called Orville's wife, and their grandson was working with him," she says. "His grandson stayed with Josh and Ruth so I could go with Steve. He is in the back of a pickup truck with the snow, and the neighbors come out and give us an umbrella to hold over him so we could wait for the ambulance." Orville and Nellie's grandson stayed with Josh and Ruth the entire ten days Steve was in the hospital. When he was released, the neighbors came to Charleston to get him. They had made a sled to pull Steve up the driveway because the snow was so deep. "There was such an outpouring of love from our neighbors who would come and take our laundry because they knew that I had to help take care of Steve," Gail says. From January, when the accident occurred, until the end of August,

Steve Balcourt explains his "no-mold" candlemaking technique.

neighbors brought dinners. Their church held services at the Balcourts' home so Steve could worship with them. Their doctor even traded his medical services for candles and a ham.

Eventually, however, the success of Steve's candles proved their home-based industry's undoing. He began receiving more orders than he could fulfill. They poured in from Tiffany & Co. and Macy's, from California, and all over the country, but the quantity they demanded was too great for one person to produce. Unable to manage both the farm and the business, he had to cut back. That shift, the inability to properly ship the products, and the rising cost of materials finally caused the Balcourts to rethink their lives after almost fourteen years.

Steve says it was the hardest decision of his life. "I just couldn't make enough money. I reached a point where I was only making X amount, and it just wasn't enough. Besides, at that time, the market was changing as well. People who were wealthy were willing to pay a lot of money for high-end items, but the middle-class working person, who was our bread and butter, didn't have extra money to lay out for a nice evening dinner centerpiece. They loved the work but just couldn't afford it." The craft scene was changing too, from artists who actually worked with their hands to commercial operations that could hire staff. It frustrated Steve to know that the public wasn't aware of the difference. "Here I am doing the best work of my life. I was using the best materials and had perfected my dyes, but people just didn't realize that I was making the things they were looking at. They just kinda walked past me, and it was just breaking my heart to experience that. I said, 'I've had enough; I'm going back to school.'"

Before Steve could make good on his threat, Gail beat him to the punch. When their children opted for public high school, rather than continue being homeschooled, Gail decided to become a teacher, the career choice of her youth. Steve knew he wasn't the type to stay home while his wife supported the family, so after one more year of pouring his heart and soul into the candle business without a profit, he, too, reluctantly returned to the classroom. He says, "I didn't want to give that up. That was really my vision: to live off the farm and off the craft business." Ironically, however, his decision allowed them both to fulfill their earliest dreams.

Because of their financial situation at the time, they received Pell grants, got financial aid, and took out student loans that they are still repaying. One year, because she couldn't afford personal transportation, Gail rode the county school bus to Glenville College, where she obtained her teaching degree. Now totally immersed in the field of education, she holds a graduate degree from Marshall University in school administration and was named special education teacher of the year in Braxton County in 2004. Steve went back to the University of Charleston when he was thirty-eight to become a registered radiology technologist. He has been working a weekend tour at a small rural hospital in Gassaway, doing all the x-rays and CT scans since 1990. His schedule allowed him to return to his earlier passion—large-format photography—both in his profession and at his home-based photography studio.

Although radiological technology feels a bit like photography to Steve, it still wasn't precisely what he'd loved previously. "I got into x-ray because it was kinda photographic to me. I was working in a dark room. I was developing films. I was taking pictures, but . . ." He trails off and Gail resumes the story. "Steve pulled out his old cameras and was playing around with them because he wasn't doing anything artistic anymore. Then I saw an opportunity for him to take a workshop with one of Ansel Adams's last assistants at a university in Maryland that had a scholarship program." Gail convinced her husband to apply. He gathered a portfolio of his work, sent it off, and was accepted into the week-long intensive workshop with Rod Dresser, a well-known, black-and-white, fine-art photographer who had worked with Adams near the end of his life.

That workshop rekindled the fire. Steve radiates as he talks:

I said, "You know, I'm going to do this. I can do this. This is my passion." I got a bigger camera so I could have bigger negatives because I didn't want to use an enlarger. It's hard to explain why. When you look at 35mm contact strips, the contact prints always really glow, and then when you blow them up, everything changes, so I wanted a negative the size of my print. I got a camera that will actually make an eight-by-ten-inch negative. Now I am currently building a body of work in black-and-white images using traditional, old school methodology: platinum and palladium printing, hand coating my own paper, and producing silver chloride eight-by-ten-inch contact prints. I had a nice article published in the September 2005 issue of *Wonderful West Virginia* magazine, and I do exhibit occasionally. But I make images primarily for my own pleasure, with the hope that others will find a connection and appreciation of my work.

It's the dream of long ago, reborn. Not surprisingly, what Steve captures through his viewfinder often invokes nostalgia—abandoned vintage cars, wooden screen doors, gnarled roots, a lone metal porch chair—and they have a hauntingly beautiful quality. He says he finds a deep appreciation for nature as he searches for his subjects, and then he responds on an emotional level. It shows.

Yet after all those years as successful homesteaders, the Balcourts feel they copped out when they sold the farm and moved to town in 1990. Although they still live on five acres in a rather rural setting in Exchange and get their mail at the only somewhat larger town of Sutton, they no longer garden, raise livestock, or live by candlelight. Steve does, however, make beer. And he has awards attesting to its quality. Nevertheless, the boy who wanted to be an art photographer and the girl who wanted to teach are now both doing so. After eighteen years and a lifetime of back-to-the-land experiences, Steve and Gail may no longer be living in a homesteader's utopia, but coming to West Virginia allowed them to fulfill their own personal dreams. And they found a community of neighbors who nearly adopted them. Gail again recalls the support they received when Steve was injured. After she'd spent days at the hospital without money or a checkbook, Gail needed desperately to get cleaned up and get some fresh clothes. She walked to the Cultural Center and asked the craft shop manager, Rebecca Stelling, for help. Without hesitation, Rebecca gave her what she needed. She says simply, "I love West Virginia. If there was only one place to live, that's where we'd [choose to] be."

7

Finding Utopia in Floe and Chloe

Keith Lahti – Potter

According to *Back From the Land* author Eleanor Agnew, America's strain of Puritanism also may have fueled the back-to-the-landers' desire for shedding themselves of material goods. She says that because self-denial and moderation are imbued with virtue, by renouncing possessions and technologies, they announced their superior level of integrity. When Detroit native Keith Lahti left Michigan, he did just that, even though his newly launched pottery business had begun to provide him a modest income.

A graduate of Albion College, a small liberal arts school in southern Michigan, Keith says he plundered through several majors before doing what he always dreamed about: becoming an artist. Although he didn't take pottery until his senior year, once he got his hands in the clay, he was hooked. At Albion, Keith also was actively opposed to the war in Vietnam and attended the 1969 March on Washington, a scene he calls "crazy with millions of people, cops, soldiers, and tear gas." That event bolstered his belief that the military-industrial complex had gotten out of control and solidified his decision to move as far from society as possible. After the march, he spent the rest of his college years working with the Quakers as a draft counselor. While he had no quarrel with those who did want to serve, he counseled others to help them avoid service, if possible, and if not, tried to help them adjust once they returned.

Following his draft-counseling days, Keith and his bride, Julia Cassells, settled down in a farmhouse outside Albion while he drove a truck for six months in order to build his first kiln and buy a potter's wheel. Still, his philosophy, and that of his fellow hippies, was to be as self-sufficient as possible and to live in an ecologically sustainable manner. He felt he could do more to reach that goal if he left Michigan. In 1972, he and Julia took off to pursue that dream.

Like searching for a chocolate-covered cherry in a Whitman's Sampler, he considered other states first. North Carolina, Kentucky, and Tennessee were on the list, and he almost bought property in north Georgia. But it wasn't quite right, either. Keith admits West Virginia wasn't on his radar screen until he came to the state by chance. "I really didn't think about West Virginia because no one knew anything about it. It was considered by northern ideas a coal-mining wasteland back in that time. No one knew what kind of beauty and culture was here, and still is. It's the best kept secret, as they say," he states emphatically. Yet one of his wholesale customers knew of Keith's quest and suggested West Virginia. He told him about a guy named Mike Roundhouse who had bought land and was seeking like-minded folks to form a craft community. Curious, Keith and Julia headed through Ohio, over US Route 33 and down US Route 16. It was the spring of 1973, and I-79 was under construction.

Keith recalls the day they found Roundhouse and their new home. Directed up and over the hill by a local boy, they were stunned by the condition of the unpaved road ahead. "It was during the spring thaw and it was a sea of mud. We said, 'That's a road?' We were from Michigan; we had never seen West Virginia roads. They were way worse than they are now. We churned our way up and down the other side," Keith recalls.

Mike Roundhouse was living in an old two-story log house, nestled at the foot of the hill under a hemlock tree, along with some hippie friends from California who had stayed on when their van broke down. "We pulled up to this driveway. The leaves were just budding on the trees and the redbuds were blooming. Here's this overgrown place in these hills, up this driveway, which was horrible too. You could get stuck walking in the driveway. But I just looked around and thought I'd died and gone to heaven. It was just the most beautiful place I had ever seen. Two weeks later I owned it." Keith paid three thousand dollars for the ancient log house and thirty acres of Mike's land, although he'd never set foot on West Virginia soil until he got out of the car that afternoon. After working another year in Michigan to save enough money to build a pottery shop on his land, Keith moved to Clay County, to Floe, a town that no longer exists.

His family had gardened in Michigan, but Keith says he didn't inherit or absorb a lot of their knowledge. Although he grew up with an appreciation for the vegetables his parents and grandparents harvested each year, learning to survive on what he grew was a life skill he gained in West Virginia. He is still learning, he admits. "I took notes again this year, after thirty-five years of gardening. I want to do it differently next year. Usually, I set aside August every year for preserving the garden. I can and freeze, and I grow a big garden. I was out picking the raspberries today. I've got a big fall garden planted, so that's been a part of my lifestyle."

Keith believes he never was destined to stay in Michigan, but his youthful dreams didn't include precisely how he would survive in the mountains. "When I was in kindergarten, they had us draw a picture of what we wanted to be when we grew up," he says. "Believe it or not, I drew a picture of an artist living in a log cabin in the mountains. From my earliest memories, I would check off on the calendar, starting in March, when school would let out and my family and I could go to the country. I just always knew that I was going to live in the country somewhere."

Perhaps he should have planned better, though, because carpentry was not a skill he brought with him, either. Undaunted, Keith taught himself by reading books and learning from the neighbors who had lived on the land their entire lives. "Our neighbors were mostly older people at the time, traditional West Virginians, some of whom still farmed with horses and stuff. It was really neat that I came in time to get exposed to that. They helped some with the gardening skills too, and they instantly accepted us." He says they formed an instant bond because he was interested in the skills they had that their own kids didn't care about. "We wanted to know how to work the land, and their own kids were leaving it, so they were actually tickled to death to have us here. They got a laugh

out of us, too, out of some of the ways we tried to do things," Keith says with a chuckle.

Keith likens those early days to living on the frontier:

It took a lot of hard work, ingenuity, and persistence to overcome our own stupidity. We learned everything from scratch because there wasn't anyone else to do it. Any building project that came up, we'd go around the neighborhood to all the different back-to-the-landers and ask, "How would you do this?" By the time we got done, we had a pretty good set of skills between us. We had cooperative work crews for a while. Once a week, or once every couple of weeks, we'd get fifteen people together, converge on Joe's farm, and do some big job. Then we'd all get together on John's farm and do the same thing over there. We had to learn to fix vehicles, too. We tried to do everything for a while.

It was that sort of ingenuity that built the house in which Keith now lives. Over coffee, steaming in a mug from those early days, Keith tells the story:

During the first couple of summers there were hippies from all over coming in barefoot. They were just having a ball picking the apples off the trees, and then winter came. My old log house was *the* coldest house in the world. We'd sit in the living room with a wood stove glowing red hot, with down jackets on, warm in the front from sitting around the wood stove and cold in the back, just like sitting around a campfire outside.

A good friend of mine and his woman, who was going to have their baby that winter, didn't have a warm place to stay. He said, "Hey, how about if we scrounge up some material, rebuild that old house over the cellar, stay in there for the winter, have our baby, and see what happens?" So he got a hippie carpenter who was drifting around looking for a place to stay. He was a pretty good carpenter, and my friend is an expert scrounger. He scrounged up the material to frame it up, side it, and put in old, used windows.

Keith Lahti throws on the wheel, 1985.

Originally, Keith had no plans to leave his log home, despite its frigid conditions. However, when the couple went on to find a place of their own, Keith realized how much warmer this new house was and moved in. For a while, he still summered in the log house and lived in the new house each winter. Ultimately, after Keith added on to the new house, re-floored it with flooring from an old Clendenin roller rink, and completed its interior, he abandoned the log home altogether. It's this house that Keith now lives in and where we are having coffee. Since then, he's put on a two-story addition, built a room with a garage underneath it, and cut off part of one finger in the process of trying to build some cabinets.

In the early years after Keith's arrival, West Virginia suffered some vicious winters. He recalls 1977 vividly. "When it went above zero, we declared a heat wave. For weeks and weeks, it didn't reach zero during the day, and there was three feet of snow on the ground. We couldn't drive anywhere for a couple of months. A friend and I put on backpacks and walked to the Nebo General Store once a week. We had saddlebags for the dog and brought back supplies for the two families," he says. His daughter was born that January.

Not everyone who came to Clay County in those early years was as willing to learn, to work, or to endure such hardship. Keith confirms the disheartening conclusion of Eleanor Agnew's book when he says only 5 percent of the original homesteaders he knew are still in the area. "A lot of people came to just be back-to-the-landers," he says, "but with no particular skills and no particular desire to do physical work, so that sorted things out real quick. The fact that it took a lot of physical work to cut all that firewood, hoe the gardens, and do all that stuff was a huge factor. And people need *some* money to live. A lot of people came with no thought for how to do that. How do you make money in 1970s West Virginia? There were no jobs—zero. Either you had a skill, you went back to school, or you left."

Keith believes there's something about being successful at one skill that enables you to be successful at another. According to Keith, those who were successful liked to learn, applied what they learned, and did the hard work. "It's the old American ethic," he says. Keith's talents as a potter didn't hurt, either.

Once he established his pottery shop, Keith soon realized that flying solo was tough, so he started going to a lot of workshops, some at Cedar Lakes Conference Center, where the annual Potters' Gathering was a big influence on him. He also credits Tim Pyles, Cedar Lakes Crafts Center director, who brought in workshop leaders from across the country to teach budding West Virginia artisans new skills or suggest ways to sharpen those they already had. He still seeks out potters whose work he admires, often traveling across the country to work with them. A trip to China with West Virginia University ceramics professor Bob Anderson exposed him to dozens of new skills, some of which he now incorporates into his work.

For over thirty years, Keith has earned his living as a potter, selling to shops and at craft fairs. For nineteen years he sold regularly at in-state shows and festivals large and small, but one of his best markets was a summer show in Ann Arbor, Michigan. Only briefly did he "work out," as taking a job off the land was called. For a few years, he worked part time at Shawnee Hills Mental Health Facility doing art with the developmentally disabled and the chronically mentally ill, a job he found very rewarding, before returning to pottery full time. He's still at it. But it's a modest living; folks don't get rich working with their hands, Keith cautions. In general, however, Keith firmly believes West Virginia is a great place to be a craftsperson. For one thing, the living is affordable: low property costs, relatively low tax rates, and a lower cost of living make it possible for craftspeople to live their dream.

He also recognizes the support from the West Virginia Division of Culture and History as instrumental to the success of the artist community in those early days. Banding together, potters found support among themselves as well. "Naturally we gravitated together. I started the unofficial potters' gathering here, where we got probably fifteen potters that spent a long weekend here, and we fired raku and cooked and talked all about pottery and drank wine. We didn't have out-of-state experts or anything, but we shared what we knew, so there was a sense of community. Now MountainMade, Tamarack, and the Central Appalachian Guild have

(Overleaf) Keith Lahti in front of his studio, 1985. His log home is to the left.

offered a lot of opportunities for networking, business training, and training in our crafts." A founding craftsperson at Tamarack, Keith says, "I was one of the very first. When Rebecca Stelling and Cela Burge had the idea to test market in just one little room at one of the travel plazas, I was one of the first craftspeople in there. I've been selling to the Tamarack system before Tamarack. Yeah, Tamarack has been wonderful." Keith is on the board of directors of the Tamarack Foundation, the nonprofit arm of Tamarack that provides support and training for artists.

Keith's work has evolved from the functional cups, mugs, and vessels he sold in the early days to a more stylized form with lots of intricate carving and inlays. He often uses a soft blue glaze that seems to fade into the brown clay of his graceful forms. His three decades of immersion in various cultures is reflected in many of his earthenware urns that he calls "twenty-first century ritual vessels." Often the matte-finished pieces from his current line of memorial cremation vases and urns feature clay tusks, branches, tails, or deep carvings and embedded jewels. Keith's work is regularly chosen for exhibition in the David L. Dickirson Art Gallery at Tamarack.

Now the original log house is gone, but the hemlock that towered over it thirty years ago still stands. Several years after he stepped out of his car on his soon-to-be-property, he bought thirty additional acres just to preserve the space. Gone too is Keith's long hair; now it recedes at the temples and barely touches his collar. His sixty-acre homestead includes the refurbished two-story house, which is now filled with guitars and the recording equipment that fuel Keith's second passion—playing lead guitar and electric slide in the two-man group, "Holy Cow!" His pottery shop and showroom, an extensive garden, and the stand of pine trees he's been planting by the score in areas he no longer wants to mow complete his personal utopia.

Despite his comfortable surroundings, he feels those early days were the best time of his life. Perhaps it was the feeling that he had shed himself of unimportant things to learn how to appreciate what really mattered. Perhaps it was the sense that he was living in an ecologically sustainable manner. Whatever it was, Keith says he misses it:

We all lived incredibly primitive lives for a while and enjoyed the heck out of it. I was very naïve when I came here. We were just going to run barefoot and live one with nature, but we had no idea what that meant. Now, as you can see, with the satellite dish out on the porch and the room of electric guitars and all this stuff, it's changed some, but the same spirit of idealism is still there. In a way, I kind of miss that, living on a couple thousand dollars a year. We didn't have health insurance, and car insurance wasn't required back then. My property taxes were thirteen dollars a year when I had the old log house. You'd grow your own food. I was healthier, happier, and had more free time then than I ever have had since.

Nevertheless, Keith's roots now run deep in Clay County, and he has no intention of leaving. He's spent thirty years carving out his homestead and making a name for himself. "I love it here. I love the space, the lifestyle. You're fed here. I think the capacity to see that and rejoice in it is one of the things that was a common denominator of the back-to-the-earth movement," he says. "Every time I come back after a couple of weeks gone, just seeing these green hills again makes me relax. It feels good."

Tom and Connie McColley – Basketmakers

Across the ridge in Chloe, the town that has swallowed Floe, world-renowned basketmakers Tom and Connie McColley have retired to their mountaintop utopia. Their story is similar to Keith Lahti's: both couples left home to find land and live as self-sufficiently as possible; both searched other states before landing in West Virginia; and both admit to being very naïve when they arrived.

The McColleys' farm in Calhoun County is a bit harder to reach than the Lahti homestead. Tom's directions read: "Go about ten miles to Chloe. There is a sign, but Chloe is one hardware store, so don't blink or you will miss it. Take the first paved road to the left and follow it for two miles, then turn left again. When you pass the riding ring and old barn, bear to the right and head straight up the hill." What he didn't say was that the second

(Overleaf) Figure 7.3: Tom and Connie McColley making baskets. (Photo by Ric MacDowell)

road isn't paved, that it snakes back and forth in sharp switchbacks, and that if another car approaches, one has to risk the ditch on one side or the drop-off on the other to allow polite passage. It's been a dry summer; dust billows from beneath my car, obliterating where I've been.

Navigating the undulating surface, bouncing from bedrock to deep ruts, praying for the wellbeing of my oil pan, I continue to climb in the gathering September dusk. A half-dozen precariously balanced rock towers that Tom must have constructed stand like watchful sentinels along the road. Eventually I find the flat spot Tom mentioned, park, and turn off the motor. I'm struck by the total silence. Over the lush valley the sky is turning the navy blue that signals impending darkness, and a scrim of fog is beginning to edge around the hillside. Soon, both will cut us off from civilization below. The lights that beckon from the McColleys' house just over the hill break my feeling of acute isolation.

As I start toward the lights, barking signals my arrival. Tom appears on the porch a dozen yards down the steep hill from where I parked. "They won't hurt you! Come on down," he says. Although the porch light is faint, I can see that he has barely changed since we last met over twenty years earlier. Spare and lithe, with almost no body fat, he stands with arms crossed, clearly comfortable in his jeans, T-shirt, and plaid flannel shirt with rolled up sleeves. He grins and his face lights up. "Gosh, it's good to see you," he says. He opens the door and shoos the dogs aside, motioning me inside with a flurry of greeting and questions about my trip.

Connie McColley comes toward us from the kitchen, her arms open to offer a welcoming hug. She too is little changed. Her blond, straight hair still skims the middle of her back, although it now holds a hint of gray. She looks as if she works out daily, but her exercise more likely consists of tending their garden than lifting weights. The smile that begins in her dark brown eyes takes over her entire face as we embrace. "It's been a long, long time," she says. Indeed it has. We last crossed paths when they taught basketmaking at a summer art camp for high school students I directed in 1984, but they greet me as if they've missed me terribly in the intervening years.

Settled at the oval table that dominates one side of the McColleys' multipurpose great room, I feel right at home in the warm, inviting space. A well-worn oriental rug covers the polished pine floors on the seating side of the room, and an overstuffed couch beckons me to curl up with a book or to simply enjoy whatever lies beyond the large window it faces. Behind me, a handsome shelving unit of bare trees supporting sleek wooden planks covers the length of the room. The unique piece holds all sorts of art, pottery, baskets, sculpture, small photographs, glass, and paintings both native and foreign. I spot the work of several artisans I know and some I've yet to meet, but whose style I recognize. As I admire the display, Connie delivers a running commentary on each piece, including the fact that Tom originally designed and built the shelving for Poplar Forest, the cooperative craft shop she managed for several years before it closed. It's clear that they've filled their life and home with the art they love. And it's clear they've come a long way from their early homesteading days.

Coffee poured, small talk finished, the couple begins to spin a tale of two naïve Ohio kids who met in the bakery department of a Columbus department store, fell in love, married, and, in 1970, decided to take up the simple life touted in *Mother Earth News* and the *Whole Earth Catalog*. Both had been struck by the mounting turmoil afoot in the country. Although Tom once was in ROTC, he began to reassess the course his life was taking after his brother was drafted and sent to Vietnam. Soon he was protesting the war at Ohio State and was an active participant in the demonstrations that brought in the National Guard and closed that university on the heels of the killings at Kent State. Tom left school shortly thereafter, abandoning his earlier plans to become an architect. He credits Richard Nixon, as much as anyone, with his change of heart. "When Nixon was reelected, it was like, 'Well, we can't change the system. The only thing we can do is change ourselves.' I think that was a lot of what inspired people to move back to the land. There was a point where I thought, 'This thing is too big. We'll

(Overleaf) Tom McColley pulling white oak splits for basketmaking. (Photo by Ric MacDowell)

never change it. The hell with it. I'm getting off this train.' That's pretty much what we did."

With their homesteading bibles on the coffee table, Tom and Connie dreamed for two years of going to the country and living simply. They'd done their research and learned, through national realty company catalogs, that land in Appalachia was cheap. They had no specific location in mind, but they knew they wanted a region with few cities; the more remote the better. With their search narrowed to eastern Kentucky, West Virginia, and western Pennsylvania, like the Appalachian settlers before them, they set out. When their truck broke down in Hazard, Kentucky, they considered staying, but the reception was less than hospitable. Connie laughs. "Of course, we were the hippies in a van," she says. "No, it was a pickup truck," Tom corrects her. Regardless, they left, drove into southern West Virginia, and headed toward Morgantown to visit Connie's uncle while they redirected their search.

As they consulted the map for the best route, they found US Route 33 and noticed that the surrounding area had very few cities. Intrigued, they left the state highway near Ripley, West Virginia. Their strategy: stop at every county seat along the way, get a newspaper, and visit the local realty companies to see what they had to offer. The first piece of property they stumbled onto had fifty acres way up the hollow, an abandoned house with no furnace and no glass in the windows, and was extremely difficult to reach. But in their eyes, it was fabulous. The farm near the tiny town of Orma cost the couple only $2,250, but it was theirs, free and clear. Before they could move in, they had to chase out a groundhog that had taken up residence in the house. Tom runs his hands through his curly hair. "When Connie and I moved to Calhoun County, we knew no one here. We came and looked at property, and we met the neighbors, but that was it. We didn't come here with any connections whatsoever, and when you think about that, that's a pretty brave thing to do," he says. Then, less seriously, he adds, "We've always thought it was appropriate that we arrived on April Fools' Day, 1973."

Surprisingly, their parents were supportive. Connie smiles when she recalls her mother's reaction:

She accepted the decision that I had made and pretty much didn't give me a hard time about it. In hindsight, I really appreciate that. We had no jobs. I think we might have had a thousand dollars. But we had our land paid off. We just came with this invincible I-can-do-anything attitude. We wanted to live on the land and live as cheaply as we could. It was like an experiment. We got all the books on how to do everything. When I would go out to plant, first I'd stand on the porch. I'd think, "Peas, OK, now you plant them this deep and the rows are this far apart." Then I'd close the book and go out and plant.

The McColleys actually kept detailed accounting records to see how little they could spend and how self-sufficient they could be. Nevertheless, Connie admits it was tough. The notion of making baskets to sell hadn't occurred to them yet. From time to time, they took seasonal jobs to buy new equipment or to improve their house. For two summers Tom cut gas rights-of-way with a scythe, and Connie once worked for six or eight months at the hubcap factory in Spencer, but for the most part, they lived as they'd dreamed they would—on the land. "We had a real crappy diet and our shoes were worn out," says Connie. "We were really living pretty much to the bone, but that was what we wanted to do. We sold our truck and re-placed it with a backpack and a garden way cart. We hitchhiked. For shopping trips into Orma, we hooked a pony onto the cart so we could bring home our grain. We'd carry the other supplies on our backs. We lived on fifteen hundred dollars our first year here. It was all very carefully thought out, though."

A few years after they settled in Orma, Tom and Connie were in Spencer when they spotted a group of fellow hippies in a van. The couple turned around and followed them to a gas station, where they introduced them-selves. That chance meeting led to the purchase of their second farm—the one in Chloe, where they now live. "One of the couples lived over in the Grantsville area and we ran into them at different times. At one point, they had another couple staying with them who were looking for land. How-ever, the first couple had company coming, and they had to send them

(Overleaf) Connie McColley weaving a basket. (Photo by Ric MacDowell)

somewhere else. So they [the second couple] came and stayed with us. I think they spent a month with us. They just, you know, moved in," says Tom, laughing at the memory.

After four relatively isolated years, the McColleys had a family again. Connie describes how it grew:

Everyone needs family, so all of us outsiders became our own family. It was part of the survival thing. We needed each other, and we grew up together. We cooperatively took care of our children. We bought things from the health food store; we bought fertilizer for our gardens; we worked on the land together. For instance, if you were building a house or ripping down a building or clearing land or building a fence, we'd go to your house on Saturday, and we'd work all day and have a big potluck. Next week we'd go over to somebody else's house and work on their project. No telephones at this point. Tom and I hitchhiked from our place to the next place lots of times or walked because it was just over the hill. We created our own family.

Ultimately, the couple that had moved in and was now like family found 171 acres they wanted but couldn't afford. They turned to Tom and Connie, who agreed to purchase it with them.

Tom continues the story. "When we first moved to this property in 1978, we all lived in the house that's now our neighbor's house. I don't know how many years we lived there—a couple, I think. It started to get a little bit tense, so I built what we call 'the little house,' which is just a tiny little building, only twelve by twenty feet, with a sleeping loft in it. We lived in it for several more years," he says. Eventually they moved again, to their current house, which Tom also built. In order to have a bit of cash, they sold vegetables. They raised a pig or two and sold the extra ones. The cooperative spirit thrived in those days. Work parties were common and so were joint sales efforts. Soon after they bought their current one-hundred-acre farm, several other couples joined the McColleys to sell farm produce and baked goods at a road crossing. "I made gingersnap cookies; we sold gladiolas and produce. We'd keep the books and divvy out the money when we'd get to the end," says Connie. She rises to get more coffee while Tom finishes the tale.

"When we moved up here we became more of our own family unit. The other couple was raising horses at the time, and we were farming with them. We cut and baled the hay with horses. But when Connie and I had to build a house, we had to have money, so we had to generate income. Even though we built our first building very inexpensively, we had to focus on making money," he says. And that's when the basket business took over. By then they also had two small children, so working "off the land" was not an acceptable option.

They'd discovered basketmaking in their early homesteading days, but had only made them for their own use or for gifts. Encouraged by a neighbor, Scott Bailey, who remembered the traditional skill his uncle had practiced, Tom and Connie essentially taught themselves. Scott's kids had moved away, so he eagerly embraced these neophyte homesteaders. Connie says he was excited that they cared about the same things he did: planting by the moon, gathering wild greens, and having a big garden. He became their best friend. As she hands me their first attempt—a simple, white oak, less-than-perfectly-round, utilitarian-style basket—she says:

Scott and Tom and I would pick every piece [at shows] apart trying to figure out how things were done. Then we'd go back and do it. Tom split out all the white oak, and I figured out how to weave. That was another thing where there weren't any books. Tom made the handles. We had to take care of our kids. That was part of the reason for staying home, not doing any more work outside of the farm. It wasn't until the kids were two and four that Tom really started doing more carving, the thing that made our work stand out more. This first basket was probably made in 1974. We only made three baskets that year; the next year we made twenty; and the year after that, maybe thirty. Our skill level was growing. By 1979 or 1980, we were really trying to market our work.

A basketmaking workshop at Cedar Lakes Conference Center taught by Bryant Holsenbeck changed the way Connie looked at baskets. Holsenbeck made colorful baskets, which she often turned over to form into a hat. That simple inversion gave Connie a new perspective: baskets didn't have to function solely as a basket. Soon their style began to move into more contemporary forms, although they still made their perennial favorite, a traditional "muffin basket." They continued making it because Connie says she was always worried about paying the bills, while Tom was always pursuing grand basket projects.

Over the next fifteen years, Tom and Connie's baskets gained museum status and were coveted by collectors. They sold at the Mountain State Art & Craft Fair for a few years and were honored with a solo show at the Stiffel Art Center in Wheeling, where, alongside their fine baskets, they displayed their very first one encased in Plexiglas. As their work became more complex and less functional, the prices rose. Winterfair in Columbus, Ohio, proved to be a good sales outlet for fifteen years, until the price point of the baskets drove the McColleys to seek even more prestigious shows like the Philadelphia Museum of Art Craft Show and the Smithsonian Craft Show. From the latter, their work was chosen for the Smithsonian Institution's permanent collection. In the 1990s, it was nothing to find a McColley basket with a two thousand dollar price tag.

The McColleys made a name for themselves in the basketry world for more than their skills. For over fifteen years and beginning in 1979, Connie, Tom, or both taught basketmaking at the Cedar Lakes Conference Center at sold-out workshops. For ten years they operated a basketry school on their farm, sharing their techniques with hobbyists and professionals alike. Finally, after twenty-seven years of steady production, they literally worked themselves out of a market. As Tom says, "The baskets had evolved into a fine art thing, and the market was really thin. I mean, it's just miniscule." Ultimately, they simply stopped. For a few years, both worked in the marketing end of the craft industry. Connie managed the craft cooperative, Poplar Forest, and Tom helped other West Virginia artisans develop and expand their businesses. Eventually, though still relatively young, they retired altogether.

Reflecting on their career choice, Connie says, "Being in West Virginia was probably the only reason our paths followed that direction at all. I certainly had no interest in baskets before I came here. And if I had moved to any other place at any other time, I would have been somebody different. I am who I am because of West Virginia." Tom concurs. "Basically we got pushed into baskets because there weren't a lot of other options. Calhoun County is Calhoun County. The reason Calhoun County is like it is is because there are no jobs here. The choices were leave or find something and work it out. And we chose to find something and work it out. We certainly didn't want to leave. Connie and I both love it. We love West Virginia and we love Calhoun County," he says.

Observers of the back-to-the-land movement say that by the 1980s the tide had turned and most wannabe homesteaders had had enough. Many of the McColleys' friends were among them. Connie says, "I have so many friends that moved into places, just like I did, that were very, very inaccessible. Their houses were difficult to live in. Yet what Tom and I did was to move just a little closer to the road. A lot of my friends stuck it out until they were crazy. Then they went back to the city. So they went all the way to the other extreme. I always felt like they could have made it a little easier, gotten just a little more comfortable."

For Connie, however, the more remote, the better:

Even Braxton County, where I worked for a while, has too many people. That sounds ridiculous because it doesn't have that many people, but I've gone to friends' houses up there and you can hear the traffic, the interstate. I really like the crickets, the fox, and all these other animals. And I like silence. I like looking out into the night sky, seeing the moon and the stars and maybe lightning, but not that haze from lights off in the distance. I don't have to look at that. I don't have to listen to that. I worked really, really, really hard to be isolated. And I succeeded. I've been able to make a living and raise my kids out here in this wonderful spot. That was worth it to me.

Perhaps there's something about being a successful artisan that translates into being a successful back-to-the-lander, or vice versa. Connie believes that's true. "I think you have to be really brave to take your soul, your art, and lay it out on the table to let the world see. You also have to be very brave to move into West Virginia with very little knowledge or planning. It's like you have to be somewhat fearless, or maybe stupid. There's a fearlessness that dares you to do those things, and not everyone is willing to put himself or herself at such risk. Really, that is what it is. Both those things just take a lot of guts."

Their original land partners are gone, but Tom and Connie remain. And although they've left the basket business behind, they've remained true to their homesteading ideals. Tom points to the flat of seedlings he'll nurture over the winter. They sit near the window, protected by plastic. "We've had a garden every year we've been here. We had a garden this year. It's not as grand as it used to be, but it's still got vegetables, fruit, and flowers. We've never abandoned it completely," he says.

And they never abandoned working with their hands, either. After the baskets, Tom began turning wooden bowls that he sent to Tamarack, where they had sold their baskets at the end of their production run. Connie missed making things too, and in the last few years has turned to handcrafting jewelry fashioned in sterling silver and gold. While they often return to the craft show circuit, the couple is not solely dependent on that income like they were in the days of the basket business. Wise investments during those years afford them a more relaxed lifestyle. Admittedly, now cell phones, computers, and four-wheel-drive vehicles do make life a lot easier than it was in the 1970s. Nevertheless, it's the hard work they were willing to expend back then that has enabled them to have it "their way." They went back to the land, lived simply, worked hard, and created their own utopia.

8

Communes and Intentional Communities

Living in Harmony

"Once upon a time, a tribe of people went off into the woods, and nobody ever heard of them again." These words, from the 1972 commune journal of West Virginia filmmaker, dancer, wood sculptor, maskmaker, and teacher, Jude Binder, could describe many communes from the 1960s through today. And in the instances where the commune did not survive, her quote is certainly prescient.

Both the precise definition of a commune and the extent of the phenomenon are hard to pin down. For some, the term has a religious connotation; for others, it screams socialism. Most folks agree, however, that they are planned communities whose members have common interests and in which property is often shared or owned jointly. Within this clear definition, their *raisons d'être* varied widely. However, from the well-chronicled Drop City commune in southeastern Colorado, where the dwelling of choice was a Buckminster Fuller-inspired geodesic dome, to the rural Virginia entrepreneurial hammock enterprise at Twin Oaks Farm, communes of the period usually shared the values of cooperation, nonviolence, equality, and ecology. For some, common interests were not enough. Strict governance ruled some communes, while others were highly amorphous. Some disintegrated over adherence to those rules, others over the lack thereof.

While a scene of pot-smoking hippies engaging in nonstop orgies springs to many mainstream minds when a commune is mentioned, that was not the norm, according to Timothy Miller, chronicler of the 1960s-era communes. Most set no rules about sexual activity, neither promoting free sex nor requiring abstinence; instead, they let members work it out for themselves. Thus, while frequent partner switching was rare, and group sex even more so, about anything imaginable did happen at one time or another in some commune, somewhere, he says.[1]

Drugs may have been another matter, though. Some believe that West Virginia's soil was conducive to growing marijuana, thus providing a draw for the youth of the period, but there's little documentation to prove this. Indeed, the communards and other back-to-the-landers had enough trouble growing food to sustain themselves; a pot crop would have taken up valuable land. This is not to say that some drugs weren't tolerated, if not advocated, in the communes. But there was, according to Miller, a distinction between marijuana and other psychedelic drugs, and hard drugs like heroin or cocaine. The former, usually referred to as "dope," was acceptable, while "drugs" were often banned.[2]

Timothy Miller, in his documentation for *The 60s Communes: Hippies and Beyond*, readily admits that a true count of those living communally in the 1960s and 1970s is impossible to achieve. He cites a New York Times article in 1970 that claimed nearly two thousand communes could be found in America, but admits the author did not justify how he arrived at his number.[3] Miller also cites other articles of the time that reported two hundred communes in Philadelphia, two hundred Jesus communes in California, a thousand communal houses in New York City, two hundred to eight hundred in or near Berkeley, California, and two hundred in Vermont. On the other hand, he notes that scholars working on defining the movement gave much greater numbers; some said up to five thousand or ten thousand communes existed in rural America, with more in urban areas.[4]

Miller personally identified over one thousand communes in his own research, but he said he also heard of a great many others he could not name and that did not appear on any lists. If the common estimate of typical commune membership being between twenty and fifty persons is correct, and the number of actual communes is closer to several thousand—

probably tens of thousands—the real population of communards could have been several hundred thousand, Miller calculated.

Poet, literature professor, and former communard Judson Jerome, whom Miller called the most careful commune counter of all, arrived at a different number. According to Miller, in Jerome's book on the subject, *Families of Eden: Communes and the New Anarchism*, he concluded that perhaps 250,000 persons had lived in urban communes not centered on any specific creed. Given that the creed-based communes probably equaled the non-creedal ones, the total number of urban communards equaled half a million by his count. Adding evidence he found pointing to approximately 30,000 rural communes, Jerome then calculated that closer to 750,000 to 1,000,000 persons lived in communes by the early 70s. Ultimately, Miller said his math agreed with that of Jerome.[5] Nevertheless, given any of those numbers, even if they are hard to prove, it is difficult to argue with the enormous impact the movement made on the country.

In *Back From the Land*, Eleanor Agnew identifies quite a few well-known communes and chronicles the story of at least one West Virginia homesteader who has since left the state. Although she does not mention any specific communes in the Mountain State, the Fellowship of Intentional Communities, a national nonprofit organization, currently lists a dozen, and not all are throwbacks to the 1970s.[6] Arguably the most famous among them is The New Vrindaban Community in Moundsville. Founded in 1968 by a band of Hare Krishna followers who bought a small farm and lived in a rundown shack with no running water, heat, or electricity, the community now covers five hundred acres. The elaborate temple, built as a home for their leader, Srila Prabhupada, attracts millions of visitors each year. While it was built around the dream of an ideal society based on Krishna Consciousness, or love of God,[7] the community has a checkered history. Accounts of child abuse, drugs, and murder in the 1980s caused it to be removed from the officially sanctioned list of Krishna temples and communities. Now it draws both devout pilgrims and the curious alike.

While on paper the idea of living in harmony and sharing the wealth sounds to some like bliss, the act of doing it day in and day out wearied many communards to the breaking point. It wasn't necessarily the physical depravation created by the more than occasional lack of heat, water, electricity, reliable transportation, or ready food supply that wore folks down. Indeed, many stayed on the land in similar hardscrabble circumstances even after they left the commune. Instead, it was the personal conflicts with those whose ideas or methods differed from their own that usually caused the dream to evaporate and the commune to disband.

However, one of the state's oldest, Sassafras Ridge Farm—founded in 1972 by three friends who lived together for almost two years in a slightly fixed-up outbuilding on the property—seems to have avoided many of the pitfalls that doomed other intentional communities. Located on a mountain above the Greenbrier River in Summers County, about ten minutes from historic Hinton, it was not originally intended as a commune, according to one founding member, Larry Levine. However, less than two years later, six adults were living together in one large house. The group expanded and lived communally for several years, while maintaining a cooperative farming industry. Then some decided that while they still wanted to be around the group, they preferred a separate family household. At its apex, Sassafras Ridge had about thirty-two residents, including the dozen or so children they raised there.

While farming, growing, and selling vegetables and raising dairy goats and beef cattle was enough to sustain the group and make a bit of money, it was never their total income. From the beginning, some worked off the land and others had home-based craft businesses. As more residents began commuting to work, rather than working on the farm, the move to establish individual family households on the property quickened. Folks still wanted to have some involvement, but not as much as when they had lived communally. Though issues were never brought to a formal vote, the group decided by consensus to build more family homes, and in some cases to sell off parcels of land for private residences. Levine believes that flexibility is the key to the intentional neighborhood's longevity. "There was nothing rigid, and our planning was open to discussion and a range of possibilities. We allowed flexibility to change with peoples' basic needs, interests, and economic situation. There was no formal membership process. There were voluntary dues for upkeep of some of the property," he says. "It's been primarily a stable population with people being here a long time, but it has also served several of our friends in transitional times in relationships."

Sassafras Ridge now has four hundred acres, multiple privately owned residences, and some jointly held farm equipment. Currently it has nineteen full-time and four part-time residents. Folks in the broader community around the farm often join them in celebrating the earth holidays (the equinoxes, the solstices, and the midpoints of each) in events that combine some elements of Celtic culture, Native American culture, and traditions that grew out of the 1960s back-to-the-land movement.

And for about five years in the late 1960s and early 1970s, another commune existed adjacent to Sassafras Ridge on Hix Mountain outside of Hinton, West Virginia. Called The Isle of the Red Hood, this infamous group was rumored to be either an enclave of pot-smoking hippies who lived in a makeshift Sheetrock shelter with a baby grand piano perched precariously on the second floor; a community of talented craftsmen; or the owner's acreage in a "trust fund gift" from a coal baron to his rebel son. Stories also have circulated that it was part of a larger organization out of New York City, and that they did truck farming, made yogurt, and sold fine leather clothing at the direction of a well-dressed, handsome Greenwich Village entrepreneur. Descriptions of fifty people living in an uninsulated, fourteen-room farm house heated by only one coal stove; five brand-new tractors stored in a barn but never used; a shirtless young man building a stick-and-string model geodesic dome in anticipation of constructing the real thing the following spring; and walls covered with exquisite quilts are also part of the Summers County commune's lore.

What seems clearer is that Ronald Goodman, a civil rights activist, poet, and native of Huntington, West Virginia, formed the community in 1968. Allegedly, he was fascinated by anthroposophy, a spiritual belief founded by Rudolf Steiner, the late-nineteenth-century original thinker who was greatly influenced by the German philosophers Hegel and Goethe. Steiner called anthroposophy a spiritual science that investigates and describes

(Overleaf) Solstice celebration at Sassafras Ridge Farm.

spiritual phenomena with a precision and clarity approaching that with which natural science investigates and describes the physical world. Steiner described his approach as "soul-observations using scientific methodology."[8] According to some, Goodman was a mystical, esoteric guy who spent five years of unremitting toil trying to make the commune work. Under him, anthroposophy was more about the use of the land, space, and gardening and farming techniques than about soul-searching.

According to several sources, when the group arrived on the mountain, a bunch of red car hoods lay abandoned in the grass, and the name, The Isle of the Red Hood, simply evolved. But the owner of the neighboring farm, Geneva Bragg, says the name was selected by commune vote. Membership was also somewhat fluid, she recalls, with up to twenty-five living there at one time. A trained nurse, Bragg and her husband taught them how to farm, plant seed, create good fertilizer, and how to shell, cook, and can what they grew. According to her, they had books, but her instructions were better. She also delivered a baby at the commune and doctored its members, sometimes with moonshine, sometimes with antibiotics. In return, they often treated the Braggs to big dinners, serving what she'd taught them to make. And as thanks, the artisans made things for her. She still treasures a batik silk scarf she once received for her birthday.

Goodman had invited several artisans to join him, with the idea that craft sales would help support the community. Sources say he put one member in charge of the farming and another in charge of the building. His goal: to make the commune self-sufficient. Although a leatherworking business provided its primary income, there were other artisans: a potter who built a studio and a gas-fired kiln, a woman who did batik, a flute maker, a clown, an artist, and several drama teachers as well. Their business did well for about three years, producing leather and suede fashion items sold to boutiques in New York and Philadelphia. One year, the group went to the Mountain State Art & Craft Fair (MSACF) to sell their goods. But because they had not paid the booth rental fee, they set up teepees around the lake and were considered "unofficial craftsmen" until they were escorted off the fair grounds, according to Don Page, who was on the fair board at the time.

The Isle of the Red Hood was a loose confederation of like souls with perhaps ten permanent members. They tried to keep a low profile, going to town only to do laundry or go to the doctor, but even on those trips they did not find the local community friendly. Some believed there were drugs up there, but that was never substantiated. Nevertheless, they thought "those hippies" were a bad influence on their teenagers. Eventually, active hostility ensued, and the commune moved to Friar's Hill at Renick, outside of Lewisburg in Greenbrier County.

These two communes, while well known, were certainly not the only ones mentioned by those who came to West Virginia and stayed. The Farm in Putnam County, where most of the *Mountain Stage* house band (formerly The Putnam County Pickers) lived, was a commune of sorts, although each family had its own dwelling. Near Spencer, the commune that indirectly brought potter and painter Joe Lung to West Virginia was home to about sixteen hippies when he arrived in February 1972. And that spring, multi-talented Jude Binder arrived in the state as well, bringing a commune of fellow artists with her.

Joe Lung – Potter, Painter, Jeweler

By Labor Day, West Virginia's lush vegetation has taken on a tired, dusty look, as if it has simply been green for much too long. In the hollows of rural Roane County, this aging seems to advance more slowly, however. Along I-77, the trees do have that weary look, but as the car burrows deeper into the county's valleys, the hue deepens and it's full summer again, despite the calendar's reckoning. Similarly, the transportation infrastructure outside the county seat of Spencer seems an anachronism, bearing little resemblance to the two interstates that bracket it. Instead, the road narrows markedly from eight lanes to four, and then squeezes into two lanes as you head toward the communities of Clover, Looneyville, or Left Hand. From there, it branches off onto dozens of unnamed gravel roads. Ceramic artist Joe Lung lives at the end of one such road.

As I jolt along beside a now-dry creek bed that hugs the road, I recall vividly the hot July afternoon thirty-some years earlier at the MSACF when

I first saw Joe. A white slick of mud coated his arms to the elbows. His left hand, thrust deep into the rising lump of clay, was invisible. This slight, bare-chested Chinese man bent over the potter's wheel was oblivious to the droplets of watery clay rhythmically spinning off the metal wheel and onto his chest. A dried smudge of white across his high cheekbone and across his long black dreadlocks was the only sign of the effort his art took, for his face was as serene as if he were deep in meditation. I was at the edge of the crowd gathered to watch his demonstration.

Within his booth, dozens of striking black-and-white bowls, vases, dishes, bottles, and cups were arranged for sale. Most were intricately covered with crisp line drawings of abstract nudes nestled among dense, feathery backgrounds. Joe Lung's booth was as different from the neighboring display of sock monkeys and wooden folk toys as he was from the bonneted lady across the fairway stirring a vat of lye soap. I remember wondering then what had brought a Chinese man to West Virginia.

Now, at the insistence of his dogs, barking to warn him of a stranger, Joe appears on the porch. My mental snapshot of him is twenty-five years old, but except for a receding hairline and a touch of white at the temples, Joe hasn't changed. His face is unlined; one hank of braided hair reaches below his hips; his body is still spare and angular; and his arms are well muscled. Thick bushes surround his weathered clapboard home, tucked comfortably into a hillside. Old-growth trees block the distance behind the aging farmhouse, while a carefully tended rock garden climbs the foreground hill toward a pergola towering over it. It's as if he's made peace with the environment, allowing some natural beauty to dominate, while taming another plot to his own liking.

Once inside, I know immediately that Joe's soul hasn't changed either. He's still a hippie at heart. The walls are covered with the outsized abstract oils he now prefers to ceramics; a set of bongo drums occupies center stage beside the batik-covered window seat, banked with tied-dyed pillows. As we settle onto his couch, I feel like I've returned to the 1970s, but with a new perspective. Back then, Joe was the artist and I was merely

Joe Lung at the wheel. (Photo by Ric MacDowell)

the administrator of a crafts group; now I'm also an artisan, and a ceramist at that. We share the bond of clay. He begins to talk, and the tape recorder between us becomes invisible.

"I was born in Beijing, and then after the Chinese Revolution, because my father was working for Chiang Kai-shek in the air force, we had to flee to Taiwan," he says. Throughout his childhood and college life, Joe lived under Chiang's rule. Despite all his years in the United States, Joe's English carries traces of odd syntax. "Since I was a kid, I really liked art, but for the family pressure and the education system, it end up, I went to engineer," he says. Joe earned a civil engineering degree in Taiwan and worked for six months in an office calculating numbers all day, but he was miserable. At twenty-five, Joe applied to Missouri State University for an advanced engineering degree, but once he was in the United States and away from his family's pressure, he switched to fine arts.

For almost four years, he studied there and worked each summer in New York. Then, with one semester left, Joe dropped out of college, confident that his success as an artist would not be dependent on a degree. He wanted to paint or make ceramics, but without the money to set up a studio, he headed for Greenwich Village, where he planned to "hang out" in the art scene. It was a tremendous struggle, for now he had a wife and a child. Joe credits his parents with sending him to the United States, but he knew they couldn't continue to support him once he quit school. And without any money, he found the city too difficult to manage. Comparing West Virginia to New York, he says, "If you don't make it here, at least you can get by doing something like gardening. But in the city, if you don't get by, you don't get by." He liked city life from the artistic point of view, but the hustle and bustle, especially in Manhattan, made him wary. He shrugs as if the memory is too much. "The danger, just violence, all those things. I just couldn't take it," he says.

Actually, Joe's wife—now his ex-wife—drew him to West Virginia. Because she had been at Kent State when the shootings occurred there in May 1970, she had wanted to go back to the land as a protest. They had married and lived in Missouri before he left school, but when he went to New York, she came to the commune outside Spencer. When he finally joined her and their daughter in February 1972, the group consisted of only sixteen members. He recalls:

Everybody is pretty educated. That was kind of typical—1960s leftover, antiwar, very idealistic, spiritual-seeking kind of hippies. A lot were from real rich families. I remember they wouldn't take any money from their parents. Every month they would send money and the members would tear up the checks. Nobody wanted to go out to society to work—basically just doing farming and everything. We only had one car that everybody drives except to take some long trips. Every day, just to go to town, just ride bicycles. It didn't last because I think it's just very idealistic, but there is not a special one purpose to hold to. It's not like they followed a certain religion or one strong belief or a guru. Everybody was just pretty free-minded. So it was not very organized. After two or three years a lot of people just burnt out.

Joe and his family were there only three months before the commune broke up.

Some returned to school, others moved away, but Joe hung on. A young Cleveland couple he had met at the food co-op in Spencer owned a farm nearby. Since they only visited a few times each year, they offered to let him live at the farm rent-free, as a caretaker. This allowed Joe to begin painting, but in less than a year, he realized his abstracts were not providing an adequate income for his family. Although he did sell some work, it was slow going; he soon realized that making and selling ceramics would be more practical. After he bought his current home, Joe's situation was stable enough to borrow the money to build a kiln and set up his ceramic studio.

Ironically, while coming to West Virginia fulfilled his desire to be a hippie, switching to ceramics took Joe back to his Chinese roots. As he explains it, "I always liked ceramics when I was in school. I grew up in a culture in China where a lot of people still consider ceramics as a fine art." Joe's early porcelain pottery followed the Chinese tradition of simple forms with a lot of cobalt blue oriental decoration, rather than the American ceramic tradition of relying mostly on straight glaze techniques. But once he paid

(Overleaf) Joe Lung trims a vessel form.

229

off his farm and didn't have as much financial pressure, he slowly began to develop his own style of surface decoration, and his work became more modern. Using the traditional Chinese brush stroke techniques, Joe decorated his pots with black slip painted directly onto the unfired pot, creating a maze of nature-inspired forms. He also employed sgraffito—the art of carving through a layer of black slip to reveal the white surface below—and often included the human figure. The nudes he fused into these intricate abstract designs became Joe's signature style for nearly twenty-five years. But because it was labor intensive, he could produce only about one hundred pots a year.

Joe's move to West Virginia was opportune. He says that coming to the country, to West Virginia, also kept him more centered, as did making pottery:

In doing paintings, the attraction for most artists is more like a mind thing. You deal with certain kinds of emotions and visual fantasies. The ceramic is totally different for me. I always wanted to be a hippie because it's kind of back to the nature, back to the earth. When you put your hands around the clay, the first thing you do is center, and the centering itself is very attractive because it's kind of like a meditation. You have to center yourself before you can center the clay. If your mind is wandering every way, you can't center the clay. The process itself is so physical; it takes you to a different kind of state of mind, which is very pure because, for me, that's the beauty about throwing pots.

While the concept of centering oneself has Eastern roots, living simply and stripping away the metropolitan trappings of life also seems central to the success of many a back-to-the-land artisan or musician.

After ten or fifteen years on the craft fair circuit, Joe gained a reputation as one of the state's premier potters. But like Tom and Connie McColley, as his work evolved from highly functional to larger and more abstract pieces, it took on an art gallery quality and the prices went up accordingly. Eventually his market narrowed, he stopped traveling to craft shows, and finally, after twenty-six years, he quit making ceramics altogether and resumed his painting career.

Now his work is even more deliberate; one oil painting may take months to complete. He points to the large abstract across the room. "My passion is towards painting. I just feel like I'm getting older and I really want to do something where I don't have to worry about sales. I think the money itself corrupts some part of your spirit and your belief in some ways. That's what I'm really trying to get away from. I think it is a sad thing even for a lot of famous artists because they start to be controlled by the money, by the galleries," he says. Living simply in West Virginia has allowed Joe to dodge that trap and to retain his sense of artistic integrity. And like the McColleys, he's found other ways to express his creativity. Lately, jewelry by Joe Lung has appeared in several sales venues. According to Joe, "Being in a peaceful place helps my mind too." If the paintings sell, that's great; if not, Joe still paints. He's a humble, contented man. He tends his garden, he plays his drums, and he paints. Perhaps this inner tranquility is what I saw on Joe's face that long-ago July as he bent over the clay.

Jude Binder – Dancer, Maskmaker, Teacher

Jude Binder came to Calhoun County, West Virginia, full of dreams. She wanted to establish a school for the arts that would provide an underserved, rural population an environment for learning, healing, personal growth, and community building. Heartwood in the Hills is the realization of that dream. According to its own publicity, the school provides students from at least nine counties, regardless of age or income, the opportunities and resources to develop cognitive and creative skills, self-confidence, and self-expression through the arts. Heartwood sits on the mountaintop above a wide spot in the road known as Five Forks, near the rural communities of Grantsville and Sistersville. Built in 1982, without any public financial assistance, by her partner and Heartwood's co-founder, Frank Venezia, the sprawling building includes a dance studio, classrooms for art projects, and their home.

On this October day, twenty-some years later, the crisp air holds a touch of the winter ahead. On Jude's mountaintop, when the sun breaks through the clouds, the knee-high field of golden grass beyond the house shimmers.

A quick breeze kicks up and the grass comes to life, waving, inviting me to explore. From the deck that fronts the house, Jude throws up her arms and waves excitedly, as if competing with the grass for my attention. She wins. Inside, as we tour the house, art room, and dance studio, she talks about the school's latest performance project, about her upcoming documentary on domestic violence, and about her students. Her energy is barely contained, as if mere talking isn't expressive enough. I expect her to *pirouette* at any moment.

In the workshop—a jumble of works-in-progress, supplies, and paint-splattered tables—the creativity is palpable. Life-size masks of all shapes stare from the walls, shelves, and tables: masks with sharp beaks, furtive eyes, and wild raffia hair; masks with heart-shaped, jewel-edged, green leaves for eyebrows; and masks with gold eyelashes as long as your fingers, feather-like ears, and iridescent butterfly-wing hair. Rhinoceroses, cats, unicorns, pigs, and deer seem to watch as we pass by. They seem to smile, shout, leer, laugh, and frown at us. The workshop feels alive. In contrast, the paneled dance studio next door is uncluttered, and the clean, expansive floor gleams. Here, only the floor-to-ceiling mirror wall reveals faces—ours.

After a simple meal, we sit in the dining area of her home, fifteen miles from her original commune farm, while she tells me of the convoluted path to her dream's realization. Unquestionably, she is a tiny, energetic woman who looks and acts younger than her years—think Shakespeare's Ariel or *Peter Pan*'s Tinkerbell—yet she says her size has always been a drawback. "People always think they have to help me," she says. As I listen, it becomes evident the opposite is true. This woman of fiercely held convictions can accomplish anything she desires. Her once-strawberry-blonde hair appears steel gray until fingered by a shaft of light, and then a coppery sheen ripples across the wiry waves, which tumble onto her shoulders. Spread before her among the dishes are her photo albums and the commune journal, mementos of those early years.

"I was totally blissed out and convinced that all these people in this book were going to live together forever and have our grandchildren

Jude Binder, 1976. (Photo by David Katz)

together," she says. She hands the journal to me with a wry chuckle. As I study her watercolor sketches of commune members and their daily activities, I'm reminded of Peter Max's posters. Sunbursts, flowers, pan flutes, beards, long hair, and granny glasses cover the pages. These images still live in Jude's memory and in her masks. "Of course, within the first year most of them left. The commune lasted five years. I don't know how many people must have come the first year. It created havoc because you never knew when a truckload of people was going to arrive," she says. Some members took it in stride, while others, like Jude, felt limits should be set, especially when they started coming with children for the others to raise and educate.

Jude admits she's always been a rebel, but it took the death of her mother for her to finally break out of the mold girls of the 1960s were expected to follow: husband, kids, home-making. Born Judy Kendall—she replaced the *y* with an *e* as an adult—Jude had an extraordinary exposure to the arts as a child growing up in Washington, D.C. At nine, the talented ballet student danced as an extra with the Sadler Wells Ballet Company. Artistically gifted as well, at ten, she studied watercolor at the Corcoran Gallery, but quit when the teacher put his own brush on her work.

In 1960, following high school graduation, she attended George Balanchine's ballet school in New York, but chafed under the strict regimen imposed on the students. Moreover, she found the starvation, self-loathing, constant criticism, and competitive cruelty among the students excruciatingly painful. She calls it one of the worst experiences of her life.

A year later, at the Pennsylvania Academy of Fine Arts in Philadelphia, she became friends with black students, taught a children's ballet program at a black dance school, and, in an Afro-Cuban dance class, found the free-spirited style of dance she had longed for. "For the first time in my life," she says, "I just let loose and danced like crazy." Like others in the 1960s, her thinking and her art were becoming increasingly political. That often brought her teacher's condescension, however. She frowns at the memory. "They would say, 'You are so cute. Why are you doing such ugly things?'" she says.

By 1965, she and her husband were living in Ann Arbor while he pursued a graduate degree at the University of Michigan. Jude calls this move "serendipitous." When the university's student newspaper editor, Tom Hayden, wrote a list of goals—subsequently called "The Port Huron Statement"—for the Students for a Democratic Society (SDS), the protests against the Vietnam War were just beginning. According to Hayden, his 1962 list represented the first deviations from the mainstream.[9] With participatory democracy as its credo, SDS had been formed three years earlier in Ann Arbor to focus on civil rights and community organizing, but as the war intensified, opposition to it overpowered all other causes.

Against this background, Jude's husband was on campus when the first teach-in occurred there in March 1965. It consisted of nonstop guest speakers, seminars, and films geared to "constitute a clear, factual, and moral protest against the war."[10] Over three thousand students attended, and two hundred faculty members showed their support. Although the teach-in was momentarily disrupted by a bomb scare, it proved overwhelmingly successful.[11] Jude took note, was impressed with the growing SDS movement, and set about to meet its super stars: Hayden, Rennie Davis, Carl Oglesby, and Todd Gitlin, all based in Ann Arbor at the time. She succeeded, and in time became both an artist for the movement and a close friend to many of its leading spokespeople. After moving to Austin, Texas, the following year, Jude participated, along with activist Helen Garvy, in the women's sit-in at the draft board office and helped produce an underground newspaper for the local SDS chapter. Garvy's 2000 documentary about the movement, *Rebel With a Cause*, featured two of Jude's posters from those early days.

After her son Gideon was born in 1966, Jude continued to dance, but found herself drifting deeper into the routine of housewife and mother. Although conflicted about her changing self-image, she did not yet consider herself capable of breaking that traditional woman's role. Wherever she went, she danced, immersing herself in different genres and new forms of expression like clowning, mime, and clogging. After a move from Austin to Rockport, New York, she became an associate professor of dance at the State University of New York. Over the course of that year, her rebelliousness erupted into action. Following a stellar dance performance, one review condescendingly held her diminutive size up to ridicule. Increasingly unsatisfied with her artwork as well, she began to question what she was doing on both artistic fronts.

The final straw was the death of her mother in 1971. "My mother died from an overdose of prescription drugs. I had seen her decline, but I still thought, 'Well she's just going to stop taking them. She'll be fine and everything that she's ever taught me about my *real work*, which was to make a man happy and have children and make a nice home, will be reinforced, and I'll know that I'm on the right track.' Then she was gone, and my whole world just exploded. I had just turned thirty," Jude says. She knew she had to make a change to survive. Her son was nearly six and she didn't want him in public schools. She had tried to form a school based on her own principles, but after that year she gave up. "I came to my husband and I said, 'I'm moving to a commune. I'll have a school on the commune. I want to go to West Virginia,'" she says.

Neither cheap land nor the homesteading movement had anything to do with that choice. As a child, Jude's family had vacationed at Cacapon Springs, and throughout her youth, the trees and the mountains of the state had beckoned. A cherished wooden box, a gift her father bought in West Virginia, symbolized that magnetism for the young girl. Jude says, "It just never left me that if I was really going to be myself someday, I would live way out in the heart of the country in West Virginia. So I got all these people to move in with us, and we started trying to make money to get land." Doggedly, Jude and a male friend hitchhiked to West Virginia, found a farm they wanted the group to buy, and, as she says, they "bullied the rest into a group decision to settle in the hills of Calhoun County."

Like on so many other communes, reality often did not measure up to the dream. Jude recalls, "People came for different reasons, and they left for different reasons. Some people just couldn't stand being on a commune. We began to realize that this idea that we disappeared into the woods and nobody ever heard of us again wouldn't work. We needed to try to make a life; we needed to follow our dream." Although it upset Jude when her aunt predicted the commune would not succeed, she was right. Jude describes some of the conflicts that led to its dissolution. "Living on a commune, you're anything but free. You're beholden. You're in a family. You're sharing economics and childrearing," she says. The latter was the subject that caused a huge uproar. She believed that if rearing and educating the children was a communal effort, the decision about having children should also be made by the group. "I stood up at one of our meetings and I said that. All hell broke loose, but I was right. Of course, I wanted to start a school. I thought I needed to be a revolutionary, and I was turning into a homesteading wife instead. There also were some meetings that would last all day about whether or not the sesame seeds should be ground, or how to treat children, or how to discipline," she says. Her frown now turns to a wistful, nostalgic smile. "*When* the commune worked, it was *the* most exhilarating and powerful thing in my life, ever. And it did work, often," she says. Her journal ends with a drawing of the birth of the first child. Surrounding the laboring mother are several men and women. I close the book and return it to Jude, who reopens it, absently caressing the pages.

Although Jude's husband also came to West Virginia, they divorced soon thereafter and he left the commune. Ultimately, she and fellow commune member Frank Venezia became partners. When a career-ending dancing injury sustained in 1976 also prevented Jude from working on the farm, she took up wood carving, mentored by an old man named Talmadge Roy Geeho, who offered to teach "the whittling woman" about wood. "That's when my apprenticeship started. He taught me everything I know about wood. This wouldn't have happened if I hadn't come to West Virginia. West Virginia gave me the wood," she says.

In 1977, after her injury healed, Jude began teaching a class called "Movement for Health and Centering" at the train depot in nearby Spencer. Her first two students were women who had heard there was a dancer living on a commune in Calhoun County. "It was a three-hour class, and it was one dollar, or you could barter," says Jude. Soon others who drummed or played flutes joined them. It was a beginning.

When the commune dissolved, the property was sold and the money divided among the members. Jude and Frank found themselves adrift for a few years. Homeless at one point, caretakers of a farm at another, they even crashed at a friend's house for a time. In 1982, Frank found the land on which Heartwood now stands and began to build. There were walls when they moved in, but not much else. When the school opened, there was no plumbing and no running water, only a composting toilet. But Jude didn't care. Her dream was finally going to come true. Since its founding, Heartwood in the Hills has provided hundreds of students a way to express themselves and to develop self-confidence. In after-school classes and on Saturdays, the children learn dance, movement, maskmaking, theater, and visual arts. Partial and full scholarships are available according to need. Adult movement for health and dance are also offered.

Jude closes her journal. "It was a fabulous time, a phenomenal experiment, and I wouldn't trade that experience for anything. Frank and I agree that what we learned on the commune made it possible for us to build what we've built here, and for him to work his law practice," she says. Of those dancers, actors, and artists who came, only Jude, Frank, and one other man remain in West Virginia. Jude realized that in order to live out what she wanted, she had to come out of the woods and take a stand.

Today, Jude Binder is nationally recognized on many levels for work on issues that matter: poverty, peace, child labor, homelessness, domestic abuse, and women's rights. Her 2006 film, *Field of Flowers*, which deals with domestic abuse, premiered at the Culture Center in Charleston. Empowered by a 1996 grant from the Benedum Foundation to travel the state listening to stories of battered women, Jude was driven to artistically create their collective story. A collaborative project of the West Virginia Coalition Against Domestic Violence, Heartwood in the Hills, and Jude, the film took over eleven years to complete. That same evening, West Virginia's secretary of education and the arts recognized Jude with the Star Award for her lifelong commitment to arts and education.

Ron Swanberg – Leathersmith

During college, Michigander Ron Swanberg rented a house in a West Virginia community, Rivendale Farm, for about two years after a long-term relationship ended. In the early 1970s, he had abandoned academia on his way to a master's degree in biology at Western Michigan University, saying he looked down that road one day and didn't like what he saw. His brother, father, and grandfather were all self-employed butchers, and like them, he was more comfortable working with his hands. After dropping out of college, a job with a moving company, where he could simply work instead of thinking, gave him a much-desired, simpler life. That changed, however, after he spent several days helping some friends open their leather shop; they gave him a piece of leather in lieu of payment and suggested he make a belt. He enjoyed the process and kept at it, despite the meager fourteen-dollar take from his first show in Kalamazoo, Michigan.

Ron says he often makes decisions based on what seems right at the time. He also says he never consciously decided to be a leathersmith or the people's belt maker, but it happened because it was the path of least resistance. All he really wanted to do was go to the woods, have his freedom, and work the way he wanted to work. But as he continued to hone his leather skills and sell his work, a sudden decision to hitchhike to Washington, D.C., in 1971 to see the Lincoln Memorial proved fortuitous. The two people from Durham, North Carolina, who gave him a ride happened to be leathersmiths, and as he got out of their car, they invited him to visit them some time. Soon after, Ron and his partner at the time went to Durham and found the leathersmiths at a craft show in the university's student union. They secured a space in the show for Ron, and he sold all of his stock—three to four hundred dollars worth. It was enough to finance his entire trip and gave him the confidence to continue making leather goods. "It was pretty gratifying," he says, "making something and people liking it and handing me money so I could take care of my needs."

Unlike Keith Lahti, Ron's decision to live with few possessions stemmed less from idealism than from frugality. "I just did not see the need to have all that stuff. Partly it was ecological and partly it was just being tight," he says. "If time is money and money is time, which would you rather have?" That answer came to him quite easily. Although it took Ron a while to realize he didn't want to work inside, he always felt that the self-reliance he learned as a child would support him. He'd always figure out how to make it. Therefore, his new livelihood was more a personal rejection of academia or a future in the corporate world than a conscious decision to embrace leatherwork. Although he says he did all the stereotypical hippie things—

wearing sandals and growing a beard—he was really searching for his personal identity after a divorce from the mother of his two oldest children.

Soon the hippie in the tie-dyed T-shirt began showing at prestigious Michigan shows—the Birmingham-Bloomfield Fine Art Show, the Ann Arbor Show, and one in East Lansing. But in 1973, as Ron was thinking of moving to North Carolina, his friend Stan Crawford invited him to come along on a visit to his family's home in Hinton. He went and camped in a cow pasture along Madam's Creek outside of Hinton. Ron fell in love with the land and they immediately decided to stay. He and Stan and a friend bought a farm in Raleigh County where Ron and Sue eventually lived for ten years as they raised their three children. The hoped-for community never materialized.

Although the purchase was another snap decision, both were familiar with life on a farm. Ron's family owned a 125-acre farm in Grant, Michigan, and Sue had grown up farming and gardening near Kalamazoo. They figured their inherited self-reliance would help them figure it out as they went along. On the property were two houses: one log, the other frame. In the spring, Ron and Sue cleaned out the log house, added a wood stove, and settled down. Neighbors Bill and Sadie Bragg, who were in their seventies and eighties when Ron arrived, treated them as surrogate grandchildren, helping them learn what *Mother Earth News* didn't teach. "The sobering effect of being mostly around older people who worked all their life was good, humbling stuff," he admits. He also says that, in turn, the Braggs and the other old folks must have been endlessly amused by their naiveté.

As they began homesteading in earnest, Ron cut back on the number of shows he attended, concentrating on those in West Virginia. The couple built a log barn, grew a lot of their own food, home schooled the kids, and as he puts it, "lived on air." "If we needed a little bit of money, we'd go to the bank and the bank official would give us a loan on a handshake for five hundred bucks, and that would be seed money to start in the spring," he recalls. "Life was simple. It wasn't about money; it was just about being on a piece of land, being responsible for that, and life was simple."

The MSACF was one of those in-state shows that Ron attended. Fairgoers became familiar with the heady scent of rich leather that filled the air around his booth, and with the sight of his three small children napping on a bed under his counter, tucked behind a burlap covering held open by a clothespin for ventilation. When he wasn't talking to customers, Ron, in a tied-dyed T-shirt, shorts, and Earth shoes, often juggled leather balls to amuse his children, or pulled them across the grounds in a wagon. Customers, enchanted by the children, often mailed Ron pictures they'd taken of them. Clearly, his family mattered. Even his sign declared it: "Ron Swanberg and Family." Thirty-five years later, the sign is the same, and it's still largely a family affair. Two of his daughters occasionally come to the MSACF to help their dad sell his wares.

After a number of years, Ron and Sue went their separate ways, however. And although they tried co-parenting for three or four years, the girls finally moved with their mom back to Michigan. Shortly thereafter, Ron fell out of a tree while visiting them, broke five ribs and his collarbone, crushed some vertebra, and had a partially collapsed lung. He says it was life changing. After several days of intensive care, he stayed in Michigan for several weeks so his sisters could care for him. Soon he itched to get back to West Virginia, however. With the help of some friends, he returned and stayed at their farmhouse. He says it was a wonderful expression of community. "That is one of the reasons I'm still here," he confesses. They were fellow back-to-the-landers, and Ron believes that sharing that experience of living frugally bonded them. They knew what it took to survive and were willing to help others do it.

Nearly forty years later, Ron still works hard, but on his own schedule. His last show is in November so he can finish his orders before Christmas. From January through April, he builds up his inventory, and then begins the show circuit again in May. However, he can choose how and when he wants to work. Now he leaves plenty of time to ski, ice-skate, read, or travel. If, on the way to his shop—five hundred feet from his house—he decides to spend the day in the garden, he can make that choice instead. It works for him, satisfying his need to be self-sufficient while still providing for his meager needs and wants.

9

Passing it Down

Although most of the back-to-the-land migration happened in the late 1960s and early 1970s, its impact was still evident in the 1980s. Stories of the work parties, the social gatherings, and the community spirit became lore and were passed down to folks half a generation younger. These young adults were not old enough to fight in the Vietnam War or to participate in the protests against it, but they watched both on television. They weren't necessarily children of Depression-era parents, but they read *Mad* magazine and saw *The Graduate* lampooning their parents' mindset all the same. These hippie-wannabe adolescents didn't work in big cities, but they felt the crush of urbanization vicariously when others complained of it.

Glenn Singer – Performer

One artisan, Glenn Singer, came to the Mountain State ten years later than most, but spiritually he says he feels at one with those he followed. I never heard Glenn speak in the first few years I knew him, but he communicated eloquently with his expressions and actions. He was performing as a white-faced mime in the Marcel Marceau tradition at the Mountain State Art & Craft Fair, where he strolled the grounds juggling and clowning. Today, over lunch at his log home in Lewisburg, he's full of conversation, telling me how a friend's yarns of her life in West Virginia caused him to come in 1980 to see for himself. He and Mikki Burrows had lived in the same apartment complex in Glenn's hometown, Newark, Delaware. Yet Glenn was looking for something he hadn't found in the rolling Andrew Wyeth countryside around Pennsylvania's Brandywine River Valley. He was entranced by Mikki's tales of West Virginia's natural beauty, the laid back lifestyle among the homesteaders she had known there, and the possibility of getting back to the land to live cheaply. When she returned to the state, Glenn came to visit her and then moved to West Virginia a few months later.

It took a few tries before he found what he was looking for. First, he stopped in Hinton, where he parked his car in front of the high school, took out his camp stove, and made his dinner. He hoped someone would come by who could tell him about the town, to help him decide if it was for him. No one came. Next, he went to Renick in Greenbrier County, where his friend lived, but stopped along the way when he saw a real estate sign. He called the broker, and she told him of a farmhouse in nearby Friar's Hill, which he subsequently rented for the next four years. There he found a whole community of people who had arrived in the 1970s, and he felt at home. Because Glenn had saved two thousand dollars working as a cook before he arrived, and had a car, he was free to just settle in to decide what he wanted to do with his life. Now he tells his own stories of the work parties, the gardening, the communally built houses, and the social life that echo those of his predecessors. Earlier settlers Bob Zacher, Carli Mareneck, and others are still friends from those halcyon days.

The son of a rocket scientist and a Catholic church administrator, he knew he didn't want to be either of those things. Instead, he wanted to be a performer, to become a mime. When he told people that and they asked how he planned to do it in West Virginia, he said he didn't know, but would figure it out. And figure it out he did. "I wasn't here for two or three months until I heard that just three hours north of me in Elkins was the International Mime Festival," he recalls. "The entire world of stuff I cared about was in West Virginia. They were all coming from all over the world to West Virginia, where I had run away to, to be close to nature, so I went."

Later that year, he returned to Elkins to attend dance classes during the Augusta Heritage Festival and studied there for the next two years. And he practiced. "I lived on this beautiful fifty-acre farm in Friar's Hill," he recalls. "Across this field, about a football field away from me was a big stand of

beautiful maple trees. They stood on the edge of this field like the front row of a crowd. I would dance for those trees. Those trees had energy. They had an ambient quality about them. They had an inherent integrity in the way they stood there. It was very much like front rows I've stood in front of all over the world since then."

Glenn eventually settled in Lewisburg, where he served for a time on the town's planning commission, and where he recently made a bid for a seat in the West Virginia House of Delegates. Now known the world over as "the horse guy"—an apt moniker, as his current costume mimics a man riding a horse—he's still a mime. As he says, however, the mime now hides inside his character. Many of his audiences include children. That's fitting, because a performer who entertained for his school when Glenn was a kid sparked his initial interest in mime. He travels the world with his show, often acting on the streets at festivals. Interestingly, West Virginia has fed his success. As he puts it, "I came to West Virginia because I was running away from stuff I didn't like in places that were more crowded, and I came here to hide from that." He admits, "I came here to hide from the harsh aspect of the anonymous, impersonal machine world, and I have hidden here successfully—so successfully that I became strong and deeply rooted in natural rhythms that I then took back out into the city and was successful with."

Glenn Singer is only one of those youthful, naïve college kids who came to West Virginia, remained, and made an impact on the state. While hundreds came and subsequently left, those who succeeded came with ideals, determination, and dreams that were similar to those of the elders they encountered in the hills. This alignment of values may have been a strong contributing factor in the success of those who stayed. Loyal Jones, noted expert on Appalachia, enumerates and applauds those principles in his book, *Appalachian Values.* He believes that many strengths like neighborliness, love of place, independence, and self-reliance have been lost in much of America, but still exist in Appalachia.[1] The artisans I know saw

---

Glenn Singer mimes at the Mountain State Art & Craft Fair. (Photo by Carter Seaton)

and admired these traits in the older Appalachians they met. They recognized that the elders' determination to survive with meager resources on an often-stingy plot of land matched their own. Correspondingly, the elders must have seen themselves mirrored in the youth, despite their long hair, odd accents, and college ways. Indeed, they often befriended them as if they were family or surrogate children who helped fill the void created by their own kids' departure for the big cities.

On the other hand, the author of *Yesterday's People*, Jack Weller, who worked as a preacher in Hazard, Kentucky, for thirteen years, saw the traits of the Appalachians as sometimes negative and often the cause of the region's poverty. Many of the characteristics he viewed disparagingly, however, were positive influences that contributed to the back-to-the-landers' successful assimilation into life in the West Virginia mountains. For instance, Weller spoke of individualism as creating a stumbling block to the Appalachians' ability to fit into society. Yet the newcomers were delighted to encounter that trait, for those individualistic elders allowed them to be who they were as well. As one person put it, "I've had the freedom I wanted to have, and the culture here promotes it. It's not something that I have to explain to people. My neighbors around here . . . if I'm doing something different, they're different too."

Weller also denounced traditionalism as keeping the Appalachians hidebound to the past, unable to move into the future. Again, however, this is precisely what forged the bonds between newcomer and elder. The newcomers had eschewed the looming disaster they saw in the future and fled for the hills, only to find themselves almost totally ignorant about how to live off the land. Fortunately, they found the advice and "old ways" of the elders just what they needed. Many "stupid pioneers," as Sandy Sowell called herself and her fellow communards, admit owing their survival to the assistance of the elders who befriended them. This sense of community that came naturally to the rural people often amazed the newcomers. Chuck Wyrostok is still awed by those who fed his children or offered a helping hand when he was stuck in the mud. "They just did it," he marvels. Many artisans also admit that those neighbors, by their example, made them better neighbors as well.

Like the original pioneers, these new settlers were willing to work, and to work hard. Although their older neighbors often didn't understand why these young couples chose to live in poverty when they didn't have to, the newcomers were determined to stick it out. Despite their naiveté, they knew it wouldn't be easy. The fearless transplants that succeeded were willing to do what was necessary to have their dream. According to basket maker Connie McColley, those unwilling to work hard eventually left. Those who stayed figured out a way to survive. This trait, too, is like that of the elders whom Weller termed "existence oriented."[2]

This similarity between the values of settler and newcomer is but one of the forces that may have made West Virginia's back-to-the-land migration so successful. The nurturing solitude of the mountains is another. Escaping from the pressures of urban living, the newcomers wanted a place to just live, a place that gave back, that nurtured. In that almost solitary life, they were free to create, to be inspired. Here, they were able to create a spiritually satisfying existence. Joe Lung, the Chinese potter, believes living here allows one to center one's self, to avoid the distractions that inhibit artistic expression. That lifestyle—uninhibited by societal pressures—contributed to the success of many of the artisans who stayed. Connie McColley says she's who she is because of West Virginia. Potter/musician Keith Lahti says he's "fed here." Bob Zacher called them "loving mountains." Jude Binder wanted to go into the hills and never come out. And Adrienne Biesemeyer says West Virginia really is an enchanted forest. Like the transplants, many native West Virginians come home to its hills to recapture that loving, nurturing feeling. Moreover, it's often said that West Virginians may not live in the state, but they know they'll be buried there.

The traits the artisans brought with them contributed to their success as well. As Don Page theorized, the reluctance of the native artisans to try new styles or methods of working was both a curse and a blessing. While it kept the heritage crafts pure, it didn't allow for changes that market forces sometimes demanded. The college-educated artisans who came, however, were willing to make those changes, and even brought some new ideas with them. They willingly learned what they could from the best older practitioners, then improvised until a new design or technique emerged. Those products are the ones for which demand increased, and that ultimately brought greater attention to the state's handcraft tradition.

When the artisans' need for cash and the state's desire to encourage economic development merged in the 1960s and 1970s, success was far from assured. Yet when the state brought government resources to bear on the arts and crafts scene during the precise period of the new artisans' arrival, things began to change. Don Page says it was a wonderful time to be involved in the craft movement. This push for economic development through the tourism draw of crafts may have happened in West Virginia primarily because of the impending centennial, but at the very least, the state appears to have been one of the first to support its artisans so whole-heartedly. According to Don, "We didn't just tell them about markets in New York, Chicago, Washington, Baltimore, or Atlanta; we went with them and footed the bill." Artisans regularly accompanied the Department of Commerce staff to national trade shows where handcrafts were showcased as one of the state's prized industries. "No one else did it this way, no matter how much they loved their craftsmen," he says.

From Don's perspective, this wasn't happening anywhere else. "There were cottage industries all over Appalachia," he says, "but to be able to use them as an economic development tool . . . improved our state." While neighboring Kentucky had a long-standing craft tradition in association with the Southern Highland Handicraft Guild, the state was not heavily involved in marketing products made by its citizens. Indeed, most of the economic development efforts in other Appalachian states focused on building expensive craft training facilities that ultimately failed, or they followed a self-promotion business model without state support.

For many years, the Mountain State Art & Craft Fair was the largest outdoor craft festival in the country. It regularly drew huge crowds and brought significant income to many of its two-hundred-plus exhibitors. In the 1970s and early 1980s, out-of-state license plates were as common as those from West Virginia. This influx of outside dollars was later largely spent in state by those artisans whose work the tourists purchased. Additionally, when the visitors bought gasoline, food, and spent the night to attend multiple days of the five-day fair, they fed the economic engine again.

In 2006, the West Virginia Division of Culture and History commissioned a study to determine the economic impact of the arts and crafts industry, which revealed that more than fifty-four million dollars is contributed to the state economy each year through the sale of arts and crafts in West Virginia.[3]

When Tamarack became a reality, it began to help fuel the state's economic engine. In 2008, the Tamarack Foundation released data showing that since its opening in 1996, it had generated in excess of $86 million in gross sales and collected more than $4.5 million in tax revenue. In a single year, the resulting $18.6 million in total economic impact, the $5.9 million in additional income to West Virginia workers, the 240 new jobs, and the generation of $1.4 million in-state and local taxes collected occurs without the expenditure of any state tax dollars.[4] In May 2012, Tamarack welcomed its seven millionth visitor.

The state's involvement in the arts created ripples that affect its artisans today. Don Page and dozens of the artisans speak of it as a "craft community." He recalls, "Those people stayed. They were successful. They remember the forces and the people of West Virginia that made them what they are today. They were appreciative, and they tried to turn back around and contribute themselves." Over the years, those artisans have taught hundreds to dance, perform, weave baskets, throw pots, or play music. They've handed down heritage crafts that might have died otherwise. And they've brought attention to the state with the sale of each product, with each performance.

Given the number of talented artisans and musicians discovered during that period, it is no surprise that West Virginia was the first state to build an artisan center, Tamarack, to showcase their work. Additionally, these artisans helped develop the center and were among the first to have their work sold there. Today, they mentor new artisans to ensure the tradition is passed down. Furthermore, the internationally famous *Mountain Stage* radio program was another early result of the state's support. After thirty years, it continues to be the longest-running live performance program on public radio. It, too, nurtures new musical talent, giving them a worldwide performance platform they can find nowhere else. Tamarack and *Mountain Stage* are arguably the state's best advertisements. These two cultural icons fly in the face of the stereotypical image of West Virginia as an isolated backwoods and argue strongly for it as a haven for creative living.

Still, the conventional image of West Virginia artists is that they were born in the state but made their career and found success in Nashville, New York, or Hollywood. Yet these back-to-the-land artists turned that formula on its head. They came to the state and found success here. That success should be championed and copied. These events, these shared values, these artisans' stories hold lessons for the state's future. As the megacities become more oppressive, with their attendant problems of crime, pollution, and urban sprawl, the nurturing mountains of West Virginia look inviting once again. For that reason, the eastern panhandle of the state already has become a bedroom community for the nation's capital. The same elements that drew both the early settlers and the back-to-the-landers to the mountains exist still: the beautiful mountains, the possibility of solitude, relatively inexpensive living, a laid back lifestyle, creative communities, and Appalachian values. Add to that the opportunity to live rurally and work anywhere via the Internet, and you've got a new recipe for success—a new cash crop—for the people and the state.

Bibliography

Agnew, Eleanor. *Back From the Land: How Young Americans Went to Nature in the 1970s, and Why They Came Back.* Chicago: Ivan R. Dee, 2004.

AmeriCorps. AmeriCorps Vista, 2006. http://www2.illinois.gov/serve/documents/Factsheet_americorps_vista.pdf.

Anderson, Colleen. "Tamarack at Ten." Tamarack, The Best of West Virginia, 2006.

————. "West Virginia Chose Me." 1990. Lyrics used with permission.

Bauerlein, Mark and Ellen Grantham, eds. *National Endowment for the Arts: A History 1965– 2008.* Washington, DC: National Endowment for the Arts, 2009. http://www.nea.gov/pub/nea-history-1965-2008.pdf.

Beaver, Patricia D. *Rural Community in the Appalachian South.* Prospect, IL: Waveland Press, 1986.

Becker, Jane S. "Craft Revival." In *Encyclopedia of Appalachia,* edited by Rudy Abramson and Jean Haskell. Knoxville: University of Tennessee Press, 2006.

————. *Selling Tradition: Appalachia and the Construction of an American Folk 1930–1940.* Chapel Hill: University of North Carolina Press, 1998.

Braunstein, Peter and Michael William Doyle, eds. *Imagine Nation.* New York: Routledge, 2002.

Budds, Michael J. *Jazz in the Sixties.* Iowa City: University of Iowa Press, 1978.

Caudill, Harry M. *Night Comes to the Cumberlands.* Boston: Little, Brown and Company, 1962.

Cook, Lakin. "West Virginia Commission on the Arts." In *The West Virginia Encyclopedia,* edited by Ken Sullivan. Charleston, WV: West Virginia Humanitites Council, 2006.

Deidzoeb, G. Roberto and David Conway. "War and Protest – the U.S. in Vietnam (1972–1975)." In *h2g2: The Unconventional Guide to Life, the Universe, and Everything,* April 19, 2002. http://www.bbc.co.uk/dna/h2g2/alabaster/A715060.

Fellowship for Intentional Communities. Intentional Communities in West Virginia. http://directory.ic.org/intentional_communities_in_West_Virginia.

Fike, Rupert, ed. *Voices from the Farm.* Summertown, TN: Book Publishing Company, 1998.

"Getting It All Together In the Name of Action." *Time Magazine,* June 7, 1971.

Gitlin, Todd. *The Sixties: Years of Hope, Days of Rage.* New York: Bantam Books, 1987.

Goldsmith, Lawrence H. "Locating and Buying Low Cost Land." *Mother Earth News* 3 (May/June 1970). North Madison, Ohio: John Shuttleworth.

Groce, Larry. "A Simple Song," the *Mountain Stage* theme song. Camp Run Music. Lyrics used by permission.

Grun, Bernard, ed. *The Timetables of History.* 3rd ed. New York: Simon Schuster,1991.

Hayden, Tom and Dick Flacks. "The Port Huron Statement at 40." *The Nation,* August 5, 2002.

Insua, Glenda and Teresa Hebron. A Decade of Dissent: Student Protests at the University of Michigan in the 1960s. Accessed January 29, 2008. http://www.bentley.umich.edu/exhibits/dissent/teachins.php.

International Society for Krishna Consciousness. New Vrindaban, West Virginia. http://content.iskcon.org/worldwide/centres_detail/moundsville.html.

Jacob, Jeffrey. *New Pioneers.* University Park: Pennsylvania State University Press, 1997.

Jay Rockefeller for West Virginia. About Jay. http://rockefeller.senate.gov/about/.

Jerome, Judson. *Families of Eden: Communes and the New Anarchism.* New York: Seabury, 1974.

Jones, Loyal. *Appalachian Values.* Ashland, KY: The Jesse Stuart Foundation, 1994.

J. R. Clifford Project. http://www.jrclifford.org/The Carrie Williams Case.htm.

King, Mary E. "Vista: A Vision of Social Change for the Future." In *A History of National Service in America,* edited by Peter Shapiro. College Park: University of Maryland Center for Political Leadership and Participation Publications, 1994.

Larry L. Rowe, Attorney at Law. Last modified 2013. http://larrylrowe.com/History-of-Malden/King-Salt-History.shtml.

Leen, Jeff. "The Vietnam Protests: When Worlds Collided," *The Washington Post.* September 27, 1999.

Lipton, Michael and Dan LeRoy. *20 Years of Mountain Stage.* Charleston: Friends of West Virginia Public Radio, 2003.

LyricsMode.com. "Going Up the Country Lyrics." Used by permission. http://www.lyricsmode.com/lyrics/c/canned_heat/going_up_the_country.html.

Maslow, Abraham. "A Theory of Human Motivation." In *Motivation and Personality.* New York: Harper & Row, Publishers, 1954.

Miller, Timothy. *The Hippies and American Values.* Knoxville: University of Tennessee Press, 1991.

————. *The 60s Communes: Hippies and Beyond.* Syracuse: Syracuse University Press, 1999.

Nearing, Helen and Scott. *Living the Good Life: How to Live Sanely and Simply in a Troubled World.* New York: Galahad Books, 1970.

Purdy, Jedediah. *For Common Things: Irony, Trust, and Commitment in America Today.* New York: A. A. Knopf, 1999.

Rich, Louise Dickinson. *We Took to the Woods.* Camden, ME: Down East Books, 1942.

Salstrom, Paul. "Back to the Land in the 1970s," unpublished article used with permission of author.

————. "The Neo-Natives: Back-to-the-land in Appalachia's 1970s." *Appalachian Journal* 30, no. 4 (Summer 2003): 312.

Schulman, Bruce J. *The Seventies: The Great Shift in American Culture, Society, and Politics.* New York: The Free Press, 2001.

Shapiro, Henry D. *Appalachia on Our Mind.* Chapel Hill: University of North Carolina Press, 1978.

Southern Appalachian Archives website (Hutchins Library, Special Collections & Archives, Berea College). Guide to the Appalachian Volunteers Record. http://community.berea.edu/hutchinslibrary/specialcollections/saa02.asp.

Tamarack. The Economic Impact of Tamarack and the Tamarack Foundation. Economic impact study prepared by the Marshall University Center for Economic and Business Research. https://tamarackwv.com/shared/content/TF_Report.pdf.

Unger, Irwin and Debi. *The Times Were A-Changin': The Sixties Reader.* New York: Three Rivers Press, 1998.

United States Census Bureau. Population by Poverty Status in 1959: 1960 (Excel file). All West Virginia Counties. http://www.census.gov.

Weller, Jack E. *Yesterday's People.* Lexington: University of Kentucky Press, 1965.

West Virginia Coal Association. Coal Facts 2009. http://www.wvcoal.com/201012192464/2009-coal-facts.html.

West Virginia Division of Culture and History. http://www.wvculture.org/index.aspx.

The West Virginia Division of Culture and History, Arts & Crafts Industry Contributes $54.5 Million Annually to State Economy. 2006. www.wvculture.org/arts/artsindustrystudy.html

West Virginia Department of Education. History of Cedar Lakes: Planning Stage Through 1962. http://wvde.state.wv.us/cedarlakes/documents/CedarLakesHistoryPlanningthru1962_002.pdf.

Whisnant, David E. *All That Is Native & Fine*. Chapel Hill: University of North Carolina Press, 1983.

Whitcover, Jules. *The Year The Dream Died*. New York: Warner Books, 1997.

Whyte, William H. *The Organization Man*. New York: Simon and Schuster, 1956.

Wikipedia, The Free Encyclopedia. Draft Evasion. Last modified September 2, 2013. http://www.en.wikipedia.org/wiki/Draft_dodger.

———. Eleanor, West Virginia. Last modified September 13, 2013. http://www.en.wikipedia.org/wiki/Eleanor,_West_Virginia.

———. Nancy Hanks (NEA). Last modified October 10, 2012. http://www.en.wikipedia.org/wiki/Nancy_Hanks_(NEA).

———. Rudolf Steiner. Last modified August 29, 2013. http://www.en.wikipedia.org/wiki/Rudolf_Steiner.

Wilson, Kathleen Curtis. "Crafts." In *Encyclopedia of Appalachia*, edited by Rudy Abramson and Jean Haskell. Knoxville: University of Tennessee Press, 2006.

Wolfe, Tom. *The Electric Kool-Aid Acid Test*. New York: Farrar Straus Giroux, 1968.

———. *The Purple Decades*. New York: Berkley Books, 1983.

Notes

Chapter One

1 Wilson, "Crafts," 770.
2 Ibid., 771.
3 Becker, "Craft Revival," 853.
4 Becker, *Selling Tradition*, 85–89.
5 Ibid., 89.
6 Wilson, "Crafts," 772.
7 *Wikipedia*, "Eleanor, West Virginia."
8 Becker, "Craft Revival," 98.
9 Population by Poverty Status in 1959: 1960, All West Virginia Counties, U.S. Census Bureau, www.census.gov.

Chapter Two

1 WV Dept. of Education, "History of Cedar Lakes," 12.
2 Bauerlein and Grantham, *National Endowment*, 6–7.
3 Ibid., 17–18.
4 Ibid., 51.
5 *Wikipedia*, Nancy Hanks (NEA).
6 Bauerlein and Grantham, *National Endowment*, 36.
7 Cook, "West Virginia Commission on the Arts," 762.
8 West Virginia Division of Culture and History, www.wvculture.org/index.aspx
9 Anderson, "Tamarack at Ten."

Chapter Three

1 Agnew, *Back From the Land*, 6.
2 Jacob, *New Pioneers*, 3.

257

3 Agnew, *Back From the Land*, 5.
4 West Virginia Coal Association, Coal Facts 2009.
5 Salstrom, "Back to the Land in the 1970s."
6 Salstrom, "The Neo-Natives," 30.
7 Goldsmith, "Locating and Buying Low Cost Land."
8 Whitcover, *The Year the Dream Died*, 186.
9 Ibid., 187.
10 Leen, "The Vietnam Protests."
11 Grun, *The Timetables of History*, 548.
12 Leen, "The Vietnam Protests."
13 Unger and Unger, *The Times Were A Changin'*, 80.
14 Whitcover, *The Year the Dream Died*, 316–335.
15 J. R. Clifford Project. Page about Carrie Williams.
16 *Wikipedia*, "Draft Evasion."
17 Ibid.

Chapter Four

1 Americorps, AmeriCorps Vista.
2 King, "VISTA: A Vision of Social Change,"
3 Jay Rockefeller for West Virginia. About Jay.
4 U.S. Census Bureau, Population by Poverty Status.
5 *Wikipedia*, "Mary Harris Jones,"
6 Larry L. Rowe, Attorney at Law.
7 Southern Appalachian Archives website, Guide to the Appalachian Volunteers Record.

Chapter Five

1 Groce, "A Simple Song."
2 Deidzoeb and Conway, "War and Protest."
3 Anderson, "West Virginia Chose Me."
4 LyricsMode.com, "Going Up the Country Lyrics."

Chapter Six

1 Miller, *The Hippies and American Values*, 15.
2 Whyte, *The Organization Man*.

3 Gitlin, *The Sixties*, 17.
4 Ibid., 35.
5 Budds, *Jazz in the Sixties*, 6–11.
6 Ibid., 90–92.
7 Jacob, *New Pioneers*, 3.
8 Agnew, *Back From the Land*, 90.
9 Ibid., 120.

Chapter Eight

1 Miller, *The 60s Communes*, 202.
2 Ibid., 205–206.
3 Ibid., xviii.
4 Ibid., xix.
5 Ibid., xx.
6 Fellowship for Intentional Communities, *Intentional Communities in West Virginia.*
7 International Society for Krishna Consciousness, New Vrindaban, West Virginia.
8 *Wikipedia*, Rudolf Steiner.
9 Hayden and Flacks, "The Port Huron Statement at 40."
10 Jack Rothman to William Haber, 1972, "Teach-in" vertical file, pp. 11–12, Bentley Historical Library, University of Michigan, quoted in Insua and Hebron, *A Decade of Dissent.*
11 Insua and Hebron, A Decade of Dissent.

Chapter Nine

1 Jones, *Appalachian Values*, 138.
2 Weller, *Yesterday's People*, 35.
3 WV Division of Culture and History, "Arts & Crafts Industry Contributes $54.5 Million Annually."
4 Tamarack, *The Economic Effect of Tamarack.*

Index

D

N

About the Author

Carter Taylor Seaton is the author of two novels, *Father's Troubles,* and *amo, amas, amat . . . an unconventional love story,* numerous magazine articles, and several essays and short stories. In her earlier life, she directed a rural craft cooperative, Appalachian Craftsmen, Inc.; was nominated for the *Ladies Home Journal* "Woman of the Year 1975" Award; and ran three marathons—Atlanta, New York City, and the United States Marine Corps—after she was fifty. A ceramic sculptor living in Huntington, West Virginia, she is a 2013 Tamarack Foundation Fellowship winner, an award given to artisans in recognition of their lifelong achievement in the arts.